Praise for *New Hope for People with Depression*

"Marian Broida has written a clear and sensible guide for better under-standing the complex and sometimes controversial issues associated with depression. She makes her point clearly and convincingly that there really is good reason to be hopeful about overcoming depression."

—MICHAEL D. YAPKO, PH.D., clinical psychologist and
author of *Breaking the Patterns of Depression*

"This is an outstanding publication for the lay reader but with enough depth to be an excellent reference and resource for physicians, nurses, and other health-care professionals working in primary care or mental health settings. As a family physician who teaches medical students and physicians in train-ing, I thoroughly enjoyed Broida's perspective on depression and associated disorders. Her book will be a tremendous benefit to patients regarding the ability to "partner" with their health-care providers for the best possible outcome. The section on treatment options takes much of the "mystery" out of how antidepressant medications work (or sometimes don't work). This book may truly be a lifesaver for those people suffering from unrecognized and untreated depression."

—JEFFREY T. KIRCHNER, D.O., associate director,
Family Practice Residency Program and associate professor,
Family and Community Medicine,
Temple University School of Medicine

"*New Hope for People with Depression* is an excellent, up-to-date resource on depression. It provides an organized review of the current knowledge on depression. It is a must read for the layperson and professional."

—LINDA STURDIVANT, M.ED., CEAP, president,
International Employee Assistance Professionals Association

In memory of my brother,
1952–1996

Contents

Foreword

SERIOUS DEPRESSION HAS only recently come to be recognized as one of the leading causes of disability in the world. Depressive disorders afflict millions of people, but are nevertheless underdiagnosed and undertreated. How can this be? Why do so many people with such a widespread illness go without treatment?

One answer is that depression can be subtle, difficult to recognize and diagnose, and a challenge to treat effectively. Another factor is that the shame many people feel about having a "mental" illness like depression prevents some people from seeking treatment. This stigma remains, despite the fact that scientists have shown that certain areas in the brain are underactive in people who are depressed and have found other evidence of changes in brain chemistry associated with mood problems. Serious depression is a real illness: The fact that it is still a very poorly understood illness doesn't make it any less real.

Serious depression is probably not just one illness but a group of many related disorders, now usually called *mood disorders*, that psychiatrists and brain scientists simply have been unable (so far) to separate out from one another for the kind of intense study that illnesses like diabetes or heart disease have received. We still don't know what is "broken" in depression and related mood disorders, a fact that makes "fixing" them one of the most challenging tasks in all of medicine.

Perhaps you are someone who suspects that a family member or you yourself have depression, and are wondering about the current treatments. Perhaps you or someone you love has just been diagnosed with a mood disorder and you want to understand this illness better and its treatment more completely. Or perhaps you have been treated for depression for a while and are discouraged and frustrated by an incomplete response to treatment or medication side effects and are interested to know more about the full range of available treatments, including treatments still in the experimental stages.

This excellent book addresses all these questions in clear and easy-to-read language. Read every word and have a pencil or highlighter on hand to focus your thinking, mark the points you think are relevant, and, most important, to remind yourself of things you want to ask your doctor.

Knowledgeable patients are able to make more informed decisions about their treatments and better use of their time with their doctors. Although I always ask patients, "Do you have any questions?" at the end of a discussion about a new treatment or a change in medications, I often hear back from them later that they were confused or in doubt about something but couldn't really think of a question that would express their uncertainty. The complexities of diagnosis, common medication side effects, details about experimental treatments you may have read about in the news—all these topics are addressed here, and many more besides. This information will help you to ask better questions and *more* questions and to understand the answers better, too.

I'm very pleased that this book stresses the importance of psychotherapy and counseling. Too many people with serious depression put all their hopes in medications and think that psychotherapy is only for "neurotics," or that it's too "touchy-feely" and won't help them. On the contrary, talk therapy and various forms of counseling are invaluable, probably even essential, ingredients in the treatment of serious depression. The unique healing powers of psychotherapy have something to offer everyone being treated for this often difficult-to-treat problem.

Only fifty years ago, there were so few effective treatments for serious depression that its sufferers were miserable for years at a time; some of them would spend many weeks, even months in psychiatric hospitals until their illness had run its course. The suicide rate for one of the most serious forms of depression, bipolar disorder (then called manic-depressive illness), was on the order of 30 to 60 percent. Those bleak days and grim statistics are, thank goodness, very much over for good. We have dozens of effective medications for the treatment of depression. We understand much better how psychotherapy helps and, even more important, what types of therapy best help people with depression. Experimental treatments like transcranial magnetic stimulation (TMS) and vagus nerve stimulation hold the promise of even more effective new approaches to the treatment of depression in the very near future. This is indeed a time of new hope for people with depression. My wish for you is that this book, by sharing this good news, will give you new hope, too.

—Francis Mark Mondimore, M.D.
Johns Hopkins University School of Medicine

Acknowledgments

I WISH TO THANK the many people who helped with this book: the brave souls who consented to be interviewed about their personal battles with depression; those close to my brother, who were willing to reopen wounds to share their thoughts, feelings, and memories; and the numerous professionals who shared their expertise with me, in particular, David Avery, M.D.; Larry Beutler, Ph.D.; Steven Bratman, M.D.; Douglas Jacobs, M.D. and Joelle Reizes, from Screening for Mental Health; and most especially, Francis Mondimore, M.D. These individuals generously gave their time for the betterment of this book. Any errors in the book are my own.

I would also like to thank a number of other individuals: Robbie Sherman, Megan Abbott, Mercedes Lawry, Matt Glover, and Ken Clark, for putting me in contact with people to interview; Elaine Way, for elegantly transcribing those interviews; and my editors at Prima Publishing, especially Marjorie Lery and Alice Feinstein. Finally, I would like to thank my friends Sara, Laurie, Pat, Ann, Gail, Lynn, and especially, Jeremy, for their loving support.

Introduction

A BLACK HOLE, some call it. A season in hell. A monster. A beast. People use many terms to describe the experience of depression. At its most severe, depression can make people long for death—and even accomplish it. Yet the condition is so widespread that doctors sometimes call it the "common cold" of mental difficulties. Nearly 19 million adults in the United States alone spend at least part of any given year sunk into turmoil and despair as a result of depression.[1] Many teens and even children suffer from depression, too. So serious are its effects, and so common the condition, that authorities rank just one form of depression, major depressive disorder, as the *leading* cause of disability in the United States.[2]

Isn't it time we took depression seriously?

In fact, thousands of researchers, hundreds of thousands of health care providers, and millions of ordinary people *have* been taking it seriously—by developing, providing, and receiving treatment.

But there's a key ingredient to recovery from depression. People with depression need to seek help. If you suffer from depression, that's sometimes hard to do. Depression, by its nature, drains people of hope—the very hope that they need in order to seek treatment and to stick with it.

The message of this book is simple: There is hope, new hope, for people with depression. Scientists and compassionate health-care providers have revolutionized the treatment of depression in this generation: from the first antidepressants discovered by accident 50 years ago to the latest varieties on pharmacy shelves; from the older forms of psychotherapy to newer, short-term therapies specifically targeting depression; from early, disparaged forms of electroshock treatment to cutting-edge enhancements of the technique. Moreover, the likelihood of yet further improvements in treatment is high. Today, researchers are plumbing the mysteries of intercellular processes in depression, seeking new, radically different drugs. Others are exploring the wisdom of the ancients, scientifically validating the effects of herbs, meditation, and other complementary forms of care. Many others are seeking the best ways to prevent or treat the disorder with psychotherapy or other methods of treatment.

If you've suffered from depression in the past, or are suffering from it today, or if you love someone who's depressed, be aware: There *are* things people can do to tame the monster, defeat the beast, and emerge from the black hole into daylight. What's needed is an accurate diagnosis, access to informed and compassionate health care providers, up-to-date information, and the determination and support to keep trying until treatment works. Even if you're feeling hopeless, keep putting one foot in front of the other. Eventually, hope will dawn.

In writing this book, I interviewed dozens of experts, ranging from eminent psychiatrists and psychologists to authorities in complementary medicine and depression's social aspects. Their words appear on these pages, describing their research, their experiences, and their perspectives in treating people with depression. Alongside their words appear the words of brave individuals who've gone through depression themselves.

As the author, I bring my own perspectives to this book. I write it as a nurse who has worked with adults in a mental health setting; as a person with a lifelong interest in complementary medicine; as someone who suffered two episodes of depression in the past, and recovered; and as the sister of a man who died from it. It is the last experience that gave me the emotional imperative to write this book.

My brother survived a very difficult, complicated depression for many years, but at last succumbed to suicide, despite the efforts of his wife and family to help. Although my brother didn't survive, my hope is that others might benefit from the information I've gained. My brother wasn't able to take advantage of the many treatments available, despite receiving care for years from highly competent mental health professionals. Who knows if additional treatments might have helped, had he been willing to try and had used them consistently? For those of you battling this monster in your own lives, I can only repeat: Help is available. Reach for it, and don't give up.

CHAPTER 1

An Overview of Depression

❧

Depression, for me, is like putting on gray sunglasses.

—JOHN, A TEACHER WITH RECURRENT DEPRESSION

If you can look at things in a good light, a neutral light, and a negative light, I would look at things in a negative light. It was very difficult to get myself out of that perspective.

—PHILIP, A COMPUTER PROGRAMMER WHO HAS RECOVERED FROM DEPRESSION

I F YOU'VE EVER had a bout of depression, you may recognize what these people are describing. With depression, things that used to seem fun no longer do. Pessimism and guilt rule. Living can seem a chore, even a cause for anguish. Worse, we often see no hope, no way out. This state can seem to be our fate in life, our just desserts, or even part of our personality—who we really are.

This book is here to say that depression is not who we are. If you are currently depressed, there's hope: Multiple treatments are available, and there is much you can do at home to support recovery. If you've been depressed in the past, there are things you can do to help

1

keep depression from returning—and to quickly recognize and stop it if it does recur.

Depression saps our will and our energy, making it hard to get motivated and to take the steps necessary to improve. It also depletes our self-esteem, making it hard to believe that we, with all our faults and inadequacies, are somehow still worth helping. Like an unwelcome guest, depression uses various tricks and manipulations to keep us from evicting it from our minds. But remember, it's *your* mind—you get to decide what goes on in it.

This book is here to give you tools to push depression out.

WHAT IS DEPRESSION?

Although we may say we're depressed when our team loses a game, or a movie gets us down, true depression is more than a passing feeling. True depression—sometimes called clinical depression—is a *mood disorder:* Our mood does not respond normally to the ups and downs of life.

"A normal mood is reactive," says Francis Mondimore, M.D., a psychiatrist and faculty member of the Johns Hopkins University School of Medicine. "In other words, people react to what's going on in their lives. When nice things happen, they are in a good mood; when bad things happen, they are in a bad mood."

In contrast, with clinical depression, our mood drops and stays down. "The person's mood is constricted, unresponsive, and relentlessly the same," explains Dr. Mondimore.

Clinical depression can zap our self-confidence, destroy our decision-making power, derange our sleep, and turn us irritable or grim, unable to appreciate life's pleasures. It can fill our minds with self-criticism, reminding us again and again of our failings, sometimes even harking back to childhood. Physical symptoms, such as weight gain or loss, can arise. Far too often depression can even make us seek death, so painful does it become to drag ourselves through our daily existence.

Symptoms of Depression

Common symptoms of depression include:

- Feeling blue, sad, or down in the dumps
- Losing interest and energy
- Feeling tired
- Trouble concentrating and making decisions
- Feeling hopeless, helpless, worthless, or guilty
- Feeling irritable or anxious
- Believing life isn't worth living
- Sleeping too much or too little
- Eating too much or too little
- Slowing down physically, or moving around restlessly
- Experiencing multiple aches and pains; worrying excessively over physical health
- Thinking about death or suicide, or attempting suicide

Most people with depression experience only some of these symptoms. Some people may feel empty rather than sad. People from different cultures may experience different patterns of symptoms; for instance, people of certain ethnicities are more likely to experience physical symptoms (fatigue or aches and pains) than others.

"I am now the most miserable man living," wrote Abraham Lincoln, who suffered from bouts of extreme depression.[1] In this century, author William Styron described his experience with depression thus: "My brain, in thrall to its outlaw hormones, had become less an organ of thought than an instrument registering, minute by minute, varying degrees of its own suffering."[2]

Depression Differs from Mourning

Depression is different from grief, although both can share certain qualities: sad thoughts, easy tears, and changes in appetite or sleep. The cause of the greatest grief is bereavement. "Bereavement is a process that is tied to a specific kind of event in people's lives—the loss of someone close to them," says Dr. Mondimore. During bereavement, people go through stages: shock, anger, bargaining, depression, and finally acceptance. People can have "wellings of emotion" for a long time after the loss, and still find themselves in the realm of normal grieving, notes Dr. Mondimore.

Unlike grief, which usually has a clear origin, clinical depression sometimes seems to arise from thin air. It can also follow bereavement, however. "When the mood begins to contaminate lots of other areas of life so that people find that they're preoccupied with the death, maybe feel responsible for what happened, or are troubled by feelings of regret and self-blame that affect the way they think about themselves and how they see the world—at that point, the grief becomes depression," says Dr. Mondimore.

A Treatable Disorder

Depression is not a character flaw or a sign of personal weakness, despite the pervasiveness of this myth. Professionals consider depression a disorder—or rather, a group of disorders, since different types of depression exist. "These are brain-based disorders," says Alexander Young, M.D., director of the health services unit at the Los Angeles Veterans Administration Mental Illness Research, Education and Clinical Center, and assistant professor of psychiatry at the University of California at Los Angeles. "They have specific symptoms. They represent real diagnoses. And there are specific treatments in terms of counseling and medication."

In precise scientific terminology, depression is not a disease. Scientists reserve the term *disease* for conditions in which they have pinpointed damage to specific tissues or organs. So far they haven't confirmed such physical damage in depression. Some of the most stunning recent advances in neuroscience, however, have begun to identify changes in function, and perhaps even structure, in different areas of the depressed brain. Someday scientists may identify these changes more clearly. When that day arrives, it will be much harder to view depression as a character flaw or a sign of moral weakness. We are all likely to take depression more seriously—and deal with it more compassionately—in both ourselves and others.

> *Some of the most stunning recent advances in neuroscience have begun to identify changes in function, and perhaps even structure, in different areas of the depressed brain.*

The Author's Own Experience

I was a college sophomore when depression hit. It began with the breakup of a romance on my birthday. Normally a dedicated student, I found myself having a hard time concentrating on my studies. Instead, I ruminated on what I could have and should have said, things that just might have saved the relationship. As the semester wore on, I felt worse and worse. I dropped out of two of my classes, and still found myself barely finishing my schoolwork. Everything I wrote seemed like garbage. Nothing I'd cared about seemed to matter—and I didn't think that I mattered, particularly, either. I began staying in bed, avoiding friends, periodically bursting into tears out of sheer unhappiness.

After several weeks of increasing misery, I found I couldn't focus my eyes on my textbooks. I took myself to the school clinic for my "eye problem," where a savvy nurse referred me to one of the school's psychologists. He was a kind man who truly seemed to care. He gave me his phone number in case I wanted to call between sessions, and once, overwhelmed by despair, I did. To my astonishment, he arranged for me to see him right away. His availability made me feel the world was a little warmer, and my despair lessened.

After a number of sessions, I felt a little better, enough to finish out the semester and arrange an internship over winter break. Free from the stresses of schoolwork, in a new environment, I began to recover a sense of optimism and even excitement about life.

For me, the visits to the school psychologist helped enormously. They helped me place my experience in context, and taught me that there were things I could do to recover from depression. One of the main benefits of treatment was simple: learning that I was not alone.

Mine was a relatively mild depression. But it was enough to give me a taste of what depression is all about.

TYPES OF DEPRESSION

The psychiatric profession's official manual of mental difficulties is the *Diagnostic and Statistical Manual of Mental Disorders, Fourth Edition*, or *DSM-IV*. The following sections describe some of the types of depression listed in the *DSM-IV*. Before describing these individual disorders, the *DSM-IV* first describes a *major depressive episode*, whose symptoms can occur in more than one type of depression.

Major Depressive Disorder

The first category of depression in the *DSM-IV* is major depressive disorder, sometimes called by its older name, major depression. People with a major depressive disorder have at least one bout of a major depressive episode (see sidebar, "Criteria for a Major Depressive Episode," page 7).

Major depressive disorder is both common and debilitating. According to the National Institute of Mental Health, it is the *leading* cause of disability in the United States. In a given year, it affects about 9.9 million adults—that is, about 5 percent of American adults. About twice as many women experience major depression as men.[3] Approximately 17 percent of all Americans—about 13 percent of men, and

Criteria for a Major Depressive Episode

According to the *DSM-IV,* five or more of the following symptoms, including one or both of the first two symptoms, must have been present nearly every day during the same 2-week period:[4]

1. Depressed mood most of the day (in children or adolescents, this can be an irritable mood).

2. Markedly diminished interest or pleasure in all or almost all activities.

3. Significant weight loss when not dieting, weight gain, or decrease or increase in appetite.

4. Insomnia or increased sleeping.

5. Restlessness or slowing down of body movements.

6. Fatigue or loss of energy.

7. Feelings of worthlessness or excessive or inappropriate guilt.

8. Diminished ability to think or concentrate, or indecisiveness.

9. Recurrent thoughts of death (not just fear of dying), recurrent thoughts of suicide, or a suicide attempt.

about 21 percent of women—will have at least one episode of major depression during their lifetime.[5]

Usually, major depression develops slowly, over days or weeks, although it can attack suddenly after a job loss or other shock. Early symptoms may include mounting anxiety and minor, off-and-on depression. Left untreated, major depressive disorder tends to last at least 6 months. A. John Rush, M.D., professor of psychiatry at the

University of Texas, says, "Typically, people get out of the episode spontaneously, but there are about 10 percent of people with a major depressive episode where the episode lasts beyond 2 years." Treatment can shorten its span significantly. Researchers estimate, however, that 80 to 90 percent of people who have an episode of major depression will experience it at least once more.[6]

The author William Styron chronicles his experience with a major depressive episode in his book *Darkness Visible: A Memoir of Madness*. Early on, he writes, "I felt a kind of numbness, an enervation, but more particularly an odd fragility—as if my body had actually become frail, hypersensitive, and somehow disjointed and clumsy, lacking normal coordination." Later, he describes "an immense and aching solitude." Of his worst period, he writes, "I experienced a curious inner convulsion that I can describe only as despair beyond despair. It came out of the cold night; I did not think such anguish possible."[7] Yet Styron recovered. His powerful depiction of his experience inspired others, including *60 Minutes* host Mike Wallace, to come forward with their own stories, motivating thousands more to seek care.

Bipolar Disorder

The second type of mood disorder in the *DSM-IV* is bipolar disorder, sometimes called by its older name, manic-depression. People with bipolar disorder have abnormal moods reflecting two opposite poles: depression, on the one hand; and mania, a state of abnormally elevated energy, on the other. The *DSM-IV* notes two types of bipolar disorder, involving different degrees of mania. True mania, and states of mixed mania and depression, occur in *bipolar type I*. A milder form of mania called *hypomania* occurs in *bipolar type II*. Most people who have bipolar disorder have long periods of normal mood interspersed with their highs and lows.

According to the National Institute of Mental Health, 1.2 percent, or about 2.3 million, adults in the United States are living with bipolar disorder in a given year.[8] Unlike virtually every other type of depression, bipolar disorder affects men and women in equal numbers. Untreated, it tends to worsen over time, with episodes of mania and depression rising in frequency. Numerous actors, artists, writers, musicians, and politicians have shared this disorder, including actress Carrie Fisher, composer Robert Schumann, poet Ralph Waldo Emerson, and, possibly, Alexander the Great.

One well-known person with bipolar disorder is actress Patty Duke. Born Anna Marie Duke, Patty Duke rose to fame at age 12 playing the deaf and blind Helen Keller in *The Miracle Worker*—a stunning portrayal that later earned her an Oscar. Unfortunately, spells of depression increasingly disrupted her life as she grew older. In her mid-teens, she would stay in bed from Friday night until Monday morning. Later, she had periods of tearfulness, indecision, and terror.

Mania and Hypomania

Mania and hypomania are the hallmark features of the two main types of bipolar disorder, bipolar I and II, distinguishing these conditions from other types of depression. While manic, people talk faster, think faster, and lose some of the judgment that keeps behavior within normal bounds. They may burn through credit cards, buying everything in sight; develop grandiose business plans; start a dozen creative projects at once; or initiate frequent sexual encounters with different partners. Once the mania passes, this behavior stops.

The milder hypomania, found in bipolar type II, can resemble a giddy exuberance, and may be difficult to identify because it's closer in range to a normally elated mood. People with bipolar type I may also have periods of hypomania. In addition, people with type I may have so-called mixed episodes, where the abundant energy of mania combines with the low mood of depression.

Beginning in her late teens, Patty reports having occasional periods of intense high energy and rage when she would scream insults, barely sleep, and spend huge amounts of money she didn't have. Although some may argue that this is normal behavior for a celebrity, in Patty's case it wasn't. Although she didn't know it, she was being driven by periodic bouts of mania.

At one low point in her life, she recalls, she would go into her closet to dress. Hours later, her husband would come home and find her still standing there. Over the next 15 years, she tried numerous times to kill herself by overdosing on pills.

It was not until 1982, when she was in her mid-thirties, that a doctor diagnosed Patty Duke with manic-depression (the term for bipolar disorder at that time). Her periods of rage and her spending sprees, along with her struggles with depression, were the keys that allowed the doctor to make the diagnosis. Patty began taking lithium, a mineral the Food and Drug Administration (FDA) approved in the 1970s for this disorder, revolutionizing treatment for this condition. From that point on, Patty recounts in her book, *A Brilliant Madness*, her life changed.

"In about ten days I started to feel easier," she writes. "For the first time in my life I felt 'normal.'"[9]

For a year, Patty toured the country, talking to groups of people interested in learning about depression. "It thrills me to talk to someone and see in her eyes that a connection has been made," she writes. "And when I get a letter saying, 'I took the bull by the horns and now my husband has been diagnosed,' I feel all through me a moment of exhilaration."[10]

Dysthymic Disorder

Less familiar to many people is dysthymic disorder, also called dysthymia, a chronic form of low-grade depression. "Dysthymia is a smoldering depression that can go on for years at a time," says Dr.

Mondimore. "These are the people that, when you ask them how long they've had a problem with depression, will say 'as long as I can remember.'" In dysthymia, he says, "people are troubled by many symptoms of serious depression, including low moods. They have low energy, will lose interest in things, really have to push themselves and motivate themselves to get things done." From time to time, some may experience a major depressive disorder on top of their dysthymia, a situation that doctors term *double depression.*

About 10.9 million, or 5.4 percent of adults in the United States have dysthymia at some point during their lifetime. In a given year, about 40 percent of people with dysthymia also have major depression or bipolar disorder.[11]

Bruce's Story: A Lifelong Depression

Bruce, manager and part owner of a small graphics business, isn't sure exactly when his depression began. "A good deal of me thinks back and feels that I've always been depressed," he says. "I do, however, think that in later life it's become more pronounced." Bruce's symptoms have flared up on occasion. "I would get very quiet—didn't want to talk to anyone—didn't have a lot of interest in doing much of anything. Just wanted to be left alone. My wife is very good at being able to spot it coming on." He also has symptoms of anxiety.

Bruce is doing better since he began taking an antidepressant. "I'm currently using Zoloft, and I've had pretty good success with it," he says. "I would describe it as taking the anxiety down a few pegs. I seem to be able to deal with things on a more even keel." His bouts of lower mood are also less frequent.

Other Types of Depression

The following are other types of depression listed in the *DSM-IV.*

Cyclothymic Disorder

Sometimes called cyclothymia, cyclothymic disorder "is probably a type of bipolar disorder," says Dr. Mondimore. With it, "the individual has unexplainable changes of mood on a day-by-day basis." People still have abnormal ups and downs of mood, but their mood swings are closer to normal in range compared to those in bipolar type I or II. Accurate statistics on the frequency of cyclothymic disorder may be hard to come by. "Most people think that this is very underdiagnosed," says Dr. Mondimore. It's rarely included in counts of people with bipolar disorder.

Adjustment Disorder with Depressed Mood

This term applies to those people depressed over life circumstances—job loss, family upheaval, breakup of a relationship—who don't meet the criteria for a major depressive disorder. This condition is presumably quite common, although estimates vary considerably (and most people with this disorder are probably never diagnosed). Unlike conditions discussed above, the *DSM-IV* doesn't categorize this diagnosis as a mood disorder. Although people with this condition benefit from treatment, their responses to their situations are relatively normal—it's the situation that's making their lives difficult.

Premenstrual Dysphoric Disorder

Premenstrual dysphoric disorder (PMDD) is the *DSM-IV* term for premenstrual depression, and it's not yet considered an official diagnosis. In the manual, the category is buried in an appendix set aside "for further study." According to the *DSM-IV,* this condition typically causes a sad mood, anxiety, tearfulness, irritability, difficulty concentrating, or other symptoms for at least one week before a woman's period. PMDD is more severe than the premenstrual syndrome that many women experience. To fit a diagnosis of PMDD, emotional symptoms need to be severe, interfering with relationships or on-the-job functioning. The cause of PMDD is unclear. Shifting levels of female hormones such as progesterone may play a role, perhaps by affecting levels of brain chemicals.

Postpartum Depression

Depression occurring after childbirth is not listed in the *DSM-IV* as a separate kind of depression, but as a "modifier" to another diagnosis of mood disorder. Most women have some emotional symptoms after childbirth, which is not the utter, unmitigated joy that popular culture assumes. These symptoms range from relatively mild *baby blues* to the more severe postpartum depression to the rare postpartum *psychosis*, which includes hallucinations or delusions.

Theorists often link these conditions to the enormous and sudden change in female hormones. Levels of estrogen and progesterone in a woman's body plummet by 90 to 95 percent in the first few days after delivery.[12] But hormonal transitions in themselves don't tell the whole story. "All women have these hormonal changes, but not all women have postpartum mood disorders," notes Dr. Mondimore. "Why *some* women develop mood changes in reaction to these hormonal changes is unknown." Other factors also play a role in postpartum depression. New mothers may have to cope with enormous psychological and social changes brought on by the family's newest member. In addition, sleep deprivation can be extreme.

Most common are the baby blues, a period of low spirits, easy tears, irritability, and confusion that usually peaks 4 to 7 days after childbirth. Postpartum depression and postpartum psychosis are respectively more severe, but less common.

Women who have previously had a major depression are most at risk for postpartum depression, and having postpartum depression increases the risk of a major depression later in life. Women with bipolar disorder are also more at risk for depression immediately after childbirth.

Substance-Induced Mood Disorder

Chemical causes of depression include drugs (both prescription and recreational) and poisonous substances in the environment. The following is a list of some of the more common substances causing depression. Of all of these, alcohol is one of the greatest culprits.

Alcohol
Antabuse (a drug used to treat alcohol dependence)
Antianxiety medications
Antibiotics (some)
Antihistamines (some)
Birth control pills
Cancer drugs (some)
Epilepsy medications (some)

Seasonal Affective Disorder

Seasonal affective disorder (SAD), sometimes called winter depression, involves mood changes according to the time of year. "It's a disorder characterized first of all by a seasonal pattern," says SAD expert David Avery, M.D., of the University of Washington. Symptoms can resemble those of major depressive disorder, but typically occur "during fall and winter, sometimes even spring, if it's cloudy and dark," says Dr. Avery. "Individuals experience increased sleep, difficulty awakening, increased appetite—in particularly cravings for sweets and starches—weight gain, and then more nonspecific depressive symptoms: low energy, low mood, difficulty concentrating." He notes that occasionally people with SAD have suicidal ideas, "although these aren't as common in winter depression as they are in nonwinter depression."

People with SAD sometimes describe it as a desire to hibernate. Like bears aroused too soon in the spring, they may be grouchy and lethargic, unable to get much done. Come spring, they regain their

Heart and blood pressure drugs (some, such as
     beta-blockers)
Heavy metals such as lead (on-the-job exposure)
Nonsteroidal anti-inflammatory drugs (NSAIDs)
Parkinson's disease medications (some)
Steroid hormones
Stimulants such as cocaine and methamphetamine (as these wear
     off, or after repeated use)

If you are depressed and exposed to one of these substances, talk
to your doctor to see if it may be a factor.

Note: Many of these substances cause depression in only a small
percentage of people who take them.

---

normal energy and vitality. A minority of people experience symptoms of depression only in the summer.

In the United States, SAD is most common among people who live in northern states, where winter days are particularly short. Dr. Avery notes that women experience it much more often than men. Some studies have found that 80 percent of SAD sufferers are female.

As with postpartum depression, seasonal affective disorder is not listed in the *DSM-IV* as a distinct type of depression, but as a "modifier" of other mood disorders.

THE CHANGING *DSM*

The *DSM* has changed its categories of depression several times since its first edition in 1952. Even today, there's little consensus that each category represents a biologically different type of depression. "The *DSM* reflects the way a committee sat down and decided to slice up a pie," says Michael Gitlin, M.D., director of the Mood Disorders Clinic at University of California at Los Angeles. He believes that several of the disorders, including major depression and dysthymia, may really reflect different presentations of the same disorder. "They just differ by severity and course," he explains. "Just as you can have asthma that's more chronic versus more episodic, but really the person still has the core disease of asthma. I think ultimately we are going to find the same thing with depression." He believes, however, that some *DSM* diagnoses of mood disorders—for example, bipolar disorder—do represent distinctly different entities.

Medical Causes of Depression

Depression can be a symptom of a medical problem. The *DSM* labels such depression *mood disorder caused by a general medical condition*. In these cases, researchers believe depression results from the underlying illness—not from emotional responses to being sick or in danger of dying. Still, it's very difficult to separate these factors. The following is a list of conditions that can cause depression. Some of these—such as underactive thyroid—are quite common, while others are rare.

Hormonal Problems
Addison's disease (deficiency in adrenal hormones)
Adrenal gland tumors
Cushing's syndrome (excess of adrenal hormones)
Diabetes mellitus
Hypothyroidism (underactive thyroid gland)
Parathyroid gland problems

Infectious Diseases
Hepatitis
HIV
Mononucleosis

Other mental health professionals believe that most or all of the current *DSM* mood disorder diagnoses represent distinct clinical conditions. Only further research is likely to resolve these disagreements.

In 2000, the American Psychiatric Association released the very latest version of the *DSM*, *DSM-IVtr* (*tr* stands for "text revision"). Definitions of the categories of depression didn't change, but the text reflects more recent laboratory findings, research about risk groups, and other information.

Even with the need for more research and in the face of disagreements within the mental health professions, *DSM-IV* categories fill a

Pneumonia
Syphilis (late stage)

Certain Cancers
Brain tumor (very rarely)
Lung cancer
Pancreatic cancer

Neurological Problems
Dementia (severe memory and mental problems, usually in the
    elderly)
Huntington's disease (chorea)
Multiple sclerosis
Parkinson's disease
Postconcussion (head injury)
Stroke

Other
Anemia
Hypertension
Lupus (an autoimmune disease)
Vitamin deficiencies, especially of B vitamins

critical function: helping guide treatment. Researchers have performed controlled studies of numerous treatments for different categories of depression, as described in current and previous versions of the *DSM*. Such studies have given doctors invaluable information as to which treatments are most likely to be beneficial in which situations. In many cases, proper diagnosis can lead to a new lease on life—as it did for Patty Duke.

DEGREES OF DEPRESSION

There are not only different types of depression, there are also different degrees of depression. Odd as it sounds, someone can have a mild major depressive disorder, or a moderate or severe one.

Researchers often rate the severity of depression based on the number and type of symptoms, such as the presence and strength of suicidal thoughts and urges and the person's overall ability to function. Symptoms such as delusions or hallucinations (fortunately rare) also increase the severity of depression. Delusions are beliefs that don't reflect reality, such as thinking that the FBI has a listening device implanted in your brain. Hallucinations are sights, sounds, smells, tastes, or other sensory experiences reflecting something that doesn't exist.

Of course, any depression is likely to feel severe to the person experiencing it. Determining the degree of depression is most useful in helping your doctor select a treatment that is likely to be effective.

COMPLICATIONS OF DEPRESSION

Complications are medical conditions that occur as a result of having a primary health problem, in this case, depression. Both suicide and problems with drugs or alcohol can be complications of depression. If a suicide attempt is successful, the complication becomes fatal.

Suicide

The most dreaded outcome of depression is suicide, the eighth leading cause of death in the United States. Rates are particularly high among the elderly, more than 6,000 of whom take their lives in any given year.[13] For 15- to 24-year-olds, suicide is the third leading cause of death.[14]

Over the past few decades, most experts estimated that about 15 percent of people with depression eventually died by suicide. A recent study found this figure to be too high. The actual risk, according to this study, ranges from 2 to 8.6 percent. The study also determined that 2 percent of people treated for depression outside the hospital will die by suicide, while those who have been hospitalized have a higher risk.[15] Although these figures are lower than previous estimates, the risk is still considerable.

> **Medical Alert**
>
> If you are suicidal, have a plan for killing yourself, and have access to the equipment to do it, talk to your doctor *now*.

Substance Abuse and Dependence

Overuse of alcohol or street drugs is common among people with depression. In some cases, the combination leads to a kind of chicken-and-egg questioning, according to Dr. Mondimore. "'Am I depressed because I'm using drugs, or am I using drugs because I'm depressed?' What I tell people is that they are two separate problems," he says.

Whichever came first, the abuse of substances certainly complicates depression. It not only makes the depression more difficult to treat, but it also generates its own problems—for example, with health, relationships, or the law. The combination of substance abuse and depression can be particularly deadly: together, they dramatically increase the risk of suicide.

The overuse of alcohol and drugs in depression is sometimes a form of self-medicating—people trying to boost their moods (or the opposite, in the case of mania) on their own. Yet these "treatments" are not very good choices, for various reasons.

As a depressant, alcohol tends to worsen depression, although it may initially seem to do the opposite. Compared to prescription medications, alcohol has a terrible "side-effect" profile. Liver disease, increased rates of heart disease and cancer, bleeding ulcers, bleeding esophagi, bleeding hemorrhoids, hangovers, vomiting, and a high risk of addiction all make alcohol a destructive way to try to ease one's cares.

Some people with depression seek to elevate their moods with stimulants such as methamphetamine and cocaine. In the past, medical doctors tried prescribing stimulants to treat people with depression. They found that, in the long run, these drugs were not nearly as effective as antidepressants (although they may play a small role in some cases as a secondary medication). Again, the side-effect profile of unprescribed "uppers" is nasty: paranoid delusions, malnutrition, perennial skin infections, and eventual burnout with persistent depression. And, just as with alcohol, there's the whopping potential for addiction, including cravings that can consume one's job, family, passions, and life. Antidepressants and psychotherapy are much more benign, and instead of turning you into an addict, can turn you back into "you."

OTHER EFFECTS OF DEPRESSION

As if depression on its own weren't enough, there are other negative consequences besides the danger of suicide attempts and substance abuse. Research indicates that depression can influence the immune system, potentially worsening our health. "You're more likely to get infections, you're more likely to have heart disease, you're more likely to have a popping up of your arthritis, you're more likely to have trouble with your stomach," says John Ratey, M.D., associate clinical professor of psychiatry at Harvard Medical School and author of

A User's Guide to the Brain. Therefore, screening for and treating depression is an important part of treatment for chronic disease.

Depression also has problematic effects on other aspects of our lives besides our physical health. The impact of depression on our choices and relationships can be quite damaging. Choices we make and actions we take when depressed can, in turn, have depressing consequences, leading us on a downward spiral. If our depression tells us we are not good enough at our work and, in response, we quit our job, we then have to suffer through the difficulties of unemployment—and its impact on our self-esteem. If depression impels us to snap at our spouses or children, or be unable to participate in family gatherings, we threaten our most important relationships, and diminish our lives. Then we have even more reason to be depressed.

> *Treatment for depression can improve not only our spirits, but our life circumstances. The downward spiral can shift to an upward spiral, and our lives can take many turns for the better.*

The flip side of this, of course, is that treatment for depression can improve not only our spirits, but our life circumstances. Our on-the-job functioning is likely to improve, as are our relations with other human beings. The downward spiral can shift to an upward spiral, and our lives can take many turns for the better.

ANXIETY AND DEPRESSION

"Anxiety as a symptom is seen in many people who have depression, but certainly not everybody," says Dr. Gitlin. "You can have anxious depression," he notes, but it's also possible to have depression without anxiety.

Anxiety can also occur as a result of an anxiety disorder. Two common anxiety disorders are panic disorder—in which people experience spells of breathlessness and extreme anxiety—and generalized anxiety disorder, in which people are nervous and tense all day long, without regard to any particular situation or stimulus. Such problems can occur in tandem with major depression, and often precede it. About half of all people with major depression have an anxiety disorder as well.

Anxiety can increase the general level of distress that people feel with depression. Some researchers believe that acute anxiety combined with depression can increase the risk for suicide. Certainly it can increase people's beliefs that their situation—or symptoms—must improve *right now*.

WHO IS AT RISK FOR DEPRESSION?

About 18.8 million or 9.5 percent of adults in the United States have depression in a given year—and that figure reflects only three types of depression: major depressive disorder, dysthymic disorder, and bipolar disorder.[16] If you add in other types of depression, the numbers rise even higher.

No one is immune to depression. The talented, the wealthy, the handsome, the athletic, the famous and powerful have all succumbed. Both men and women can experience depression, although it is twice as prevalent in women (12 percent of women in a year, versus 6.6 percent of men; again, that reflects only the three types mentioned above).[17] Depression can occur in children and—very frequently—in the elderly.

While depression can strike anyone, there are some factors that make a person more susceptible. In addition to gender, risk factors include:

Previous depression. Having had an episode of major depression increases the likelihood of recurrence significantly. According to some researchers, more than 80 percent of people who have one episode will have another.

Family history of depression. Having a close relative who has been depressed raises the risk of major depression two- to four-fold.

Family history seems to be particularly significant in bipolar disorder.

Economics. According to one study, depression's favorite subjects appear to be poor young women, whether white, African-American, or Hispanic—those with the highest rates of crime victimization, sexual trauma, and financial hardship.[18] According to another study, single mothers—often struggling with full-time jobs and parenthood, or poverty and isolation—have twice the risk of married mothers.[19]

Marital status. Depression tends to affect the single, widowed, and divorced more than the married—unless the marriage is an unhappy one.

Loss or other trauma during childhood. The loss of a parent early in life increases the risk of depression considerably, as does childhood physical or sexual abuse.

Recent stress. A high level of recent stress raises the risk of depression in general, and increases the risk of relapses in people with bipolar disorder.

Just as no one is immune to depression, neither is anyone fated to have it. While multiple risk factors increase the likelihood of becoming depressed, they do not guarantee it.

Depression's Gender Gap

Women experience major depression—and all other types of depression except bipolar disorder—significantly more often than men. Scientists have yet to confirm the reason.

Quite a few experts believe the explanation may be at least partly hormonal. Before puberty, rates of depression are low and about the same in boys and girls—if anything, slightly higher in boys. At puberty, however, girls begin having remarkable increases in the rate of depression. Depression also increases

> *Women experience major depression—and all other types of depression except bipolar disorder—significantly more often than men.*

after childbirth, a time of great hormonal fluctuations. After menopause, the incidence of depression in women drops. What this pattern suggests to many experts is that the differing rates in depression between women and men has something to do with the hormonal differences.

Ellen Frank, Ph.D., a professor in psychiatry and psychology at the University of Pittsburgh School of Medicine, has her own theory—also partly based on hormones—to explain the difference.[20] She and a colleague have targeted a hormone called oxytocin, which promotes bonding between mates in animals, as well as mother-infant bonding in humans. Just before puberty, girls experience a fivefold rise in oxytocin levels, says Dr. Frank, "so their brain is kind of sitting in oxytocin soup." She theorizes that oxytocin may interact with other chemicals in a girl's body to strengthen interpersonal attachments. This poses no problems, she says, "so long as your attachment objects don't do you dirt. But should you have the love of your life tell you he's going out with somebody else, or your girlfriend tell you that she's decided to steal your boyfriend, then what we often see in the face of these interpersonal losses and disappointments is the onset of depression."

Dr. Frank's research is quite speculative at this point. Plenty of other theories exist to explain the difference in depression rates between the genders. In addition to hormonal theories, Dr. Frank notes, "there's a whole series of theories that have to do with the one-down social position of women—the reduced opportunities and that sort of thing. And certainly, along with that, there's the greater risk of various kinds of victimization—child sexual abuse and physical abuse. That's another theory." She herself doubts that hormones alone are responsible. "If it was purely biological change, then every female would be depressed, and we know that's not the case."

Depression in Teens

"Depression is quite similar in adolescents and adults," says Paul Rohde, Ph.D., a psychologist and senior scientist at the Oregon

Research Institute. "The one big difference, and it's a big difference, for teenagers is the core symptom may not be sadness but irritability. So, a teenager might never say they're really sad. Instead they're irritable, they're snapping at their parents, they're cranky, they're easily set off. That can be the core symptom of depression." In addition, he says, "the length of episodes for teenagers tends to be shorter than for adults."

In researching depression among teens, Dr. Rohde and colleagues interviewed adolescents twice during their high school years and again around age 24. "Our research suggests that if you were to go to a high school and talk to students, about 3 percent of students would be currently depressed—about 2.5 percent with major depression and about 0.5 percent with dysthymia." Ask about previous episodes, however, and rates rise. "We were really surprised that about 20 percent of our sample reported a history of clinically significant depression—so about 1 in 5 high school students," he says.[21]

Research by Dr. Rohde and colleagues also found that rates of bipolar disorder among high school students were fairly low. In any given year, they estimate that less than half of 1 percent had bipolar disorder.

People who experience depression in adolescence are at high risk of a recurrence in young adulthood, according to Dr. Rohde's and colleagues' research. "What we found is that about 42 percent of the people in our study who had depression as teenagers had a second episode during the college years. So there is already a high relapse or recurrence rate that's a big cause for concern," he says. Repeated episodes were more common in females. Risk factors for a recurrence included a history of previous recurrences, a family history of depression, and conflicts with parents.

Depressed teens may be battling on several fronts. "More so than adults, it looks like teenagers have multiple problems," says Dr.

> *About 42 percent of the people in our study who had depression as teenagers had a second episode during the college years. So there is already a high relapse or recurrence rate that's a big cause for concern.*
>
> —PAUL ROHDE, PH.D.

Rohde. "The majority of teenagers who are depressed are also struggling with anxiety or drug and alcohol problems or getting in trouble with the law or their parents." Adolescent depression, notes Dr. Rohde, is "a very serious condition."

Depression in Preteen Children

The idea of depression in children is extraordinarily sad. Nonetheless, preteen children can suffer from major depression, dysthymic disorder, and bipolar disorder as well as milder types of depression, says Jeffrey Kirchner, D.O., associate director of the family practice residency program at Pennsylvania's Lancaster General Hospital.[22] Dr. Kirchner hopes to increase his colleagues' awareness of the problem, which is frequently overlooked in medical practice.

Depressed children have similar symptoms to those of depressed adults. Like teens, many children become irritable rather than sad, but otherwise many of the symptoms are the same in adults and children: loss of interest in activities they used to enjoy, hopelessness, self-criticism, difficulty concentrating, and indecision. In children and teens, anxiety accompanies major depression more frequently than it does among adults. In major depression, children may believe that life is not worth living.

Depressed children may be afraid to go to school or reluctant to meet strangers. They may tend toward aches and pains, complaining of headaches and stomachaches, says Dr. Kirchner. Some depressed children have temper tantrums and behavioral problems. On the other hand, he says, "some children attempt to compensate for low self-esteem by trying to please others, trying to please their parents and their teachers, and actually might be doing well in school and excelling."

Children with dysthymic disorder have a chronic, low-grade depression, lasting at least one year, and on average about 4, says Dr. Kirchner. He describes dysthymia as "a mild, low-level depression off and on for days at a time." Although this description may sound benign, dysthymia is anything but. "Dysthymia is like a cancer of one's self-esteem," is how Alan Unis, M.D., a child psychiatrist and associate professor at the University of Washington, puts it. "It eats away at a kid's confidence, at a kid's hope, at a kid's drive toward mastery." It also frequently sets the stage for more severe forms of depression and other mental health concerns.

Although bipolar disorder usually first appears in adolescence or young adulthood, it can begin during childhood as well. Extreme irritability, spells of intense rage, hyperactivity, and overestimation of their abilities can be symptoms of bipolar disorder in children.

Children are more likely to be at risk for depression in certain circumstances, says Dr. Kirchner. "If there is a mother or father who has a history of a depressive disorder, it's probably the major risk factor— and one that can't be changed," he notes. Less significant risk factors include life-changing events such as "moving because of a parental change of jobs, the death of a sibling, the death of a grandparent, the death of a pet." These could trigger depression in children, he says, because "they may not have the support or the cognitive capabilities to deal with the process as an adult would."

In the past, doctors have tended to overlook depression in children. Doctors and teachers are becoming increasingly sensitive to its existence, however. If your child's behavior changes, and you are concerned about possible depression, a good place to start is the family doctor. He or she can check for illness and make a referral to a mental health care provider, if necessary. Intervening early can be helpful, says Dr. Kirchner. "Early intervention in many cases does seem to make a difference in long-term prognosis."

> *In the past, doctors have tended to overlook depression in children. Early intervention is important, however, because it can make a difference in long-term prognosis.*

CAUSES OF DEPRESSION

In ancient times, people in many cultures held demons responsible for depression. Ancient Greeks held a contrasting view, however. "The

Greeks believed that there were four basic bodily fluids, and that all medical and psychiatric problems could be explained by too much or too little of these fluids," says Dr. Mondimore. "They believed that depression, which they called melancholia, was caused by an excess of black bile." Since that time, others have seen depression as God's punishment for sin, or the result of sexual or other excesses. By the nineteenth century, theorists had identified several causes of depression still considered valid today: childbirth, loss, and a genetic predisposition, among others.

The twentieth century saw an explosion of research into various aspects of mental health and illness by numerous competing schools of thought, including psychoanalytic, behavioral, sociological, and biological. Each field developed its own theories of depression's causes. Descriptions of a few key theories—none proven beyond doubt—follow. To many experts today, these theories represent limited views of the issue.

Freud and Friends

Sigmund Freud initiated a school of thought that has since been termed *psychodynamic*. His focus was on uncovering conflicts arising in childhood between different parts of the self: for example, the conflict between anger at one's parents and the desire to please them. "He saw symptoms as usually being symbolic of underlying, unresolved personal conflict," says Dr. Mondimore. This view of depression as arising from the mind, not the brain, dominated psychiatric circles through a good part of the twentieth century, leading experts to focus on psychological explanations and treatments for depression.

Rats in a Cage: Behaviorism and Learned Helplessness

Behavioral scientists approached the study of the mind from an entirely different route: studying behavior and learning in animals as well as humans. Their research led to an intriguing explanation of the cause of depression. In one group of experiments, researchers gave dogs and rats painful electric shocks, without allowing them the possibility of escape. Eventually, the animals stopped even trying to escape during the shocks, no longer squirming or trying to chew their way out.

Later, the researchers put the same animals in new situations where they actually could escape being shocked. Instead of escaping, however, many repeated their old pattern of staying motionless. But when researchers dosed them with antidepressants, these animals learned how to escape the shocks easily.

From these and other experiments, researchers developed a theory of *learned helplessness*. Simply put, the theory states that animals (or humans) who endure inescapable trauma may come to believe that they are helpless. Faced with threatening situations later in life, they are likely to give up and become depressed.

How do modern researchers view this theory? "Certainly a feeling of helplessness is part of depression," says Larry Beutler, Ph.D., editor of the *Journal of Clinical Psychology*. He doesn't believe, however, that there is sufficient evidence that learned helplessness causes all depression. "It is one of the contributors to depression, that's the best one can say," he says.

The Power of Negative Thinking

Psychiatrist Aaron Beck, the originator of cognitive therapy, noted that extremely negative thoughts are common in depression. Traditionally, doctors have believed that depression caused such thinking, or cognition. Dr. Beck suggested that the cause-and-effect relationship might flow the other way: that distorted, negative thinking might itself lead to depression. "Beck believed that people developed beliefs that were untrue, characteristic ways of thinking about themselves and the world, that made them very prone to be depressed," says Dr. Mondimore. "In his view, people would have automatic thoughts—'I can't do anything right. I'll never amount to anything'—that they repeated to themselves, and basically talked themselves into states of demoralization." Dr. Beck proposed that people could resolve their depression, says Dr. Mondimore, "by countering those automatic thoughts, challenging them, and teaching themselves alternate thinking patterns."

In fact, studies have found that Dr. Beck's cognitive therapy is an effective treatment for depression. But does that mean that depressive thinking causes all depression? Most experts would argue no.

Neurotransmitter Deficiencies

The theories described above all fall on the "nurture" side of what is known as the nature versus nurture debate. In this basic controversy, subscribers to the "nature" side believe that depression is caused by biological factors such as genetics. Believers in the "nurture" side hold that depression is caused by factors in the person's environment, such as upbringing or traumatic experiences. In the 1950s, two startling discoveries led to a new theory on the "nature" side of the debate, specifically, that depression might arise from a deficiency in neurotransmitters—chemicals that carry messages from nerve to nerve in the brain.

One discovery was that the drug reserpine, used to treat hypertension, made some people suicidally depressed. Researchers discovered that reserpine depletes the neurotransmitters serotonin and norepinephrine.[23] Around the same time, doctors discovered that iproniazid, a tuberculosis drug, made many people taking it feel much more cheerful—and not just because their tuberculosis was improving. Iproniazid turned out to inhibit an enzyme that breaks down norepinephrine and serotonin. With iproniazid on board, more of these neurotransmitters were available for sending messages between brain cells.

After these discoveries, drug companies began madly developing the first antidepressants, medications specifically used to treat depression. They designed a group of drugs called monoamine oxidase inhibitors (MAOIs) and, later, a group called the tricyclics, to increase the store of neurotransmitters such as norepinephrine and serotonin in the brain. The drugs turned out to be quite effective at relieving depression. In a sort of cart-leading-the-horse approach, scientists developed a theory that depression is caused by deficiencies in neurotransmitters. The theory held sway in psychiatric circles for many years—at least in those circles not dominated by Freudians.

One problem with this theory is that nobody developed a very satisfactory explanation for how the neurotransmitters came to be deficient in the first place. At best, what research found was that lower than normal levels of neurotransmitters accompanied depression, not that they necessarily caused it. Recent researchers are questioning whether the original theory holds water. Says Dr. Gitlin, "We think there are certainly some abnormalities in some of the important neurotransmitters such as norepinephrine, serotonin, and dopamine, but are those the cause of the depression? Are they the effect of the depression? Are there really other brain chemicals that are even more important that we just haven't identified yet? What triggers the abnormality? What are the abnormalities? Is it really that there isn't enough of a neurotransmitter, or is it that the brain is not regulating it correctly? Those are all questions that are absolutely unanswered as of this moment."

> *One problem with the theory that depression is caused by deficiencies in neurotransmitters is that there is no satisfactory explanation for how the neurotransmitters came to be deficient in the first place.*

Genetics

Studies show that people are two to four times more likely to develop depression if they have a close blood relative (parent, sibling, or child) who has been depressed.[24] Does this information tell us that depression must be genetic? Not in itself—because genes are not the only thing passed down in families, whose members also share habits, coping styles, and many experiences. Studies of twins that have been adopted and other research, however, strongly suggest that genetics contributes to depression.

"The genetic research seems to indicate that there are probably half a dozen or a dozen genes involved in depression," says Dr. Mondimore, "and they are probably fairly common genes that a lot of people have. So genetics doesn't explain it all."

Many researchers have concluded that genetics causes some people to be more vulnerable to depression, but believe that environmental factors, such as upbringing and other life experiences, also play a role.

"If genetics doesn't explain it all, then some kind of environmental factors must," says Dr. Mondimore. "If we can find out what it is that can trigger this illness in genetically vulnerable people, then we can give people specific recommendations about various things," he notes. "There is a lot of very intensive research going on in that area."

> *When it comes to depression, heredity does not appear to be destiny.*

Bipolar disorder appears to be more closely tied to genetics than other types of depression. People who have a parent or sibling with bipolar disorder are six to eight times more likely to have the disorder themselves.[25] Here, too, however, many people who would seem to be at risk genetically do not develop the condition.

When it comes to depression, heredity does not appear to be destiny. Since our genes are (currently, at least) one of the few things we really cannot change, this fact offers hope.

The Latest Theory: Multiple Causes of Depression

After decades of disagreement, the long-standing nature versus nurture debate may be running out of gas. Some of the most exciting recent research on depression links neurochemistry and physiology with psychology. More and more, researchers are trying to find precise connections between our brains and our minds. For example, research indicates that our brains actually change structure as we develop and learn. Both negative experiences and positive ones have the potential to alter brain structure and function.

Increasingly, theorists today believe a host of factors—neurological, biochemical, genetic, psychological, and social—contribute to depression. In this *biopsychosocial model* of depression, theorists believe that different factors may account for depression to different degrees in different individuals, but no part of life goes disregarded. Research from a wide variety of fields contributes to experts' understanding. Rather than a limited, one-note approach, many believe that the biopsychosocial model holds the most hope for improving our understanding of depression.

SUMMARY

Depression is a pervasive disorder affecting the mood. Its symptoms can be emotional, mental, and physical, causing—for example—sadness or irritability, difficulty concentrating, and changes in appetite. Many types of depression exist, among them major depressive disorder, bipolar disorder, and dysthymia. These three types of depression together affect about 9.5 percent of adults in the United States in a given year.

Depression can affect people from any age group, income level, and cultural background. Many highly talented and well-known individuals—including movie stars Carrie Fisher and Patty Duke and Pulitzer Prize–winning author William Styron—have suffered from forms of depression.

Depression appears to arise as a result of a number of factors, which may be biological, psychological, and social. Many researchers today believe that people can inherit a genetic susceptibility to depression. Experiences such as child abuse, loss of a parent early in life, or extreme stress can also raise the risk.

Depression has negative consequences beyond its own symptoms. Substance abuse and suicide are two possible complications. Decisions people make while depressed may be contrary to their best interests. Sometimes, such decisions can lead to a downward spiral in their feelings, thoughts, and behavior, making it harder to resolve the depression. Yet this situation is reversible. The good news is that depression is a very treatable condition. With treatment, people can reverse the direction of the spiral, raising their mood, making better choices, and putting their lives on a positive course once again. The next chapter discusses ways to obtain good treatment.

CHAPTER 2

Getting Help:
The Diagnosis and Beyond

❧

When I first went to my HMO, they diagnosed me with just having a small problem with depression. They were just shy of worthless. I had a couple of sessions and then they said, okay, you're done. And I was just totally freaking out at that time. I ended up seeing a vocational counselor. She also worked on other things, and depression was one of them. I ended up having, at her suggestion, a test called the MMPI [Minnesota Multiphasic Personality Inventory]. And it said, in big letters, that I was clearly depressed and having a lot of trouble.

—JOHN, A TEACHER WITH RECURRENT DEPRESSION

IF YOU THINK you are depressed, what do you do next? One option is to see your doctor at once for an evaluation. Another is to take a few minutes and complete the Depression Screening Test (see page 37), developed by National Depression Screening Day Executive Director Douglas G. Jacobs, M.D. Be aware, however, that this test (or any written test) is not designed to provide an actual diagnosis of depression. For that, you need a complete evaluation by a psychiatrist or other health care professional. (If, after taking this test, you would like a more detailed screening before making an appointment with a health care provider, visitwww.mentalhealthscreening.org for the location of a free depression screening near you.)

GETTING A DIAGNOSIS

The first step in receiving help for depression is getting a diagnosis. "There are different kinds of depression. It's important to have a diagnosis so that one can have a proper treatment plan," says David Dunner, M.D., codirector of the University of Washington's Center for Anxiety and Depression.

Where should you turn first? For most people, the answer is their internist, family doctor, or other primary care provider. A primary care provider is a health care provider—physician, nurse practitioner, physician assistant, osteopathic physician, or naturopathic physician, among others—who diagnoses and treats the vast majority of common medical problems, and coordinates care with specialists. There are very good reasons for starting with a primary care provider if you think you have depression. "There are medical causes as well as psychiatric causes of those symptoms," says Dr. Dunner. "Sometimes the diagnosis leads to changing a medication that might be causing the depression, or adding a thyroid hormone if the symptoms are due to low thyroid, for example. So, a medical evaluation is very important."

Michael Yapko, Ph.D., psychologist and author, concurs. Even for children, he recommends starting with a visit to the family doctor. "It's always a good idea because there is a chance that there may be something physical going on," he says.

Most people already have relationships with their doctors, and find it relatively easy to see them for help, compared to the challenge of locating a psychiatrist, psychologist, or other mental health care specialist.

Depression Screening Test

Take the following quiz to see if you might be depressed:

1.	I feel sad most of the time.	Yes	No
2.	I have trouble doing or enjoying the things I used to.	Yes	No
3.	I sleep too little or too much.	Yes	No
4.	I notice I am losing weight and/or my appetite.	Yes	No
5.	I can't make decisions.	Yes	No
6.	I feel hopeless and/or worthless.	Yes	No
7.	I get tired for no reason.	Yes	No
8.	I think about killing myself.	Yes	No

If you answered yes to 5 or more of these questions, and you have felt this way every day for several weeks, you may be suffering from clinical depression and should consult a health care professional.

If you answered yes to question 8, seek help immediately, regardless of your answer to any of the other questions.

Source: Adapted from D.G. Jacobs, Depression Screening Test (Wellesley Hills, MA: Screening for Mental Health, www.mentalhealthscreening.org, 2000.) Used with permission.

Primary care providers are equipped to handle most health problems affecting their patients. Their time allotted for each visit, however, is typically short—often only 10 or 12 minutes—and their orientation may be more toward physical ailments than psychiatric ones. When seeing a primary care provider, it's helpful to alert him or her that you suspect you are suffering from depression. "A lot of times the diagnosis works by a patient coming in to a primary care office saying, 'I think I have depression. I have all these symptoms I read about in some magazine,'" says Dr. Dunner.

Besides primary care providers, a variety of mental health care specialists can diagnose the different types of depression. These include psychiatrists, psychologists, psychiatric nurse practitioners, and clinical social workers.

Sometimes people choose to see a pastoral counselor, addictions treatment specialist, or another type of health care provider for depression—and may feel they are receiving a great deal of benefit.

Bipolar Disorder: A Difficult Diagnosis

Bipolar disorder is one of the most difficult of the mood disorders to diagnose. People with this condition typically see several doctors over a number of years before getting an accurate diagnosis. Yet the earlier appropriate treatment begins, the better the prognosis.

Why do doctors miss this diagnosis so often? Gary Sachs, M.D., principal investigator of STEP-BD, a long-term federally funded study examining treatments for bipolar disorder, says, "Unlike depression, where patients are feeling absolutely horrible, and everybody around can see that they're suffering, with the high phase of bipolar disorder, patients do not perceive the need for any treatment. The patient's not going to come to the doctor and say, 'I'm feeling much too good today.'"

Often doctors and patients only recognize these high phases when a manic episode leads to extreme difficulties, such as indictment for embezzlement or bankruptcy proceedings. "Without those big, bold, secondary problems, it's very hard to recognize that there's a problem," says Dr. Sachs. "Unless you're systematically looking for it, you're not going to see it." For someone with bipolar type II, with milder highs than in type I, diagnosis may take even longer.

The other reason diagnosis is difficult is that during a phase of depression, when someone is more likely to see the doctor, the person

Although some of these health care providers may be trained and licensed to diagnose mental disorders—for example, with separate licensure as a social worker—many may not be. In general, don't assume that everyone providing (or claiming to provide) treatment for depression is qualified to provide a diagnosis. The safest course is to get a diagnosis from a primary care provider, psychiatrist, psychologist, or other appropriate mental health care specialist. Then, under the supervision of your doctor or mental health care provider, you may choose to seek treatment elsewhere.

---

may not recall earlier highs. "Like many psychiatric illnesses, bipolar disorder distorts the patients' perceptions," says Dr. Sachs. "When they're well, they can tell you lots of things in great detail and very reliably. But when they're ill, if you ask people with depression if they've ever been happy, let alone manic, you often hear, 'Oh no, I've been like this all my life.'"

Judith Snyder, an author and parent educator, saw a number of psychotherapists for depression before she was diagnosed with a form of bipolar disorder. Finally, after seeing one psychotherapist for many years, she burst out, "I don't understand. Why am I here every year and a half to two years for a really bad depression?" Judith's outburst prompted a much-needed discussion with her therapist. "We talked about other times of the year when I had these feelings of grandiosity, spending lots of money, needing lots of freedom, and wanting to get out of the house," she says—all symptoms, for Judith, of her high phases.

Since treatment for bipolar disorder differs significantly from treatment for other types of depression, accurate diagnosis is critical. It behooves everyone—primary care providers, specialists, and people with symptoms of depression—to be on the lookout for signs of bipolar disorder.

Information for the Doctor

To increase the likelihood of an accurate diagnosis, which in turn increases the likelihood of successful treatment, it's helpful to provide the doctor with as much relevant information as possible. Following are suggestions for information you may wish to gather and bring with you to your first appointment.

Symptom Log

Charting your symptoms in a systematic way can help you and your doctor find important patterns. You can use a diary or jot notes on your calendar (see figure 2.1). Some experts recommend rating your mood daily, using some kind of consistent scale. For example, you might rate your mood on a scale of +3 to −3, with +3 indicating euphoria (feeling incredibly great) and −3 indicating deep depression. You might also want to note symptoms such as headache, anxiety, or decreased appetite; how well you slept; and how energetic, restless, or lethargic you felt each day. In addition, you may want to jot down factors that seem significant to your moods: use of alcohol, major arguments or other stressors, important successes, or the beginning or end of your menstrual period. You can use the same log to keep track of changes in your treatment.

A log like this—the more time it covers the better—can help you and your doctor determine whether or not your moods are linked to physical symptoms, the seasons, your menstrual cycle, your use of alcohol, or particular stressors such as final exams or job changes. Even notes from a week or two may help in diagnosis. Logs can be a lot more reliable than memory.

As Bruce, manager of a small graphics business, puts it, regarding his own recurrent depression: "The problem is that, when you are not particularly depressed, it's so easy to look at things and say, 'Gosh, everything seems fine. Everything is wonderful. There is no problem particularly. How could I possibly have felt bad?' When you begin to feel good again, you can't bring those thoughts back."

Date	Mood Rating (-3 to +3)	Symptoms	Significant events	Treatment notes
6/2	-2	headache, no appetite, hard to get out of bed	skipped party due to low mood	
6/3	-2	little appetite	started period	
6/4	-1		praised at work	MD appt—upped Paxil to 30 mg every morning
6/5	-2	no appetite, slept badly		
6/6	-1	hungrier		

Figure 2.1—Sample Symptom Log

Health History

If you are seeing a different doctor from your primary care provider for your initial appointment to assess your depression, be sure to tell that doctor about any other health problems you have, including the scientific names of any diagnoses you have received. If you're unsure about your current diagnoses, you can make a quick call to your primary care provider's office and ask the nurse to look them up in your chart. Some ailments can cause depression, or make certain treatments unsafe, so you'll want your doctor to know about them before diagnosis and treatment. In addition, you might ask for the date of your last physical exam, and what blood tests were done at that time. This can reassure the new doctor you are consulting that certain health problems associated with depression are unlikely to be causing your symptoms; for example, a recent exam and blood test may indicate that your thyroid function is normal. Don't assume that your regular doctor has shared this information with a specialist you are seeing.

Current Medications

It is also a good idea to compile a list of any treatments you're using, including prescriptions, over-the-counter drugs, herbs, vitamins, and other supplements. There are two reasons for making such a list. First, certain medications, such as blood pressure medicine and steroids, can cause depression in some people, says A. John Rush, M.D., professor of psychiatry at the University of Texas. Second, although your medications or supplements may seem harmless, they can still potentially interact with treatments your doctor might prescribe for depression. The natural remedy 5-HTP, for example, may raise your serotonin levels dangerously high if combined with antidepressants in the Prozac family.

Mental Health History

If you've had mental health problems in the past, whether they were treated or not, it can be helpful to recall the dates, any diagnoses, and any treatment you may have had. If you've used medication for depression, try to recall or obtain its name, the dose, and your response. How much did it help? Did you have any side effects? If you've had psychotherapy, do you know if the therapist used a particular technique? What were the results? Write down this information and bring it with you to your appointment.

Family History

Finally, scan through your family in your mind—or call them up and talk to them. Did any of your blood relatives have problems with depression or substance abuse? Was anyone hospitalized for mental health problems? Did any of your relatives die by suicide? Again, bring the information you've uncovered to your appointment. Family history can often help with diagnosis, particularly for bipolar disorder.

Gathering all of the suggested information may seem like a lot to do. Certainly, if you're very depressed, don't feel compelled to do all of it. The most important thing is to get to a doctor. If you can take only one or two steps, try to bring with you the names of medications you are taking now, and a list of any treatments for depression you have tried in the past.

After all your work, it is possible that your doctor will ask you only a few brief questions and ignore much of the information you provided, particularly if this is your first experience with depression. If you believe your doctor isn't taking you or your problem seriously, it may be worth saying this directly—or finding another doctor.

Other Ways to Prepare for Your Visit

Before your appointment, you might take a few minutes to consider what your personal concerns are. It's surprisingly easy, in the midst of a high-anxiety visit, to forget to ask a simple question. During your visit, it's appropriate to raise factual questions about your condition,

Rebecca's Story: Getting Help Early

At age 18, Rebecca was coping well with her first year of college, which included an introductory course in psychology. Always a hard-working student, Rebecca started staying up later and later to finish her assignments. After several nights of little sleep, she noticed that she was thinking and talking very fast. She felt very intelligent, seeming to understand concepts quickly and with little effort. Her sense of humor also seemed to have burgeoned overnight; she had her friends in stitches with her nonstop jokes.

After a few days, however, she noticed that some of her friends had stopped laughing at her wit. Instead, they were looking some-what concerned. Rebecca, who had never had a mental health problem in her life, recalled the description of bipolar disorder from

and also to bring up your fears and worries—for example, if you are afraid that a psychiatric diagnosis might cause you to lose your job. Bringing a list of your questions can help ensure that your doctor addresses your concerns.

The best time to raise your questions is often near the end of the session, after the doctor has arrived at a tentative diagnosis or determined that another visit—or referral—is necessary. If your visit is scheduled to be a short one, however, it may be best to inform your doctor of your main concerns right away. That way you can be sure something important to you won't be forgotten at the end in a flurry of paper-work and prescriptions.

Finally, you may want to bring someone with you to the appointment. The presence of a family member or friend may ease your anxiety, even if he or she stays in the waiting room. Your companion may also be able to help answer questions if you are too depressed or confused to respond.

her lectures. That same day, she took herself to the student health center, recounted her symptoms, and asked, "Could this be manic-depression?"

It turned out that Rebecca's guess was correct. The doctor arranged for a brief hospital stay until her condition was stabilized with several medications, including lithium. Rebecca has been conscientious in her care and self-care ever since. Although she has not been trouble-free, she has had a relatively benign experience with her disorder. Now 34, a respected high school English teacher, she attributes much of her success to her good self-care and assertive attitude. Getting help early, paying attention to her symptoms, and voicing her concerns with her doctors have undoubtedly helped her control her illness.

WHAT TO EXPECT AT THE DOCTOR'S OFFICE

No matter what type of health care provider you see, expect to be treated with courtesy, respect, and confidentiality. If you aren't, something is wrong, and it's not with you.

Confidentiality

All licensed health care providers are required to keep client information confidential. Some jurisdictions have extra laws protecting the confidentiality of mental health records. There are exceptions. For example, the law requires that health professionals report to authorities any client's threats to harm another person. Health care providers must also report evidence of current abuse of protected groups of people such as children or the elderly. The health care provider's records may also be subpoenaed in legal cases.

If you are using insurance to pay for your mental health care, expect to sign a waiver giving the insurance company the right to review your records.

If you are a minor, your health care provider may talk about you with your parents—but even in this case you can request that certain topics be left just between you and the doctor.

If you have any concerns about what information might be shared with whom, talk about it with your health care provider. You need to feel that you can talk freely, without worrying about what information other people will obtain.

Medical History

A key part of your initial diagnosis, as noted earlier, is ruling out problems with your physical health. On your first visit, your doctor should ask about your general health, any medications you're taking, and other illnesses or physical symptoms you may have. The doctor should also ask questions specific to depression: for example, whether you have been feeling sad, blue, or down in the dumps, and whether you retain interest in activities that normally have given you pleasure. In addition, according to Dr. Rush, the doctor should ask about:

- Your sleep, appetite, and ability to concentrate, as well as other symptoms of depression

- How well you are able to function in your life

- The course of the illness—when it started, when it became more severe

- Any previous episodes

- Your family history

- Your use of alcohol and drugs

- Whether you're having thoughts about death or suicide

If the doctor doesn't ask for such information, says Dr. Rush, people being seen for depression "should definitely come up with it spontaneously." Don't be afraid to give the doctor this information, whether he or she asks for it or not.

Physical Exam

If you're seeing a primary care provider, he or she may perform a physical exam. The exam won't help to diagnose depression per se, since there is no specific finding on a physical exam that indicates depression. The main purpose of the exam is to look for signs of health problems that can cause or contribute to symptoms of depression.

As thyroid problems are common in depression, the doctor may palpate your thyroid gland, located at the front and sides of your neck. (Some primary care providers rely on laboratory tests to check your thyroid function.) Depending on your age and health history, the doctor may also take your blood pressure, listen to your heart and lungs, and palpate your belly for signs of problems with your liver, spleen, or other organs. He or she may do a neurological exam, testing your reflexes, balance, coordination, and other functions of your nervous system.

Finally, the doctor may perform a *mental status exam*, a systematic assessment of your thinking and emotions. The exam includes observing your appearance, manner, speech, and mood; looking for evidence of hallucinations, delusions, obsessions, or compulsions; testing your memory, attention and concentration; and evaluating your insight and judgment.

> *The doctor may perform a* mental status exam, *a systematic assessment of your thinking and emotions.*

Laboratory Tests

As with the physical exam, there is no particular laboratory test that definitively shows you have depression. Doctors perform such tests primarily to rule out physical illnesses that might be causing your symptoms.

Common laboratory tests for depression are a blood count to check for anemia or infection and a group of tests (usually run on a single blood sample) called a *chemistry profile* or *chem panel* (different laboratories use different names). This second group of tests screens for such problems as diabetes, liver or kidney ailments, and certain mineral imbalances. If the doctor has a particular reason to suspect a specific condition—for example, diabetes—he or she may want a more sensitive test such as a fasting blood sugar test.

As noted previously, an underactive thyroid gland can cause or accompany depression, so the doctor may suggest a thyroid test if it's not part of the chem panel. The usual test measures levels of thyroid stimulating hormone (TSH). High levels suggest an underactive thyroid.

Based on your symptoms or health history, your doctor may also suggest blood tests for mononucleosis, HIV, or other infections.

Naturopathically oriented physicians may recommend additional tests for systemic yeast infection (an overgrowth of *Candida*), digestive malabsorption, or heavy metal exposure, among others. Some conventional physicians question the value of these tests, and may even suggest that some of these conditions are unlikely to be causing your symptoms.

Before any laboratory test, it's generally a good idea to ask what the doctor expects to learn from the test and how the results might affect your treatment.

PROS AND CONS OF GETTING A DIAGNOSIS

Some people strongly resist the idea of being diagnosed with a mental health condition—even one so common as depression. "Patients aren't terribly accepting of having a psychiatric disorder," says Alexander Young, M.D., director of the health services unit at the Los Angeles Veterans Administration Mental Illness Research, Education and Clinical Center and assistant professor of psychiatry at the University of California at Los Angeles. That's often because we think of the state of our mind as being somehow more reflective of ourselves, more important to our self-image, than the state of our body. Psychiatric diagnoses can bring up stereotypes of "insanity" or memories of schoolkids' taunts. Unfortunately, some members of society still attach a stigma to mental health disorders. That stigma is fading, certainly in the case of depression. The willingness of public figures such as *60 Minutes* host

> *S*ome people strongly resist the idea of being diagnosed with a mental health condition—even one so common as depression.

Mike Wallace, or the former governor of Florida, Lawton Chiles, to publicly acknowledge their depression has helped considerably.

Although judgmental people—including family members—can misuse a diagnosis, nonetheless, having one is crucial for appropriate treatment. You don't need to share your diagnosis with anyone except the professionals who treat you (and your insurance company, if your mental health care is covered). It's really nobody's business but your own, and your immediate family's.

Knowing your diagnosis can be tremendously empowering. The knowledge enables you to obtain specific information about your condition from reputable sources (such as the resources listed in the appendixes). It enables you to question the doctor with more confidence about your condition and the options for its treatment, or to seek a second opinion, if the diagnosis doesn't seem to fit. It can also help you to assess the appropriateness of your treatment. For example, if a health care provider suggests that you continue treatment long after your symptoms have abated, you may wonder if he or she is on the up-and-up. Knowing your diagnosis can help you compare your health care provider's recommendations with those of experts in the field. You may learn that for your diagnosis, experts often do recommend continuing treatment long after symptoms have diminished.

Some mental health care providers believe in not telling clients their diagnoses, for a variety of reasons. (The classic Freudian response to any question, as parodied in the media, is "Und vy do you vant to know?") In a few cases, this reluctance may arise because the health care provider, while trained to do some kind of counseling, lacks the training or licensure to diagnose. If your health care provider doesn't tell you your diagnosis, it's appropriate to ask. If you feel the doctor is withholding the information, you might ask him or her to share the information with your primary care provider.

IS THE DIAGNOSIS CORRECT?

Since our mental states are so connected to our sense of self, it can be a shock when someone tells us we have depression or another mental health disorder. In particular, many people diagnosed with bipolar disorder initially refuse to believe it, although others—such as actress Patty Duke—receive the diagnosis with relief, finally having an explanation for their mood swings.

If you suspect your diagnosis may not be accurate, it's absolutely appropriate to get a second opinion. In today's world, requests for second opinions are commonplace. Far better to get a second opinion immediately than to harbor misgivings about your treatment, the health care provider you're seeing, or both. Trust is an important component in the success of treatment, and even the most highly qualified practitioner can make a mistake.

SELECTING A SPECIALIST

Once you receive your diagnosis, should you stay with the doctor who diagnosed you, or should you seek care elsewhere? Most people do the first, perhaps because it's easiest, because they resist the idea of seeing a mental health care provider, or because they trust the doctor they usually see. Insurance coverage of mental health care specialists

Sources of Referrals for Mental Health Specialists

If you decide to see a specialist, how do you go about finding one? The most obvious way is to ask your primary care provider for a referral. Other sources include:

- Your health insurance company

- Family or friends

- One of the national organizations listed in appendix A

- Employee Assistance Program at your workplace (if available)

- Your religious institution

- The department of psychiatry at a local hospital or medical school

- Your local community mental health association (usually listed in the front of the phone book)

can also be an issue. Dr. Young, who studied treatment of depression and anxiety disorders, found that most people he surveyed were unaware of their mental health coverage. Many people in the United States have none.

Some people choose to see a specialist because they desire services their primary care provider cannot offer, such as specific types of psychotherapy, or because they haven't improved with primary care treatment. People with bipolar disorder, who often have more complicated medication regimens, may prefer seeing a psychiatrist who, as a specialist, has more opportunity to stay on top of the latest research on their condition.

One decision that can be intimidating is the type of specialist to see. As table 1 indicates, many different types of health professionals are qualified to treat depression. If you know in advance that you will

Table 1.   Health Care Providers Who Treat People with Depression

Type of Health Care Provider	Usual Professional Degree or License	Can Prescribe Medications?	Can Offer Psychotherapy?
Primary care doctor (family practitioner, pediatrician, internist, GP)	MD or DO	Yes	Usually not
Primary care nurse practitioner (family, pediatric, or adult)	RN, usually master's degree	Varies with state	Usually not
Primary care physician assistant (family, pediatric, or adult)	PA, usually master's degree	Varies with state	Usually not
Naturopathic physician	ND (licensing varies with state)	Varies with state	Depends on training
Psychiatrist	MD or DO	Yes	Usually
Clinical psychologist	MA, PhD or PsyD	No	Yes
Clinical social worker	Usually MSW	No	Usually
Psychiatric nurse practitioner	RN, usually master's degree	Varies with state	Usually

Other psychiatric nurses	RN or LPN	No	Depends on training
Marital therapist	MA, MSW, PhD, or RN	No	Usually focuses on relationship counseling
Family therapist	MA, MSW, PhD, or RN	No	Usually focuses on relationship and family counseling
Other counselors (mental health counselor, pastoral counselor, addictions treatment counselor, and so on)	Variable; may range from MA/PhD to none	No	Depends on training; may be informal or limited to one particular approach
Other alternative health care providers (bodyworker, herbalist, acupuncturist, movement therapist, and so on)	Variable; may range from professional degree to none; best seen as providing adjunct treatment as part of health care team	No	Only with extra training

Note: Some details (such as the ability of certain health care providers to prescribe medications) vary from state to state in the United States. Statements are generalizations; exceptions may exist.

need medication, you may want to select a mental health specialist who can prescribe it—for example, a psychiatrist or perhaps a psychiatric nurse practitioner.

Often, people see a psychiatrist or primary care provider for medication and another mental health care provider for psychotherapy. Medications aside, most people find that personality, experience, and specific training (for instance, in a particular type of psychotherapy) matter more than the type of degree or licensure.

Problems with Primary Care Treatment of Depression

Most adults with depression seek care only from their primary care provider, rather than a specialist, according to a study headed by Dr. Young.[1] The study also demonstrated that this may not always be the best choice.

One study found that only 19 percent of people who received all their treatment for anxiety or depression from a primary care provider received appropriate care.

In the study, Dr. Young and colleagues analyzed data from 1,636 adults who had probable major depression, dysthymia, or anxiety disorders, based on a brief psychiatric interview. Their findings? Besides noting that most people saw only a primary care provider, they also found that only about 19 percent who received all their treatment from a primary care provider received appropriate care. In contrast, 90 percent of those who saw mental health specialists received appropriate care. People's income and type of insurance didn't seem to make a difference in whether or not they received appropriate treatment.

"Primary care providers may not have the time or expertise for their assessment or to provide treatment, particularly counseling or psychotherapy," says Dr. Young. "Rates of appropriate care are much higher in the specialty practice than in the primary care practice." His study defined specialists as psychiatrists, psychologists, social workers, psychiatric nurses, or counselors, and defined "appropriate care" for depression as at least two months of an antidepressant or four sessions of counseling—fairly generous criteria.

One reason for the gap in appropriate treatment may lie in people's acceptance of having a psychiatric disorder, says Dr. Young. "The people that are seen in specialty practices are willing to accept that they have a psychiatric disorder." In contrast, he notes, "primary care providers carry the burden of identifying mental health conditions and convincing people to accept treatment."

Some groups are at particularly high risk of receiving less-than-appropriate care. "Appropriate treatment was less likely for people who were black or male," notes Dr. Young. In addition, individuals in their twenties or over 50 or 60 had a higher likelihood of not being appropriately treated. If you fall into one of these categories, you may wish to take steps to increase your odds of getting proper diagnosis and treatment, as discussed earlier.

Much of the problem lies in underdiagnosis. If you are savvy to the possibility that you have depression, and alert your primary care provider, you are more likely to get appropriate care. "If you ask your internist for Prozac, the chances of getting it are probably quite high," says Dr. Young.

Dr. Young believes that primary care practices are capable of improving their care for depression. Until that time comes, however, many people may be better off with specialists. "If you suspect you have a psychiatric disorder and have tried to go to primary care but aren't getting better, or aren't getting what you need, I'd definitely say go straight to a mental health specialist," says Dr. Young.

If you suspect you have a psychiatric disorder and have tried to go to primary care but aren't getting better, or aren't getting what you need, I'd definitely say go straight to a mental health specialist.

—ALEXANDER YOUNG, M.D.

Fred's Story: Help from Spiritual Counseling

Different individuals can provide different kinds of help for people with depression. Fred was haunted by fears and concerns about religion during his depression. He assumed he would soon find himself in a place of everlasting, horrifying punishment. Fred first sought care for his depression from a psychiatrist. He credits much of his improvement, however, to a priest who provided pastoral counseling. For over a year, the priest met with Fred, gently talking to him about forgiveness, about opening himself to the love that was everywhere. Eventually, Fred's depression lifted, and he was able to return to work and his normal life. His fears about religion no longer tormented him.

Tips on Selecting a Specialist

Before making an appointment to see a specialist, you may want to gather some information. The following are some issues you may want to consider (not all will apply to everyone):

- Make sure the specialist is covered by your insurance plan. Find out if your insurance requires any kind of referral, and how many visits are covered.

- What are the specialist's credentials—for example, education and licensure? If a physician, is he or she board-certified? You can call the state licensing board to make sure the specialist is licensed.

- Think about convenience. How close is the specialist to home or work? Are there evening or weekend hours? Any charges for missed appointments? Is the office wheelchair accessible? You can usually ascertain this information by talking with the specialist's office staff.

- Ask the specialist or office staff about any specific treatment needs you have. Does he or she have expertise in a particular type of depression, or a particular treatment approach? Can he or she prescribe medications?

- Think about specific qualities you may be looking for, for example: male or female; a specific cultural background; willingness to include you in decisions about your care; or a preference for natural remedies. Again, you can usually ascertain most of this information with a call to the specialist's office.

- Think about emergencies. Can you call after-hours? How and in what circumstances? Can the specialist admit you to a hospital if you become suicidal or dangerously manic? Which hospital, and is it covered by your insurance plan?

- Is the specialist willing to spend a few minutes talking to you on the phone, to see if it's a good match? If not, it's generally not helpful to try to discuss your symptoms at length with the office staff or specialist before your appointment. You risk alienating both staff and doctor.

It's important to listen with your heart, as well as your head, when choosing the person who treats your depression. The relationship between you and your doctor is a critical component to getting well. It can be a comfort, when you're feeling low, to know that your doctor cares about you, and that you can rely on him or her to treat you with respect and compassion as well as clinical expertise.

When depressed, we may be more inclined to be passive, to lack self-confidence, and to have a hard time making decisions. Still, we usually retain our gut sense of trusting some people and mistrusting others. Be prepared, when first seeing a new doctor, to spend as much time evaluating him or her—either through observation or by asking specific questions—as the doctor spends evaluating you. Here are some areas you may wish to consider:

- Does the doctor answer your questions directly?

- Does the doctor make good eye contact?

- Does the doctor treat you with respect, as an intelligent person, acknowledging your right to information?

- Is the doctor a good listener?

- Does the doctor seem genuinely caring?

- Does the doctor have another specialist that he or she turns to for help in difficult situations? (Far from being a sign of weakness, this is actually a sign of professionalism.)

- Does the doctor have particular goals for your treatment? How do they compare with your own goals?

- Do you trust the doctor as a person? Do you trust him or her to do a good job treating you?

ONGOING COMMUNICATION WITH YOUR DOCTOR

A working alliance with your health care provider allows you to depend on the doctor for both treatment and emotional support. Boosting your self-esteem and self-confidence is an important part of the doctor's job. It's also the doctor's job to listen and respect your feelings, even when he or she disagrees with your choices. It's your job to be as honest as you can with the doctor.

An effective health care provider encourages you to air your feelings and concerns, even when he or she might strenuously advocate a particular approach. In her book, *An Unquiet Mind*, psychologist Kay

David's Story: Developing Trust over Time

David, a stockbroker, developed major depression following separating from his wife. He sought care from a clinical social worker. At first he was full of doubts. "The idea of therapy itself was foreign to me. So I checked it out with a lot of people, not just one." After several friends told him how much they'd gained from psychotherapy, he committed himself to the process.

After several sessions, he developed a great deal of trust in his therapist. "She didn't put me down for my feelings. So I wasn't less of a person for talking with her. She took me seriously. She was a good listener, and a good interpreter—a good translator of what I was saying. And of course I had to make sure that what she was saying was true." David's growing trust in his therapist inspired him to work very hard to get better. "If she asked me to do something, and said it was important that I do it, then I did it. She would ask me to write down what I said to myself when I was mad at myself. Then I realized of course that I'd been saying that to myself all my life."

When David's therapist suggested that he see a psychiatrist for antidepressant medication, he did. He saw the psychiatrist only once, in order to get a prescription his primary care provider could refill.

Several years after completing work with his therapist, David retains the benefits. "I'm a lot more confident. I like myself. I know my strengths. I accept myself a lot better. Basically I trusted this person to help me discover myself," he says. His depression resolved when he was under treatment and has not recurred.

Redfield Jamison describes her repeated refusal to take lithium for her bipolar disorder, even when this refusal inevitably led to bouts of mania or depression. Each time, her psychiatrist patiently worked with her until she decided to take lithium again.[2]

A Therapeutic Alliance

A good relationship between health care provider and client is essential for effective treatment, says Leslie Sokol, Ph.D., clinical psychologist and education coordinator at the Beck Institute in Bala Cynwyd, Pennsylvania. "You can't do any kind of therapy without a good relationship." She notes that psychotherapists need to have empathy, be supportive and nonjudgmental, and understand their patients. Dr. Sokol gives patients a feedback form at the end of every session, and also asks for feedback verbally. For example, at the end of each session, she asks, "Is there anything I did that rubbed you the wrong way? How do you feel about today's session?"

Jennifer's Story: The Value of Rapport

Jennifer, an attorney and mother of two, has had several bouts of moderate depression, for which she has seen different psychotherapists.

"I remember the first psychiatrist I saw," she said. "All he did was ask me questions and stare at his pencil." Jennifer never felt comfortable in his office.

She also felt a lack of rapport with the second therapist she saw, years later. The third therapist Jennifer tried, however, took a very different approach. "He didn't just sit there," she said. "He made suggestions." When Jennifer happened to mention an interest in painting lessons, he pulled out a phone book and gave her a number to call. "I called the number and took the lessons," she said. "It was very helpful. I felt I was doing something I'd always wanted to do."

When you feel the health care provider is your ally, you're more likely to follow his or her guidance, even if it means doing things that feel risky or uncomfortable at first.

Justine, a 41-year-old computer salesperson who has had several bouts of major depression, feels her psychotherapist helped her make long-standing changes that protect her against recurrences. "I've been through depression a number of times, and the kind of thoughts that used to go through my head were, 'I'm no good, nobody likes me, what's wrong with me?' Then I'd replay negative things that had happened in my life." Justine believes that such thoughts were an exacerbation of thinking patterns she'd had since childhood.

During one bout of depression, Justine started seeing a psychologist who helped her put things into a different perspective. When Justine blamed herself for problems at work, the psychologist suggested other ways to look at her situation. Justine ended up realizing that other people shared responsibility, too. The process helped Justine stop tormenting herself for things that weren't her fault.

Jennifer liked what she calls his "interventionist" approach. "I was very passive when I was depressed," she said. "For me, that kind of approach was very helpful."

She also appreciated that communication was a two-way street. Once he suggested she read *The Thornbirds,* and in response she suggested he read *War and Peace.* Years later, when she dropped by his office for a one-time visit after a relapse, "He told me he'd read it and loved it," she said. "He said I'd turned him on to classical literature."

Jennifer feels her rapport with the therapist was key in helping her recover from depression. "Of the three therapists I saw, he helped me the most."

"I really credit the counseling," she says. "Because I don't have that kind of thought pattern going on anymore—all those thoughts of how terrible I am and what's wrong with me."

Over several years of treatment, Justine had a number of conflicts with her therapist over issues such as payment. "She was really firm, really consistent," Justine said. "It helped me learn to set limits in my own relationships." Justine harbors no grudges against the psychologist for their conflicts. In fact, she says, "she provided a good role model for me."

WORKING WITH INSURANCE COMPANIES

Not every health plan covers mental health care specialists. Those that do often limit time with psychotherapists, in effect encouraging drug treatment of depression rather than effective alternatives. (Health coverage may limit the choice of drugs as well.) Some clients choose to see psychotherapists outside of their insurance system, paying for their care out-of-pocket. But not everyone who might benefit can afford this.

Some managed care organizations impose an extra layer of bureaucracy on people seeking treatment for mental health conditions. People with mental health symptoms may need to contact another organization—usually called a managed behavioral health provider—that works with their HMO in order to get authorization for treatment. In severe depression, it can be difficult for people to muster the courage to approach even their own doctors for help. Negotiating approval for therapy on the phone with total strangers may at times present too great an obstacle, and some individuals give up. On the plus side, a managed behavioral health provider may be a good way to find a specialist to treat you, notes Dr. Young. If your insurance company uses a managed behavioral health provider, the provider's 800 number should appear in your insurance materials. You can call it for referrals.

What to Do About Abuse by a Doctor

On occasion, an unscrupulous doctor or psychotherapist will make sexual overtures to clients. While these may seem flattering, they are invariably damaging. Sexual contact between client and doctor is never all right.

If you are in a situation where you're unsure whether your doctor is behaving appropriately or not, here are some things you can do:

- Listen to your feelings. Don't ignore your discomfort.

- Call him or her on it. Say directly, "I'm not comfortable when you hug me [and so on]."

- Ask a friend or family member to accompany you to appointments.

- Pull back and reassess. Time away may give you some perspective. It's okay to cancel an appointment.

- Talk to someone you trust, who will listen non-judgmentally.

- Talk to another health professional—a nurse on a hotline, a counselor at a crisis clinic, a professional at the state board of licensing—to learn if this behavior is within the norm. You don't have to report names.

- Stop seeing the doctor. You can just quit, or you can confront him or her with the reason. If you choose to confront in person, you may want to bring a friend.

- If the behavior constitutes definite sexual abuse, look first for legal and counseling support for yourself. You have many options in taking action besides a lawsuit, such as reporting the behavior to the doctor's professional association.

There are a few approaches that can help overcome at least some of these hurdles. One is learning in detail about your insurance coverage for mental health before you need it. Find out what doctors and hospitals are covered; find out what limitations the plan imposes. You may decide you want to switch plans.

For people in managed care, it's helpful to establish and maintain a strong, positive relationship with your primary care provider. This individual has the responsibility to make most decisions about referrals, often including mental health referrals. You want to have him or her in your corner. If you're too angry at the doctor about issues he or she cannot control (such as managed care policy), you may lose a potentially valuable ally. If you can't get along with your primary care provider, most HMOs give you a way to switch.

Another skill to develop is making the most of your visits to your primary care provider, particularly if he or she is the person treating you for depression. Your time with your doctor is limited; try not to waste it on chitchat or minor concerns, but get to your big issues quickly. State clearly whether you think a treatment is or is not helping. Keep track of side effects and keep your doctor informed. In some instances, the insurance plan may allow your primary care provider to switch you to a drug that is not on the plan's "approved" list, but only if the doctor thinks the second drug is likely to be significantly better. Be patient with treatment, however: It frequently takes 2 to 6 weeks for drugs to begin to take effect, and as many as 10 sessions of psychotherapy before your symptoms begin to decrease. Just because a treatment isn't working right away doesn't necessarily mean another one would work any better.

Finally, read up on your benefits, and keep track of how you use them. You may be tempted to use all outpatient psychotherapy benefits early, but these benefits may be of more use to you later if, for ex-

> *Your time with your doctor is limited; try not to waste it on chitchat or minor concerns, but get to your big issues quickly.*

ample, you need to be hospitalized for a mental health condition. Many managed care organizations maintain staffs whose job it is to calculate "trade-offs" of one type of benefit for another. If you need a psychiatric hospitalization, the staff may let you use up some of your outpatient treatment benefits to allow a longer time in the hospital. The HMO normally makes these decisions in collaboration with your doctor. It may or may not be in your interest to save up your outpatient visits, if using them might help prevent a hospitalization. But it can pay to be informed.

Working with insurance companies can be frustrating, particularly when you are depressed. If you feel too overwhelmed to negotiate for your care, see if a family member can help. Especially in emergencies, do not let these concerns become an obstacle to getting the care you need. In calmer times, you may want to consider joining an organization seeking to improve insurance coverage and care for mental health care conditions. Such organizations include the Depression and Related Affective Disorders Association, the National Depressive and Manic-Depressive Association, the National Alliance for the Mentally Ill, and the National Mental Health Association (see appendix A for contact information).

SUMMARY

Depression is so frequent that it's called the "common cold of mental conditions," yet doctors often overlook it in actual practice. It's important to tell your doctor if you think you may be depressed. It's also helpful to bring in information that can help your doctor make an accurate diagnosis. Such information can include a chart of your moods, as well as lists of medications you're taking, other diagnoses you may have, and treatments for depression you may have used in the past. One type of depression that may be more difficult for doctors to identify is bipolar disorder. Knowing your family history can help the doctor determine whether you have this condition.

Finding a doctor you're comfortable with is crucial for getting good treatment, since your relationship with your doctor is an important component of care. Although most people with depression see only their primary care providers, specialists can be helpful when depression is complex or difficult to treat. Many people see one doctor for medication and another professional for psychotherapy. Your doctor can help you decide the type of treatment that is best for you, out of the many possibilities that exist. The next chapter discusses current treatments for depression.

CHAPTER 3

Medical and Other Standard Treatments for Depression

✑

*I first started feeling better in September and felt the
"me" coming back. The next time I saw the psychiatrist
I shook his hand and said I want you to meet
me because you haven't really met me before.*

—GENEVIEVE, A 59-YEAR-OLD CHILD CARE PROFESSIONAL,
AFTER RECOVERING FROM MAJOR DEPRESSION

IF THERE IS a single hopeful message about depression, it is that
it's highly treatable. The list of treatments known to work for depression is long: more than 20 different antidepressants; several different types of psychotherapy; lithium and other mood stabilizers for
bipolar disorder; light treatment for winter depression; and electroconvulsive therapy if all else fails. New drugs, psychotherapeutic techniques, and other treatments offering further hope are under
development (see chapter 8). Moreover, these options cover only the
treatment approaches available in conventional medical care. Other
treatments exist within the realm of complementary or alternative

medicine (see chapter 4). Even exercise can significantly raise the spirits of many people (see chapter 5).

Despite this panorama of effective treatments, many people experience care that is far from ideal. "About half of patients with depression never get a proper diagnosis," says David Dunner, M.D., codirector of the University of Washington's Center for Anxiety and Depression. "Of the ones who get a proper diagnosis, only half get appropriate treatment prescribed." Even when appropriate treatment is prescribed, many people quit treatment too early, before getting its full benefits. Why? Often because of drug side effects, says Dr. Dunner. "Or they feel better and stop because they think that's all they need."

Paul Rohde, Ph.D., a psychologist and senior scientist at the Oregon Research Institute, agrees. "A lot of treatment people receive is not long enough or sufficient enough to be effective. Say they receive antidepressant medications—they don't take the medication long enough to show a clinical effect. Or if they go to psychotherapy, they're not in treatment long enough."

Yet this situation is not inevitable. Many difficulties, such as drug side effects, can be managed by better communication between you and your doctor. "Drug side effects are really a reason to be in touch with your doctor," says Dr. Dunner, noting that the doctor can help resolve the problem by adjusting medications or dosage. Many other difficulties can be prevented by a thorough, two-way discussion before beginning treatment. Ideally, you and your doctor should discuss the goals of treatment, your various treatment options, what to expect from your care, and how to know if your treatment is working. Your voice is as important as your doctor's in selecting care, for a simple reason: All your doctor can do is recommend a treatment. The real job—taking the pill, seeing the therapist, using the lightbox—is up to you. Far too many antidepressant prescriptions go unfilled, and the most common number of psychotherapy sessions people have is *just one*, according to Dr. Rohde.

If you've thoroughly discussed your specific needs and expectations with your doctor, you're more likely to find a treatment you'll be willing to follow for as long as it takes. "These things—the medicine, the psychotherapy—all take time," says Dr. Rohde.

Depressed people, who tend to feel hopeless about the future, may have a hard time putting in the time until treatment takes effect. To stay motivated throughout treatment, most people need a solid, supportive relationship with their doctor. Alan Gelenberg, M.D., professor of psychiatry at the University of Arizona, stresses the importance of this relationship—to the point of suggesting that people change doctors if they're not satisfied.

> *If you've thoroughly discussed your specific needs and expectations with your doctor, you're more likely to find a treatment you'll be willing to follow for as long as it takes.*

"If they've got a doctor who is not available to answer important questions or reassure them about problems or who doesn't seem knowledgeable, they should find someone else," says Dr. Gelenberg.

QUESTIONS FOR YOUR DOCTOR ABOUT TREATMENT

A frank and open discussion about your treatment options can help you and your doctor select the best treatment for you. As a jumping-off point for this discussion, you may want to bring a list of questions about treatment to your doctor's office. The most important questions to ask are the ones that concern *you* the most. Here are some possible questions:

Which kinds of treatment are most effective for this type of depression?

How long do they take before beginning to work? How will I know they're working?

Are they likely to bring me fully back to normal? How long might that take?

How long will I need to continue treatment after I'm feeling better?

What should I do if I don't feel better in the expected period, or start feeling worse?

For a drug:

What kinds of side effects might I experience from this drug?

What should I do if I have these side effects?

Could any of these side effects be medical emergencies?

Could any of these side effects be particular problems for me, given my medical history?

Is the drug likely to interact with any medications I'm currently taking? Over-the-counter or herbal remedies?

Can I drink alcohol while I'm on this drug? Are there foods I need to avoid? Other precautions?

How often do I take this drug? Can I take it with meals?

Is it safe to take this drug if I'm pregnant/breastfeeding/might possibly become pregnant?

What could happen if I stop taking the drug suddenly, for example, if I run out?

How often will I come in for a follow-up visit during the early phase of treatment?

For a therapy referral:

Are there particular types of therapy that might be more effective for my depression?

How can I find a therapist who practices one of these types of therapy?

What will the therapy be like?

How often will I need to go?

What will be expected of me? Will the therapist give me homework, for example?

What do I do if I don't like the therapist?

For treatment involving your child:
How will the doctor involve me in my child's care?

How often will the doctor talk to me about my child's progress?

GOALS OF TREATMENT

There are usually at least two sets of goals for your treatment: yours, and your doctor's. (Your family and friends may have goals for your treatment, too.) You might begin treatment with the goals of feeling back to normal within a few weeks, being under treatment for a few months at most, and resolving a particular symptom, such as loss of interest in sex. Your doctor may have a completely different set of goals, based on knowledge of your diagnosis, experience with depression treatments, and personal values. For example, your doctor's goals might include reducing your symptoms by 50 percent within the first 7 or 8 weeks, minimizing sleep disturbance, and keeping you on antidepressants for at least 6 months after you're better.

The American Psychiatric Association (APA) suggests the following goals for the treatment of the type of depression known as major depressive disorder.[1] They divide treatment into three phases:

1. Acute

2. Continuing

3. Maintenance

The goal of the acute phase is to bring you to back to normal. Some doctors interpret this to mean that you no longer meet the criteria for having depression; others interpret it to mean cutting your symptoms by half. This phase is expected to take at least 6 to 8 weeks. The goal of the continuing phase is to prevent a relapse, the return of symptoms during or immediately following treatment. The goal of the maintenance phase is to prevent a recurrence, or a new episode of depression in the future.

> *If you and your doctor don't discuss treatment goals in advance, both of you may be in for some nasty surprises.*

If you and your doctor don't discuss treatment goals in advance, both of you may be in for some nasty surprises. Your doctor may prescribe a particular antidepressant that tends to decrease sex drive, not realizing that a fully functioning sex life is high on your priority list. You may decide to quit your treatment if you're not fully recovered in a few weeks. Or, once you feel better, you may quit right away, not realizing that longer treatment would help prevent a relapse.

You and the doctor may be able to prevent such occurrences by discussing both parties' expectations before deciding on treatment. Together, you can decide on reasonable, mutually acceptable goals. For example, it's reasonable to expect to be fully recovered, not merely better, after completing your full treatment. It may not be reasonable to expect this to occur within the first 6 to 8 weeks, or with the first treatment you try, however.

TREATING DEPRESSION THE *RIGHT* WAY

During their education, health care professionals learn a catchy little phrase: the *right* drug at the *right* dose for the *right* patient. Let's look at how this saying could apply to depression. First, we'll alter the phrase a little, since not all depression treatments involve drugs. Instead we'll say: the *right* treatment at the *right* intensity for the *right* patient. The right treatment is one that's appropriate for a particular type of depression. The right intensity means the most appropriate dose of a drug, as well as the ideal frequency of visits to your doctor or psychotherapist. The right patient takes into account your individual biochemistry, preferences, and needs in selecting the particular treatment or treatments you use.

The Right Treatment

Certain treatments work best for specific types of depression; others are more generally helpful. One example of a specific treatment is lithium, which helps prevent mania and depression in people with bipolar disorder. (Occasionally, doctors may prescribe lithium as a secondary treatment for major depression as well.) More generally helpful treatments include antidepressants and psychotherapy, which can be useful in most kinds of depression.

The Right Intensity of Treatment

Finding the right dose or intensity of treatment is more of a challenge than it seems. Doctors use different methods to determine the right dose of a drug for an individual. With lithium, they usually determine the dose by blood testing. For other drugs, doctors usually adjust the dose to maximize the good effects of treatment while minimizing side effects. Adjusting the dose is something for which the doctor is primarily responsible. Raising and lowering the dose on your own can interfere with the effectiveness of treatment, and may pose additional health risks. Nonetheless, if a drug doesn't seem to be helping, you may need to take the initiative in asking your doctor to reconsider the dose, suggests David Avery, M.D., professor of psychiatry at the University of Washington. He notes that primary care providers sometimes prescribe antidepressants at doses too low to be effective.

Beyond the dosing issue, another issue is how often you see your health care provider. The American Psychiatric Association notes that during the acute phase of major depression, people taking antidepressants benefit from communicating with their health care provider at least once per week, whether by phone or in person.[2] This frequency probably applies regardless of whether the treatment involves medication or psychotherapy. In drug treatment, frequent visits early on help

Peggy's Story: The Importance of Communication

Peggy was 61 when she began seeing a psychotherapist for depression. For months she'd been feeling "frozen" inside, and she was having a lot of trouble coping with ordinary life. "If I was driving and had to find an address, it was an overwhelming task," she says, recalling that period. "I was also having a lot of anxiety, a lot of trouble concentrating. The therapist felt I was very depressed and that I needed to have some help with antidepressants." Since the therapist wasn't qualified to write prescriptions, she suggested that Peggy see a psychiatrist.

Initially Peggy was reluctant to consider antidepressants because she regarded them as very powerful drugs and was fearful of how they might affect her. But after her therapist emphasized how careful a psychiatrist would be in selecting the right drug, Peggy was persuaded to try. Instead of seeing a psychiatrist, however, she decided to request a prescription from her internist, in hopes that insurance would cover the drugs.

Peggy's experience with her internist was not good. The doctor hardly spoke to her, Peggy remembers. Instead, she gave Peggy "a

people cope with medication side effects and the frustration of waiting for the drug's helpful effects to kick in.

Unfortunately, people treated for depression in primary care offices often see their doctors only once every 6 weeks. Infrequent visits contribute to people's sense of isolation and despair, and often to their discarding treatments too early.

The Right Treatment for *You*

Although scientists have identified many effective treatments for depression, the truth of the matter is this: Not a single, solitary one of those treatments has been found to be effective for everyone who tries it. Nor—except in the case of bipolar disorder—are experts particu-

little written test, a fill-in-the-blank kind of test." After the doctor read Peggy's answers, Peggy remembers her saying, "Oh, yeah, I'll give you Paxil." Peggy felt the doctor's approach was far too casual. "I just felt that given the power that these drugs have, people should be a whole lot more careful about prescribing them."

Peggy took the Paxil for only 2 days. "The Paxil was horrible," she says. "I could tell at once what a powerful drug it was." Instead of giving up, though, Peggy went to plan B: seeing the psychiatrist her therapist had recommended. She and the psychiatrist talked at length, after which he prescribed a different antidepressant. She's been taking it ever since with good results. Fortunately, it turned out that her insurance covered both the psychiatrist and the drug.

Peggy was lucky in having a therapist she trusted whom she could go back to after her upsetting visit to her internist. Otherwise, she might have been tempted to give up after her first, unsatisfying attempt at drug treatment. If the only person you see for your depression is your primary care provider, which is the case for most people, establishing good communication is even more critical to your treatment's success.

larly good at predicting which people will benefit most from which treatments.

Choosing a treatment is no small matter, because every treatment has its negatives as well as its positives, and you may have to try several before you find one that works well for you. "Trying" generally means more than a day or a week; it typically means 6 to 8 weeks minimum on an antidepressant, or, according to Larry Beutler, Ph.D., editor of the *Journal of Clinical Psychology*, at least 10 sessions of psychotherapy.

Given this situation, it makes sense for doctors to discuss your treatment options with you before handing out a prescription or assigning a course of psychotherapy. Unfortunately, in actual practice, such discussions occur less often than they should. As a result, many people who seek care for depression aren't made aware of opportunities for individualizing their care—even though individualized care may result in better satisfaction and better results.

Antidepressants or Psychotherapy?

For many types of depression, people may do equally well with either antidepressants or psychotherapy. "We do know that medications do a lot of good for some people, and have a good chance of causing great benefit early if they take them," says A. John Rush, M.D., professor of psychiatry at the University of Texas. "A lot of people get totally well; a lot of people are substantially better but still have residual symptoms. For the less complicated, less severe forms of depression, psychotherapy is quite effective, too." In fact, says Dr. Rush, when you compare the effectiveness of psychotherapy and drugs for depression that is neither chronic nor very severe, the two treatments look pretty much equal. A major question is how to figure out which people will do better with which method, notes Dr. Rush. Scientists have not yet succeeded in answering that question.

> *When you compare the effectiveness of psychotherapy and drugs for depression that is neither chronic nor very severe, the two treatments look pretty much equal.*

Dr. Avery agrees. In nonbipolar depression, he says, "Some people probably do better with drugs, some people with therapy, but we don't yet know which." Your doctor may not know which will work better for you, but *you* might have a preference as to which one you want to try first. If you like the convenience of a pill and hate the idea of talking about your problems, say so. You might also prefer an antidepressant because it's likely to take less time to begin relieving your symptoms. On the other hand, if antidepressants scare you but you would love some help solving personal problems, let your doctor know. As the American Psychiatric Association advises, "Patient preference for psychotherapeutic approaches is an important factor that should be considered in the decision to use psychotherapy as the initial treatment modality."[3]

Which Antidepressant?

If antidepressants are recommended for your depression, you may face another choice—which one? Just as doctors can't readily predict which will work better—therapy or antidepressants—they also have difficulty predicting who will respond best to which antidepressant. Only 65 to 70 percent of people get good results with the first antidepressant they try, according to Dr. Avery. Switching to a different antidepressant will help about another 50 percent. Doctors can't easily predict which drug will work best for which person. "In the year 2001, we are not yet at a stage where we can say, 'Aha, you have this type of depression, therefore you need this type of antidepressant,'" says Dr. Avery. Most doctors start people on a selective serotonin reuptake inhibitor (SSRI), a group of antidepressants that includes Prozac. However, depending on your health history, you may do better to start on a drug with a different set of side effects.

> *Only 65 to 70 percent of people get good results with the first antidepressant they try.*

Psychotherapy and Medication?

Some people like the idea of combining drugs and psychotherapy in order to maximize their chances of quick recovery. Interestingly, many research studies suggest that such a combination may not be any more beneficial than either treatment alone.

There are reasons you may want to combine the two treatments, however—assuming money, time, and insurance coverage are not an issue! If you have severe or chronic major depression, some studies have found that combining antidepressants and psychotherapy gives better results.[4] You might also consider the combination if you're not getting good results with one treatment alone—or if you find that you're feeling better with treatment, but still aren't really back to normal.

Patty Duke, diagnosed with bipolar disorder, appreciates a combined approach. She notes that the most important treatment is medication—in this case, lithium or a similar drug. She suggests, however,

that psychotherapy can help "mop up" family problems or other difficulties developed during an episode of depression or mania, as well as
help you deal with resistance to taking your medication, anger at your
disease, and depression at being depressed.[5] Today, many authorities
specifically recommend a combined approach for bipolar disorder.

Who Decides Your Treatment?

Which you start with—antidepressants or psychotherapy—may have
less to do with your symptoms than with the kind of health care
provider you see. According to a survey per-
formed by the National Depressive and Manic-
Depressive Association, 97 percent of primary
care providers report that they prescribe an antidepressant for people with newly diagnosed
major depression.[6] Unsurprisingly, psychotherapists usually recommend psychotherapy, although
in addition, they may refer you to a medical doctor or psychiatrist if they think you might benefit
from drug treatment as well. Psychiatrists might recommend antidepressants, psychotherapy, or both, depending on their training and
orientation.

> *Today, many authori-
> ties specifically rec-
> ommend a combination
> of drug treatment and
> psychotherapy for bipolar
> disorder.*

NEUROTRANSMITTERS, ANTIDEPRESSANTS, AND THE BRAIN

Our brains are essentially electrical systems, jam-packed with nerve
cells sending electrical impulses to each other and to other parts of
the body. In an oversimplified image, you can think of a nerve cell as
an octopus with only two legs: one to receive incoming impulses, the
other to send outgoing impulses. The head of the octopus, in the
middle, is the cell body.

Unlike electrical wires, the "legs" of nerve cells don't actually
touch each other to communicate. Between the outgoing leg of one

Getting the Most from Your Treatment

A. John Rush, M.D., and Alan Gelenberg, M.D., have the following suggestions for maximizing the effectiveness of your treatment:

- Be candid with your doctor.
- Come in with a list of questions.
- Follow instructions.
- Tell the doctor about any side effects.
- Don't adjust the dose on your own.
- Don't borrow a medication from a family member to try it out.
- Be honest about use of alcohol and street drugs, which can affect the level of medication in your blood.
- Be an active and knowledgeable consumer.
- Be your own advocate, or have a family member advocate for you.
- If you're seeing a primary care doctor for depression and following the prescribed treatment, but not improving after a reasonable amount of time, consider getting a second opinion.

nerve cell and the incoming leg of the next is a tiny space, called a synapse. When an electrical signal passes down the outgoing leg, it signals a chemical messenger called a neurotransmitter to float across the synapse to the incoming leg of another nerve. There the neurotransmitter binds to a special docking site called a receptor.

The docking of the neurotransmitter can have several effects. It may start a new electrical impulse surging up the incoming leg of the cell where it docked. Or, it may inhibit or facilitate later electrical impulses. Each type of neurotransmitter has several different types of receptors to which it alone can dock. In theory, the same neurotransmitter might have different effects, depending on the kind of receptor it docks onto.

Once the neurotransmitter has sent its message, it detaches from its docking site and floats back into the synapse. There, it may get sucked back into the nerve cell that originally emitted it, a process called reuptake. There it's held in storage. Alternatively, the neurotransmitter may be destroyed by an enzyme.

Antidepressant drugs are designed to increase the supply of neurotransmitters such as serotonin and norepinephrine. Scientists believe that the drugs do this in one of two ways. Some drugs work by blocking the enzyme that breaks down certain neurotransmitters, so the neurotransmitters continue to be available. Since the enzyme involved is known as monoamine oxidase, such drugs are called monoamine oxidase inhibitors (MAOIs).

Other drugs increase neurotransmitters by blocking their reuptake. Prozac and other selective serotonin reuptake inhibitors (SSRIs) are in this category and prevent serotonin from being put back into storage. The result is more serotonin floating around in the synapses waiting to latch onto a receptor. Another group of antidepressants is the tricyclics, which prevent the reuptake of norepinephrine.

> *A*ntidepressant drugs are designed to increase the supply of neurotransmitters such as serotonin and norepinephrine.

Although all three groups of drugs increase the amount of neurotransmitters available, many scientists suspect that this is an oversimplification of how they work. Some believe that antidepressants may really work by altering the number or kind of receptors waiting to pick up the neurotransmitters, or changing receptors' sensitivity. Others propose that they work by increasing the supply of a particular chemical called cyclic AMP within the part of the brain known as the hippocampus. A distinguished psychiatrist recently proposed that the function of antidepressants might be simply to jolt the brain into doing something new—like kicking a machine to make it work.[7]

MEDICATIONS FOR DEPRESSION

The main groups of drugs used to treat depression are antidepressants; lithium and other mood stabilizers for bipolar disorder; and sometimes antianxiety drugs, sleep medications, estrogen, antipsychotics, or other drugs.

Antidepressants

The idea of taking a pill to treat depression arose with two accidental discoveries in the mid-twentieth century when drugs given for other problems were found to either cause, or lift, depression. Since then, scientists have developed dozens of chemicals aimed at affecting certain neurotransmitters, the chemical messengers in the brain. "All of our antidepressant medications are based on different neurotransmitters in the brain, either dopamine, serotonin, or norepinephrine," explains Rif El-Mallakh, associate professor of psychiatry at the University of Louisville in Kentucky.

Doctors today most commonly prescribe selective serotonin reuptake inhibitors such as Prozac, Zoloft, or Paxil. As their name suggests, the SSRIs affect the brain's balance of serotonin. Other types of antidepressants include the two oldest groups—the tricyclics and the monoamine oxidase inhibitors (MAOIs)—and a number of newer drugs such as Effexor, Serzone, and Wellbutrin. A list of antidepressants with their most common brand names appears in table 2.

More than 20 different antidepressants are on the market. Why such a long list of different drugs? The answer is that while antidepressants are powerful weapons against depression, none of them are perfect. Different people respond to different drugs, and some people are able to tolerate the side effects of one drug better than others. No one drug is clearly superior to the others, in either effectiveness or

Table 2.   Antidepressants

Generic Name	Brand Name(s)
Selective Serotonin Reuptake Inhibitors (SSRIs)	
citalopram	Celexa
fluoxetine	Prozac, Sarafem
paroxetine	Paxil
sertraline	Zoloft
Tricyclics	
amitriptyline	Elavil
amoxapine	Asendin
desipramine	Norpramin
doxepin	Sinequan
imipramine	Tofranil
nortriptyline	Pamelor, Aventyl
protriptyline	Vivactil
trimipramine	Surmontil
Monoamine Oxidase Inhibitors (MAOIs)	
phenelzine	Nardil
tranylcypromine	Parnate
Miscellaneous	
bupropion	Wellbutrin
maprotiline	Ludiomil
mirtazapine	Remeron
nefazodone	Serzone
trazodone	Desyrel
venlafaxine	Effexor

Note: Many of these drugs are so new that they are currently available only as brand-name products. Prozac (fluoxetine) has recently become available as a generic.

side effects. Researchers continue to search for a better antidepressant, one that will be more effective in a higher percentage of people, and that will cause fewer negative effects.

Selective Serotonin Reuptake Inhibitors (SSRIs)

Although the term "antidepressant" has been around for decades, it didn't become a household word until the advent of Prozac (a selective serotonin reuptake inhibitor, or SSRI) in the late 1980s. Prozac's popularity was early and widespread, leading people who had never before considered themselves depressed to go to their doctors and request the medication. Aided in part by extravagant media attention, some came to view Prozac (fluoxetine) as a wonder drug that could make people, in psychiatrist Peter Kramer's words, "better than well."[8] No wonder Dr. Kramer and others worried about "cosmetic psychopharmacology"—the use of medications by people who were not really depressed, but merely wanting to add a bit of oomph to their personality.

> **Medical Alert**
> Don't stop taking an antidepressant without checking with your doctor. You may be setting yourself up for withdrawal symptoms or a relapse into depression.

In the early 1990s, a few people raised concerns that Prozac might contribute to suicide because of a small number of case reports of people who became suicidal after beginning the drug. These reports took a bit of the blush off the rose, but only temporarily, as later research indicated that the risk of suicide was no higher with Prozac than with other antidepressants.

Despite Prozac's popularity with the media and the public, scientific studies have consistently found that it is really no more and no less effective than the earlier tricyclics. Where Prozac differs is mainly in its side effects. Most people tolerate Prozac's side effects a lot more readily than they do side effects of the earlier drugs. Prozac is also a lot safer when taken in accidental (or intentional) overdose.

Other drugs in the category of SSRIs include Paxil, Zoloft, and Celexa. All SSRIs affect the balance of the neurotransmitter serotonin in the brain. Each of the SSRIs has slightly different chemical effects, including side effects, "but they're all pretty much interchangeable," says Dr. Gelenberg. "Most of the time in a person with an uncomplicated depression, the drugs of first choice are the SSRIs. They are easy to use and we have the most experience with them." Usually, people need to take only one pill a day. The FDA recently approved a once-a-week form of Prozac, designed for people taking the drug on a long-term basis to prevent recurrences of depression.

> *Despite Prozac's popularity with the media and the public, scientific studies have consistently found that it is really no more and no less effective than the earlier tricyclic antidepressants.*

Prozac isn't free of side effects. Twenty percent of people taking it report insomnia, slightly more report nausea, and 13 percent report nervousness.[9] Other common side effects include dizziness, tremor, loose stools, and dry mouth, each affecting about 10 percent of those who take Prozac. Some of these side effects tend to go away as people stay on the drug; others can sometimes be tolerated, or handled with lifestyle changes or other means. It's important to remember that none of these side effects is inevitable. If 20 percent of those on Prozac report insomnia, the vast majority—80 percent—do not. In fact, 13 percent report increased sleepiness on the drug.

Sexual side effects such as impaired sex drive, arousal, or orgasm are relatively common with the SSRIs, but again, not everyone experiences them. In fact, some individuals experience the opposite effect. "For some people, Prozac actually acts as a kind of aphrodisiac," says Steven Bratman, M.D., author of *The Natural Pharmacist: Treating Depression.*

Tricyclics

Long the mainstay of antidepressants, tricyclics, such as Elavil, lost popularity once the SSRIs hit the market. The reason? Their common side effects: drowsiness, dry mouth, constipation, weight gain, dizziness, and confusion, in varying degrees, particularly with higher doses. Also, a week's supply of a tricyclic, taken at once, could kill—a serious risk for people with depression.

Still, the tricyclics have their uses. Doctors sometimes prescribe them at night for people having difficulty falling asleep. They can be effective antidepressants when other drugs fail.

Monoamine Oxidase Inhibitors (MAOIs)

Doctors rarely prescribe the oldest type of antidepressants, mono-amine oxidase inhibitors (MAOIs), as an initial treatment for depression today because these drugs (such as Nardil and Parnate) can cause blood pressure to skyrocket if taken with certain foods. The problematic foods are numerous, including preserved meats and fish, dried fruit, and aged cheese, among others. For depressed people, keeping track of what they can and can't eat poses a major inconvenience, not to mention a serious hazard if they forget.

In some cases, however, MAOIs are indicated. Studies have found that MAOIs may actually be more effective than other drugs for people with *atypical depression*, a specific type of depression that can involve ultrasensitivity to perceived rejection, overeating, and over-sleeping. If you're prescribed an MAOI, please be extra-conscientious about use of other medications. Serious interactions are common with over-the-counter medications and prescription drugs, including other antidepressants.

Other Antidepressants

Many antidepressants prescribed today don't fit into the categories listed above. Some of these newer drugs include Serzone, Effexor, Wellbutrin, and Remeron.

Serzone. Available since 1995, Serzone resembles an SSRI in its
   actions, but not closely enough to be included in that category of
   antidepressants. Compared to the SSRIs, says Dr. Gelenberg,
   Serzone is "probably a little more complicated to use because of
   the dosing schedule." It is usually taken two or three times per day.

Genevieve's Story: Persisting Despite Obstacles

When she was 58 years old, Genevieve was blindsided by depression after cataract surgery. Her surgery went fine, but soon afterward she went to her internist, saying that she just wasn't feeling herself. The doctor prescribed Celexa, an SSRI. Instead of feeling better after starting on the drug, however, Genevieve felt worse—much worse. "I just felt more and more overwhelmed, more and more like nothing good was happening. I couldn't sleep, I couldn't nap, and I couldn't rest." Over the next few months, she lost 30 pounds, and she was already slim.

Her internist wasn't comfortable treating Genevieve's depression, and referred her to a psychiatrist. For one reason or another, it took Genevieve several months to see the doctor. By then, her depression was pretty well entrenched. She couldn't even manage to answer the psychiatrist's questions. "He seemed to ask questions that I didn't even know the answers to, like how long I had felt so-and-so. He ended up having my husband come in."

The doctor put Genevieve on Remeron, a drug from a different class of antidepressants, partly because of Genevieve's weight loss. "He said it would help me gain weight," says Genevieve. Genevieve wasn't comfortable taking it, however. "I was real suspect about it, and about him, and about everything right then," she recalls. "I would read all the little things that came with these medications, and every little detail about what they could cause, and I would

Serzone's side effects differ from those of SSRIs. One of its chief advantages is that it causes less insomnia. In fact, its main side effect is sleepiness. Dry mouth is common, too. Serzone seems to cause less sexual impairment than many other antidepressants.

Effexor. Released in 1994, Effexor blocks reuptake of both norepinephrine and serotonin. Effexor's side effects are similar to those of

begin to feel that I had all these things going wrong." Instead, Genevieve wanted to take something that had worked for someone she knew. "I had a friend who was on Paxil and she felt it was wonderful for her," says Genevieve, who didn't realize at the time that Paxil, another SSRI, was chemically related to Celexa. The psychiatrist finally agreed she could try it.

During the first week or two she was on Paxil, nothing improved. On her 59th birthday, Genevieve didn't want to get out of bed. But not long after, she found her first bright spot in months—a hiking trip with her husband that she actually somewhat enjoyed. Then came a day she specifically remembers: September 9. "I got my husband sent off to work and I crawled back in bed, like I did a lot," says Genevieve. "And somehow that day something changed in me. I'm sure it was the Paxil that was finally working—I'd been on it a whole month. I just sat up in bed and thought, 'What am I wasting time in bed for, for goodness sake?' and I started thinking about my husband and how good he'd been to me, and I thought he really deserved for me to clean his bathroom. In fact, I said to myself, I think I'm going to clean the whole house."

Now, several months later, Genevieve is still on Paxil, and feeling better than she has in years. "People ask 'How are you?' and I say, 'Well, WONDERFUL.'" She looks back on her horrible 59th birthday and says, "I'm really looking forward to turning 60 because it's going to be so much better."

SSRIs, including, unfortunately, a high rate of sexual difficulties. It also carries a slight risk of hypertension.

Wellbutrin. Wellbutrin's mode of action is somewhat mysterious. It has only modest effects on norepinephrine and dopamine, according to Harvard psychiatrist William S. Appleton, and no effect on serotonin. "This makes it different from all other antidepressants in use," he writes in his book *Prozac and the New Antidepressants*, "and makes it desirable, perhaps, for people who are not helped by other drugs."[10] Dr. Gelenberg agrees with this summation. "Wellbutrin's been around for a while," he says. "It's got a different mechanism of action so it may work for people who don't respond to the SSRIs. Or occasionally, we'll use it in combination with one of those." Apart from a small risk of seizures with high doses, Wellbutrin seems to have fewer side effects, including less effect on sexual functioning, than many other antidepressants.

Remeron. One of the newest of the antidepressants, Remeron affects norepinephrine and serotonin. Compared to other antidepressants, says Dr. Gelenberg, "we know less about it. It hasn't gotten as wide a use." More than 50 percent of people taking Remeron report sleepiness, and 25 percent experience dry mouth, although these symptoms usually diminish with time. According to Dr. Gelenberg, it can also cause weight gain and fluid retention. "It's certainly not a first-line drug," says Dr. Gelenberg, noting that it might be a reasonable second or third choice if the first drug didn't work out. It does have a significant advantage over the SSRIs in causing fewer sexual side effects, however. Related to Remeron is Ludiomil, introduced a couple of decades ago. According to Dr. Gelenberg, doctors rarely prescribe it because of its high rate of side effects.

Medical Alert

Don't try to combine antidepressants on your own. Some combinations are dangerous.

Trazodone. An older relative of Serzone, trazodone is available generically or under the brand name Desyrel. Trazodone has two salient features: a tendency to cause drowsiness, and a small risk of causing priapism (painful, continuous erection) in men. According to Dr. Gelenberg, psychiatrists use it these days mostly as a sedative rather than an antidepressant. Doctors also sometimes prescribe it to women who are having sexual side effects from SSRIs.

Antidepressants and Mania

Antidepressants are not appropriate in every situation. Kay Redfield Jamison, a psychologist and expert in the field, writes that some people with bipolar disorder may actually get worse when taking antidepressants without mood stabilizers. "Their episodes may increase in frequency and intensity," Dr. Jamison writes.[11] Antidepressants carry a small risk of pushing someone with bipolar disorder straight from a depressed state into mania.

Antidepressants and Sexuality

Many people with depression lose interest in activities they once enjoyed, including sex. Often, treating depression with drugs or other means restores people's sexual interest and functioning. Sometimes antidepressants can interfere with sex drive, arousal, or orgasm, however. People taking antidepressants aren't always aware that their medications may be contributing to their sexual problems.

According to John Ratey, M.D., Harvard psychiatrist and author of *A User's Guide to the Brain*, sexual side effects are quite common with some of the newer medications. "The tricyclics can have sexual side effects, but not nearly to the degree that the new drugs do," says Dr. Ratey.

Dr. Gelenberg concurs that sexual side effects are common with many of the newer antidepressants, particularly Effexor and SSRIs such as Prozac. Asked to list drugs *least* likely to cause sexual problems, he names Wellbutrin, Serzone, and Remeron. "Wellbutrin is probably the best established as having minimal or no sexual side effects," he notes.

> *Sometimes antidepressants can interfere with sex drive, arousal, or orgasm. People taking antidepressants aren't always aware that their medications may be contributing to their sexual problems.*

Of all the possible antidepressant side effects, people have the hardest time telling their doctors about sexual difficulties. Yet if this issue concerns you, it's a good idea to bring it up. Dr. Gelenberg urges people with any kind of side effect to communicate with their doctors. "If they have a side effect, they shouldn't just stop taking the medication without discussing it," he says. "They should not take matters solely into their own hands." Expect your doctor to work with you to establish possible causes and solutions for your sexual concerns. Together with your doctor, you can develop a plan to regain a satisfying sex life.

Common Fears About Taking Antidepressants

People considering antidepressants may have a number of fears about them, says Dr. Gelenberg. "Probably among the most common is that people tend to deny that they have a psychiatric disorder. It feels devaluing, degrading—it feels like a negative statement about oneself. So someone who's depressed might say, 'I should be able to get out of it; I'm just being weak, or lazy, or passive; it'll just blow over,' or some such. It's not a fear of an antidepressant so much as, 'If I take the antidepressant, I'm acknowledging I have a problem and I don't want to do that.'" Dr. Gelenberg helps people sort through these concerns by giving people as much information as possible about depression. "The sufferer is no more at fault that someone who developed diabetes," he says. "I like to destigmatize."

"More specific to the drugs," he notes, "are fears that 'I'll be dependent on the medication, it won't make me feel like myself, or I'll have trouble stopping it.'" When someone asks if the medicine is habit-forming, "I can say absolutely not," says Dr. Gelenberg. "Yes, there are withdrawal symptoms, but we will try to use the drug in a way that gives you maximum benefit, and after you've been stable for a while, try to taper it and stop it."

Treatment-Resistant Depression

About half of those who don't respond to one antidepressant will respond to another, according to Dr. Avery. If two or more treatments don't work or produce intolerable side effects, your doctor may tell you that you have *treatment-resistant depression*. A depression that is treatment-resistant is not necessarily incurable—but can be extremely

Could a Vitamin Help Your Antidepressant Work?

An exciting piece of research suggests that folic acid may augment the effectiveness of Prozac, at least in women. Researchers studied 127 people with a new episode of major depression. They gave everyone Prozac along with either 500 micrograms of folic acid or a dummy vitamin (placebo). Adding folic acid to the Prozac made little difference for the men—about 60 percent of them did well, regardless of whether they took folic acid or not. But for the women, the difference with folic acid was dramatic, raising the rate of response from 61 percent (those taking placebo plus Prozac) to nearly 94 percent (those taking folic acid plus Prozac).[12]

The investigators suspect that folic acid may also boost the effectiveness of other antidepressants. You can bet that other researchers will be putting this to the test over the next few years.

frustrating. "People with treatment-resistant depression are clearly in the minority in the world of depressed people," says Dr. David Dunner. In the past, researchers devoted little attention to finding solutions to their difficulties. That situation has changed.

"People with treatment-resistant depression are being targeted for research studies that will help to identify pathways to get them better," says Dr. Dunner. "There are new medications, or new combinations of medications that are available." See the section "When Your Antidepressant Isn't Working" for possible approaches to this problem. A number of experimental treatments discussed later in this book, including magnetic stimulation of parts of the brain or another device that stimulates one of the cranial nerves, may also prove beneficial.

Besides treatment-resistant depression, there's another situation that should send you back to the doctor for alternative, or additional, treatment. Sometimes people improve significantly with antidepressant treatment, but still don't feel back to normal. "There are people who improve, and then there are people who get back to their usual selves," says Dr. Avery. "What we should be aiming for is full recovery." Don't settle for less. Besides the issue of your quality of life, there's another point to consider: People who have some residual symptoms of depression despite their treatment are more likely to have a relapse when treatment is stopped.

> **Medical Alert**
>
> If an antidepressant isn't working, your dose may be too low. Talk to your doctor. Don't increase the dose on your own.

When Your Antidepressant Isn't Working

If you're on antidepressants and you're still depressed, Stephen R. Shuchter, M.D., and colleagues, authors of *Biologically Informed Psychotherapy for Depression,* suggest a number of factors for you and your health care provider to consider.[13] They call them "the six D's." They appear here in adapted form.

1. Check the *diagnosis*. Could there be a medical cause for your depression, such as hypothyroidism? Might you have bipolar disorder or seasonal affective disorder? Could another medication be causing your depression?

2. Check the *dose*. Many primary care doctors prescribe the minimum dose of an antidepressant. Increasing the dosage usually increases its effects. This is not something to do on your own, however—talk to your doctor. Also, be sure that another medication, alcohol, or street drugs aren't interfering with the effectiveness of your antidepressant.

3. Check the *duration* of treatment. Doctors used to think that 6 weeks was long enough to test the effectiveness of an antidepres-

How Long Should You Take Antidepressants?

These days, more and more doctors suggest that people with non-bipolar types of depression stay on antidepressants for months—sometimes years—after they have improved. According to research, continuing treatment for a period may help prevent your symptoms from returning when you stop. If you've had several bouts of depression, prolonged treatment may help prevent recurrences (new episodes of depression).

How long you should stay on antidepressants after recovery depends on your kind of depression, says Dr. Dunner, noting that he relies on research to support his recommendations. How long is long enough? "For a single episode of depression, the data suggest 6 months to a year after recovery. The data for recurrent depression

sant. Now some specialists suggest that optimum results may take 2 to 3 months.

4. Consider *drug changes*. Studies have found that many people respond to one type of antidepressant and not another. If an SSRI doesn't work, switching to an antidepressant in a different class may relieve your symptoms. If that doesn't work, switching to another drug in the same class, for example, from Zoloft to Prozac (both SSRIs) may work better. Sometimes combining two antidepressants, for example, an SSRI with a tricyclic, can give good results. William Appleton, author of *Prozac and the New Antidepressants,* suggests you talk to your doctor about other possibilities as well, such as adding lithium, estrogen, thyroid hormone, or stimulants like Ritalin.

5. Try *different* approaches. Options may include psychotherapy, exercise, light therapy, or electroconvulsive therapy (electroshock).

6. Maintain your *determination*. Neither you nor your doctor should give up hope. The researchers now studying treatment-resistant depression are likely to publish their findings over the next few years.

suggest perhaps 5 to 7 years is in order." For chronic depression, he suggests a year and a half or 2 years. "The average duration of treatment of depression is about 3 to 3 1/2 months," he notes. "So we're not even close to getting to where we need to be."

If your doctor recommends longer treatment than you're comfortable with, it's a good idea to discuss it, rather than simply going off your medication. There may be other approaches you can try, such as psychotherapy. Several studies suggest that 3 to 4 months of cognitive therapy (or cognitive-behavioral therapy) may be more effective at preventing relapses than 3 to 4 months of antidepressants (at least the older tricyclic antidepressants).[14]

David Antonuccio, Ph.D., a clinical psychologist and professor at the University of Nevada School of Medicine, believes this makes sense. "You've heard the saying, 'You can give a hungry man a fish or you can teach him how to fish,'" says Dr. Antonuccio. "Psychotherapy is akin to teaching people how to fish—teaching them some skills they can use later."

> *You've heard the saying, "You can give a hungry man a fish or you can teach him how to fish." Psychotherapy is akin to teaching people how to fish—teaching them skills they can use later.*
>
> —DAVID ANTONUCCIO, PH.D.

Mood Stabilizers

Mood stabilizers are another category of drugs used in the treatment of depression, specifically, bipolar disorder. A mood stabilizer, according to Dr. Gelenberg, helps someone with bipolar disorder remain in a normal mood state, preventing swings into mania or depression. "Lithium is the closest to an ideal mood stabilizer, and it's the only drug with the FDA's approval for long-term maintenance treatment for bipolar disorder," he notes. "Before there was lithium there were no good treatments of any sort for either the acute phases of mania or depression, nor for the long-term maintenance of mood stability." He notes that lithium is an effective treatment for acute mania, is mildly effective in treating depression, and is an effective long-term preventive drug that doesn't push manic people into depression or vice versa.

Today, doctors sometimes prescribe antiseizure medications such as Depakote or Tegretol as mood stabilizers, in what is known as "off-label usage," since the FDA hasn't officially authorized them for this purpose.

Lithium's benefits are clear: an analysis of multiple studies of people with bipolar disorder found that lithium cuts the rate of suicide by an average of 900 percent.[15] Yet reluctance to take lithium or other mood stabilizers is common. Most people initially resist the idea of being on a drug on a long-term basis. Some people wish to avoid the possibility of side effects or drug interactions. For many people, what's most at stake is the sense of freedom and creativity they derive in mania or hypomania. Creative people may believe they do their best work when their mood is moderately elevated, and fear the loss of productivity or passion.

> *Today, doctors sometimes prescribe antiseizure medications such as Depakote or Tegretol as mood stabilizers, in what is known as "off-label usage," since the FDA hasn't officially authorized them for this purpose.*

Some of these concerns are quite realistic. For example, people on lithium need to be particularly careful to avoid certain other drugs that can cause life-threatening interactions. Other concerns may not seem so problematic once a person starts taking the drug. Many people find the life-enhancing potential of these medications is enormous.

PSYCHOTHERAPY

Although primary care doctors rarely suggest it as a first-line treatment for depression, psychotherapy can be an effective alternative to medication for many types of depression. "The treatments for simple, usual depression are generally either the psychotherapies—and there

Rebecca's Story: The Value of Self-Advocacy

Rebecca has taken lithium for 15 years. In the last few years, she's added Zoloft, Wellbutrin, and Norvasc, a blood pressure medication her psychiatrist thought might help her bipolar disorder. Although she takes her drugs religiously, she reports frequently resenting the long-term need to take medications. "It's inconvenient. In our culture, we think that it's perhaps a weakness, that it's sort of unnatural, and therefore bad." Also, she points out, not all insurance plans cover these drugs, some of which are very expensive. "That's hard to take when you think about all these hundreds of dollars that could be spent on something else. On the other hand," she notes, "if I were depressed any of that time, I might be disabled and not making any money at all."

Rebecca takes a very active role in managing her health care. Although she thinks highly of her psychiatrist, she reports an episode where she felt "snowed" by a particular dose of medication. "The psychiatrist meant well, but she was just looking at her charts and calculating the therapeutic dose. I was put on twice as much as I needed, and that caused me to be spaced out and tired all the time." Rebecca had to be extremely assertive with her doctor. "I'd say I don't feel good. This isn't just depression. I didn't have this problem before." Eventually, she ended up on half the dose, and later, she says, "the psychiatrist saw that that was right."

are new psychotherapies being developed which are quite effective—for the milder end of the spectrum, or medication," says Dr. Dunner.

Not everyone agrees that psychotherapy is effective only for mildly or moderately depressed people. Dr. Antonuccio is one who does not. "One of the current beliefs that prevails is that if someone is really seriously depressed they need to have medication," says Dr.

Even with Rebecca's initiative and persistence, she points out, "it's still easy for well-meaning doctors to overlook problems like over-prescribing something. There are so many reasons for symptoms, it's hard to say whether it's depression or it's the effect of your drugs. It's a pretty complicated matter."

Rebecca works very hard to make sure she gets good care. "I've taken a lot of energy and a lot of time," she says. During a period when she was seeing an endocrinologist for thyroid problems, as well as her primary care doctor and psychiatrist, she says, "I was ac-tually making charts. I would make a chart of what dosage I'm on of everything, just to show everybody: Look, I was on this dosage, and now I'm on that dose, and here are my symptoms. Generally doctors don't have much time to look at anything."

All of this self-advocacy has at times drained her energy. "I used to be so angry the first few years, about even going to the doctor, or having to pay doctor bills, or dealing with the insurance company. You're faced with all these bureaucratic and financial problems, in addition to feeling depressed. It's hard to stay motivated." Now, however, she says, "I'm more philosophical about it."

Rebecca definitely recommends that people with bipolar disorder seek care from a psychiatrist. "My general doctor had never heard of Zoloft when I told her I was on that a few years ago. Now she's pre-scribing it to her other patients. General doctors can't keep track of all the new developments in psychopharmacology."

Antonuccio. "I would say the existing data do not support this. That is, in comparative studies, psychotherapy does as well even for the se-verely depressed patient, and it looks like there may be some advan-tages to psychotherapy in terms of preventing relapse." He suggests an additional advantage: Unlike antidepressants, psychotherapy is medically benign.

More than 15 studies have compared psychotherapy's effectiveness to that of antidepressants. Why, then, are experts in disagreement?

Some of the controversy has to do with a fine point of research: whether people who drop out of a study for any reason are counted in the final results. Dr. Antonuccio believes that if a lot of people drop out of a study, that's not a good sign. "Controlled studies of drug treatments tend to have a higher dropout rate, an average of about 36 percent. Whereas psychotherapy studies have a dropout rate on the average of about 18 percent," he says. When dropout rates are taken into account, he notes that psychotherapy sometimes appears to work better than medication.

Although primary care doctors rarely suggest it as a first-line treatment for depression, psychotherapy can be an effective alternative to medication for many types of depression.

Those on the opposite side of the issue point out that many of these studies compared psychotherapy to the older tricyclic antidepressants, which are less frequently prescribed today, and that the dose and duration of the medications were sometimes too low compared to today's standards. The results of carefully designed studies comparing psychotherapy to SSRIs are beginning to trickle in, and may soon settle this question.

All Psychotherapy Is Not Equal

All psychotherapy is not the same. For starters, you can receive individual, couples or marital therapy, family therapy, or group therapy (the last offered to groups of unrelated individuals). Second, there are many, many different approaches the therapist can use—at least 400, according to Dr. Larry Beutler. In terms of individual therapy, researchers have repeatedly found two specific approaches effective in treating depression: cognitive-behavioral therapy and interpersonal therapy.

What do these two approaches have in common? Unlike earlier therapies, many of which helped people gain insight into their past, these therapies focus on the present, says Dr. Beutler. "They're very much in the here-and-now." Adds Dr. Antonuccio: "Usually the more active treatments that involve practice between sessions are the ones that benefit people the most." He notes that therapy focusing on gaining insight into your past seems to be less effective in treating depression. "I'm not saying that insight is necessarily bad," says Dr. Antonuccio, "but it may not be enough. Often people have good reason for being depressed, but to gain insight into those reasons may not be enough to change those situations. You need to take some action." Action-oriented therapies can help people learn to change their thoughts or behaviors or the way they relate to other people.

It may not be easy to find therapists who offer these action-oriented techniques. "Only about 15 percent of psychotherapists that are practicing in the community adhere to these kinds of more practical interventions," says Dr. Beutler.

> *A*ction-oriented therapies can help people learn to change their thoughts or behaviors or the way they relate to other people.

Even if you can't find someone qualified to provide cognitive-behavioral therapy or interpersonal therapy, other types of therapy can also help with depression, says Dr. Beutler. "The best estimate is that about 70 percent of people don't need highly specialized techniques. What is really important is having somebody who can relate to you, that you care about, who will care about you, that can feed reality back to you. And it doesn't much matter whether you go back into your past or stay in the present." He notes that most psychotherapy works "because the therapist is good at establishing this relationship, and helping people look at themselves and evaluate what they're doing."

Psychotherapy can help people pay attention to their strengths and finer qualities and stop belittling themselves and others. It can teach people to recognize what they are actually thinking or feeling, instead of what they think they should be thinking or feeling.

It can hone their decision-making skills, perhaps resulting in more constructive choices in careers, relationships, and lifestyle. Psychotherapy can also help people overcome long-standing phobias or family conflicts that have blocked their progress. At times it can give people the strength to take self-protective action, such as leaving an abusive relationship or abandoning an addiction to alcohol. Drug therapy alone may not have these effects; although by lifting people's mood and releasing them from the apathy and hopelessness of depression, drugs may help them take more positive steps in their lives.

> *Psychotherapy can teach people to recognize what they are actually thinking or feeling, instead of what they think they should be thinking or feeling.*

Cognitive-Behavioral Therapy

Dr. Paul Rohde describes the theory behind cognitive-behavioral therapy this way: "We think of a person's personality as a triangle that involves feelings, thoughts, and behaviors. *Cognitive* just means thoughts. The theory is that when you're sad, you not only feel bad, but your thinking and your actions change." Cognitive-behavioral therapy (CBT) focuses on teaching people to change their thoughts and behavior as a means toward changing their feelings. "It's almost impossible to change our feelings directly, but we can change our thoughts, and we can change our actions," says Dr. Rohde.

Cognitive-behavioral therapy sessions usually take place once a week, sometimes twice a week in severe depression. Most therapists ask clients to do some kind of homework—perhaps examining their thoughts or experimenting with changes in their behavior. The frequency of sessions typically tapers off after several months, then stops. The goal is to teach clients lifelong skills.

There are various subtypes of cognitive-behavioral therapy. One of the first, officially known as *cognitive therapy*, was developed by psychiatrist Aaron Beck. Despite its name, its practitioners incorporate behavioral techniques as well.

Leslie Sokol, Ph.D., clinical psychologist and education coordinator at the Beck Institute in Bala Cynwyd, Pennsylvania, uses the term *automatic thoughts* in explaining how our perceptions can influence our behavior and our physiological responses. An example might be thinking, "Good job," or "I really messed up," after hitting a ball or striking out in baseball. We may not be consciously aware of these thoughts, but they can have profound effects on us nonetheless.

The interesting thing about automatic thoughts is that they often have little to do with reality, particularly among people with depression. A depressed person might tell himself, "You really messed up," when onlookers thought he did very well indeed.

Cognitive therapy teaches people to identify their negative automatic thoughts, and to evaluate whether these thoughts are true or helpful. By doing so, says Dr. Sokol, "we can directly influence how we feel and how we physiologically respond." These changes can lead us to make changes in our behavior.

According to Dr. Sokol, cognitive therapy can also work from the other direction—encouraging the client to change his or her behavior, then notice the effects of these changes on feelings and thoughts. This approach can be particularly helpful in severe depression. "The key to severely depressed patients is behavioral activation," says Dr. Sokol, "educating patients to the fact that you don't have to feel like it to do something." Tools that can help get people moving include breaking tasks into very small steps. "Start with the smallest step, and move forward step-by-step, and systematically plan it out. Think through all the things that could get in the way of those steps happening." This approach, with or without antidepressant medication, can

> *Cognitive therapy teaches people to identify their negative automatic thoughts, and to evaluate whether these thoughts are true or helpful.*

Cognitive Therapy in Action

In the following invented scenario, Dr. Sokol demonstrates how she might work with a severely depressed mother we'll call Jane.

Dr. Sokol: So if I were to ask you, was there a time this week you were feeling really down and blue, when was that time?

Jane: Tuesday afternoon at 3 o'clock.

Dr. Sokol: And what was going on at Tuesday at 3 o'clock?

Jane: I was sitting at home. I was all by myself, and the kids were due home from school in about an hour.

Dr. Sokol: What were you thinking about at that time?

Jane: I was thinking that I was all alone, I had no help, the kids would walk in the door in an hour, and I wouldn't be able to handle it.

Dr. Sokol: And as you were thinking that you wouldn't be able to handle it, you're all alone, and there's no one there to help you, how were you feeling?

Jane: Really down, helpless, hopeless, and overwhelmed.

help people begin to put their behavior, thoughts, and feelings back on a positive track.

Interpersonal Therapy

"The premise of interpersonal therapy," says Larry Beutler, Ph.D., editor of the *Journal of Clinical Psychology*, "is that depression does not occur in a vacuum. It's always an interpersonal event." In the 1970s, researchers from Yale, psychiatrist Gerald Klerman and his wife, epidemiologist Myrna Weissman, sought to develop a short-term psychotherapy to fit the needs and problems of people with depression. The result was interpersonal therapy (IPT). Dr. Beutler notes that

Dr. Sokol: And what were you doing?

Jane: I was sitting on a chair, wringing my hands, doing nothing.

Dr. Sokol: Okay, let's imagine now that you get up out of the chair, you go to the refrigerator, you take out some celery, and you put peanut butter on some of the celery, and raisins on top of the peanut butter, to make "ants on a log" for the kids. You make a tray of these snacks and you set it out in the middle of the counter. Now you're looking at that tray of ants on a log and what are you thinking?

Jane: I'm thinking, wow, you know what, when the kids come home, instead of being out of control, the first thing they're going to do is sit down and start devouring that snack.

Dr. Sokol: And how are you feeling as you're thinking about that?

Jane: I'm feeling a little less overwhelmed.

Dr. Sokol notes that when Jane imagined a different behavior, she was able to realize that things could be different. Her thoughts and her feelings became slightly more positive.

IPT has become a very well-respected treatment for depression, matching the effectiveness of antidepressants in more than one study.

In IPT, the therapist looks for what was happening in the person's life at the time the depression began. Then the therapist helps the person deal with the here-and-now problems associated with the onset of depression. IPT's developers identified four basic interpersonal experiences that contribute to depression. People may choose to address only one or two of these, or all four.

One of the four basic areas is grief after the death of someone close to the person. According to Dr. Beutler, if the grief process gets "stuck," or prolonged, it can interfere with people's ability to socialize or care for themselves. IPT can help people recover those abilities.

Another focus of IPT is on skills training for people with chronic interpersonal difficulties—helping people learn what to do in certain social situations. Dr. Beutler explains: "Some people are depressed simply because they don't know how to cope with things in the world. For example, they may get depressed because every time they go into a group, people laugh at them. That may be because they say things that are inappropriate. If they are taught to be more socially sensitive and to say things in a more reserved and thoughtful way, they may be better able to handle those situations and lose their depression."

IPT also focuses on helping people resolve interpersonal disputes (the third basic experience that contributes to depression) and handle transitions in their roles (the fourth basic area). "When a person changes jobs, or retires, there is a whole new set of expectations put on them with which they're not familiar. And that leaves them confused and not functioning well," says Dr. Beutler. In these situations, he explains, IPT can help people to let go of the past set of expectations and learn new skills.

> *The goal of interpersonal therapy is to help people resolve their current difficulties and learn from their experience so they can prevent similar problems in the future.*

Like cognitive-behavioral therapy, IPT helps people actively handle their present-day concerns. The goal of IPT is to help people resolve their current difficulties and learn from their experience so they can prevent similar problems in the future.

IPT has been very successful both for acute depression and for maintenance treatment for people who are prone to recurrent depression. In one study of people who'd had at least three episodes of depression, ongoing treatment with monthly IPT helped prevent more recurrences. The combination of IPT and medication worked the best at preventing recurrences. By itself, ongoing antidepressant treatment worked somewhat better than IPT at preventing recurrences. Even people who had only IPT, however, had a longer period between recurrences than those receiving placebo or no treatment.[16]

Common Fears About Psychotherapy

"There are thousands of fears that people have about therapy," says Dr. Beutler. "One is that it's interminable—that once they start, they'll have to go forever." The truth of the matter, he says, is quite different. He notes that according to research, 50 percent of people will be symptom-free by the end of 24 sessions, and 85 percent will be symptom-free by the end of one year of weekly therapy.

Another common fear, he notes, is "that all they will hear about is their parents, and they don't want to go back and criticize their parents." According to Dr. Beutler, a number of modern-day psychotherapies "don't put much stock in going back and exploring early life. They want to talk about current, everyday, right-now problems and how you're coping with them."

A third fear people may have is that they will have to reveal all of their secrets. "Everybody has hidden secrets that they don't want to tell about," says Dr. Beutler. He assures people that they won't have to tell all their secrets. "However, therapists will ask them to inspect themselves, in all likelihood, and to talk about it. But the operative word here is *all*. No, you don't have to reveal all your secrets. What you need to be willing to do is take a risk." The risk, he says, usually requires facing some aspect of the situation or yourself that is difficult for you to face. "So yes," he says, "you'll have to uncover and talk about some things, but not all your secrets. It won't matter anyway; if the therapist is any good, then revealing yourself is going to be met with a pretty supportive ear."

LIGHT THERAPY

For people with winter depression, treatment can take a radically different form: sitting before a box generating bright light for 30 minutes or more every morning. Light therapy, sometimes called bright light therapy or phototherapy, can decrease the lethargy, overeating, and depression that mark seasonal affective disorder, or SAD.

The treatment may also aid people who are depressed year-round, but whose depression worsens in winter, explains Dr. David Avery, who is an internationally respected researcher in light treatment for depression. Lightboxes can help in such situations—as can getting out into the daylight more often.

> *Light therapy can decrease the lethargy, overeating, and depression that mark seasonal affective disorder, and may also aid people who are depressed year-round, but whose depression worsens in winter.*

Unfortunately, your doctor may be unfamiliar with light therapy. "The family doctor and the general-practice internist are faced with a rapidly expanding body of knowledge," says Dr. Avery. "It is just very difficult to keep up." If you suspect you have SAD, Dr. Avery suggests that you share information on light therapy with your doctor—including some of the research information that backs it up. He points out that researchers at the National Institute of Mental Health have led the way in conducting research on this condition. (See appendix A for a Web site with information for your doctor.)

ELECTROCONVULSIVE THERAPY (ECT)

If you've ever seen the movie *One Flew Over the Cuckoo's Nest*, electroconvulsive therapy (ECT) may conjure up horrifying images. Yet it can be a highly effective treatment for depression, says Dr. Avery. "Even though ECT is a very controversial treatment," he says, "it's very clear from the data that ECT is superior to antidepressant medications in terms of getting people out of depression." In general, he says, ECT works in about 80 to 90 percent of people hospitalized for depression, whereas antidepressants help only about 60 percent. Normally, people receive a series of 8 to 12 treatments.

In ECT, doctors administer a brief electric shock to the scalp, creating a seizure in the brain. The experience is very different today from that in decades past. An anesthetic and muscle relaxants are given to the person receiving the shock, says Dr. Avery. Due to these drugs, people don't experience the body seizure that used to accompany the brain seizure.

Still, ECT does pose some problems—particularly in its effects on memory. Dr. Avery notes that people who've had ECT may have subsequent difficulty remembering events that occurred for a month or two before and after the course of their treatment. Dr. Rush of the University of Texas notes that the effects on memory are sometimes short-term, sometimes longer-term.

Although the effects on memory can be intimidating, for people battling severe depression, ECT can be a godsend. In her book *Undercurrents: A Therapist's Reckoning with Her Own Depression*, psychologist Martha Manning writes, "In choosing the hospital and ECT, I chose to fight for my life."[17]

TREATING DEPRESSION IN TEENS

Psychologist Paul Rohde has been studying depression in teenagers for years. "What we do research on is cognitive-behavior therapy," he says. "It's the type of therapy that's been most researched for depression, and it's definitely effective. Our research suggests that 60 to 80 percent of kids are definitely helped by cognitive-behavior therapy." Studies by other researchers have found that interpersonal therapy for teens can also help.

Dr. Rohde notes that while there's no question that antidepressants work for adults, "it's been harder to show that the antidepressants, specifically the SSRIs, are more effective than a pill placebo for teenagers." He's participating in a large-scale study based at North Carolina's Duke University, which is exploring this issue. The researchers hope both to establish that Prozac is better than a pill placebo, and to determine "what's more effective: individual psychotherapy or the medication," says Dr. Rohde.

Teens with bipolar disorder may benefit from mood stabilizers as well as psychotherapy specifically oriented toward their condition. In young people with bipolar disorder, antidepressants taken without mood stabilizers may trigger attacks of mania, so accurate diagnosis is essential. Support groups for parents of bipolar teens and children may be particularly helpful.

Asked what is the most important message for families dealing with teenage depression, Dr. Rohde answers, "The biggest thing is that there are a lot of effective treatments. If you try one and it doesn't work, don't give up—try another. You could try one type of medication, and sometimes people can't tolerate the side effects, so try another. Or try psychotherapy. If you go to counseling, you might not connect with the first therapist, so try another one. Don't give up hope if the first line of attack isn't successful." He notes that both medications and psychotherapy take time to work. If you give up too soon, you may not see results.

> *The most important message for families dealing with teenage depression is that there are a lot of effective treatments. If you try one and it doesn't work, don't give up—try another.*

TREATING DEPRESSION IN CHILDREN

Treatments for a depressed child include various types of psychotherapy and medications, as well as education for the child and family, according to Jeffrey Kirchner, D.O., associate director of the family practice residency program at Pennsylvania's Lancaster General Hospital.[18] Much research is still needed, however, on the effectiveness of depression treatments for children.

When treating with medication, doctors sometimes prescribe some of the same kinds of antidepressants for children as they do for adults. "As for the proof that medicines work in prepubertal kids, there is far less information about whether that's the case," says Alan Unis, M.D., associate professor of psychiatry at the University of Washington. "But antidepressants, the newer ones, have certainly been shown to be safe in children," notes Dr. David Dunner. To date, the FDA has not approved antidepressants for use in treating child-hood depression.

Dr. Kirchner agrees about the shortage of information on the effectiveness of antidepressants for youngsters. In particular, he says, there is little scientific evidence that the older tricyclic antidepressants help children. "Some of the newer studies with the SSRI drugs show a little more promise in terms of their benefit," he says, "but I'm still a strong believer in psychotherapy."

There are multiple forms of psychotherapy that may be appropriate for children, including play therapy, family therapy, supportive therapy, psychodynamic therapy, cognitive-behavioral therapy, and interpersonal therapy. The best choice depends in part on the child's level of cognitive and emotional development.

"Medication therapy truly is indicated in many cases of major depressive disorder," says Dr. Kirchner. "But I think there are good data to show that patients do better, have fewer relapses, and have a better long-term outcome if, at the same time they are being treated with medication, they undergo some type of therapeutic intervention with a psychiatrist or psychologist. Again, there are some pediatric data to show that this improves the outcome."

Psychologist Barbara Ingersoll, coauthor of *Lonely, Sad and Angry: How to Help Your Unhappy Child*, is one who believes in combination treatment for children. "Most mood-disordered kids will probably need more than one intervention," she says, "because they're so often having problems on so many fronts." For example, she notes that many have interpersonal problems, difficulties within the family, and learning disabilities as well as depression. "I would probably call it psychosocial intervention rather than psychotherapy," she says, "because psychosocial intervention is a much broader term, and it covers psychotherapy,

> *Some studies suggest that children do better, have fewer relapses, and have a better long-term outcome if they are treated with a combination of medication and therapeutic intervention with a psychiatrist or psychologist.*

family therapy, behavior therapy, working with the schools, all of those things."

Dr. Kirchner feels that primary care doctors often don't have the time or the professional skills to do what it takes to treat depression in children. "I think that any child diagnosed with a childhood depressive disorder, particularly major depressive disorder, but even dysthymic disorder or adjustment disorder with depressed mood, should be referred to somebody who has the time," he says. He notes that appropriate treatment of these conditions requires appointment times longer than the 10 to 12 minutes the average family doctor or pediatrician can spend.

SPECIAL ISSUES FOR WOMEN: TREATING POSTPARTUM AND PREMENSTRUAL DEPRESSION

Two forms of depression unique to women, postpartum and premenstrual depression, deserve special consideration, since their treatment sometimes varies from that of other types of depression.

Postpartum Depression

Depression in the weeks or months after childbirth is common. Women coping with a brand-new infant, plus hormonal shifts and sleep deprivation, may be particularly vulnerable to depression. Often, the symptoms of low mood, anxiety, irritability, and tearfulness go away in a few days or a week without treatment. But sometimes the depression lingers and deepens, and other times it is severe from the outset. Prolonged or severe postpartum depression can affect both mother and child, as well as other members of the family.

Some of the best treatments for postpartum depression or baby blues are ones that family members and friends can provide: emotional and practical support. The following can be of enormous help:

assisting the mother in getting enough rest, fluids, and nutrition; listening to her concerns; and providing nonintrusive, nonjudgmental help with baby care. Support groups and telephone hotlines for new mothers or new parents can provide both emotional support and practical tips.

While helpful, these measures are sometimes not enough. For more severe situations, treatment with psychotherapy, ECT, or antidepressants can help. Many doctors and women are reluctant to begin treatment with antidepressants if the woman is breastfeeding, because the baby will absorb the drug. Unfortunately, no one yet knows the long-term effects of antidepressants on breastfeeding infants. Before beginning antidepressants, it's useful to discuss fully their risks and benefits, as they affect both the mother and child.

It can also be wise to have a complete checkup to look for physical causes of depression such as hypothyroidism.

Premenstrual Depression

If premenstrual depression (also known as premenstrual dysphoric disorder, or PMDD), is severe, most providers will prescribe an antidepressant. An analysis of 15 recent studies found that drugs in the Prozac family work well at reducing symptoms. Several preliminary studies have found that these antidepressants may work just as well when taken only during the premenstrual period.[19]

But there may be other options for premenstrual depression, particularly in its milder forms. Recently, a large study found calcium effective in reducing premenstrual symptoms, including emotional ones. (See chapter 4, page 128, for more information.) Cognitive-behavioral therapy, a form of psychotherapy described earlier in this chapter, may also help. Some women seem to do better on drugs in the Motrin (ibuprofen) family, medically categorized as nonsteroidal anti-inflammatory drugs (NSAIDs). Other popular treatments, some of them supported by research, include exercise, dietary improvements (less sugar, no caffeine), vitamins, and relaxation techniques.

Progesterone and birth control pills, though sometimes prescribed for PMS (premenstrual syndrome), haven't done any better than a placebo at reducing premenstrual symptoms in most scientific studies.[20] These progesterone studies didn't focus specifically on women with PMDD.

SUMMARY

Numerous effective treatments exist for depression. Two important types of treatment, antidepressants and psychotherapy, can help with many kinds of depression. For bipolar disorder, mood stabilizing drugs are the mainstay of treatment.

The Food and Drug Administration has approved more than 20 antidepressants. Antidepressants usually take several weeks to begin working. Not everyone responds to any given antidepressant. Since doctors cannot reliably predict which will be most effective for you, you may need to try more than one to find one that works. If your antidepressant causes bothersome side effects or doesn't relieve your symptoms, it's important to tell your doctor. Many alternative approaches exist, including adjusting the dose, switching medications, or using other forms of treatment.

Psychotherapy can also be effective at relieving depression. Studies have found two short-term psychotherapies, cognitive-behavioral therapy and interpersonal therapy, to be particularly effective for depression. For more severe or chronic depression, including bipolar disorder, the combination of psychotherapy and antidepressants may be most helpful. Somewhat less is known about the effectiveness of specific treatments for depression in children and teens.

Other important treatments include electroconvulsive therapy for severe depression, light therapy for seasonal affective disorder, and calcium for premenstrual disorder. In addition, many people are drawn to complementary and alternative treatments—the topic of the following chapter.

CHAPTER 4

Complementary and Alternative Treatments for Depression

❧

First thing in the morning, I take my amino acid blend right after my allergy medication, then have breakfast, wait and take my Paxil and blood pressure meds and my fish oil or borage oil because they help. B vitamins are good. I take Ginkgo biloba, *too—I feel like with these meds, at least when you're first on them, you really have trouble concentrating and ginkgo helps me concentrate and remember better.*

—GENEVIEVE, WHO SUFFERED FROM MAJOR DEPRESSION

A NATIONAL SURVEY by Harvard Medical School researchers produced fascinating results: More than half of adults reporting severe depression said they had tried treating it with alternative methods.[1] Of the people reporting severe depression, more than 53 percent said they treated it with either relaxation techniques, herbs, massage, spiritual healing, or any of nearly two dozen other approaches. Even more startling, the proportion of people using alternative methods of treatment for depression exceeded the proportion (36 percent) who saw a conventional doctor, mental health professional, or member of the clergy for treatment. Clearly, complementary and alternative treatments for depression are extremely popular.

The upside of this information is that quite a few people in the Harvard survey noted that their alternative treatments were "very helpful."[2] The downside is that many people are evidently trying to treat severe depression on their own—thereby putting themselves at risk for worsening symptoms. But using alternative treatments does not seem to make people reluctant to see their doctors—in fact, the evidence suggests the contrary. According to the Harvard survey, people using alternative or complementary treatments were more, not less, likely to see conventional health professionals compared to those who didn't use alternative treatments. Still, more than 30 percent of depressed people used alternative remedies alone.

What alternative treatments are people most often using for depression? According to the Harvard survey, the most popular alternative treatments were relaxation techniques and spiritual healing by others. Herbs and homeopathy are also popular, according to another study, this one of people receiving psychiatric care for a variety of problems.[3]

According to a number of studies, many, if not most people using alternative approaches, do not tell their doctors what they're doing. Yet more and more conventional doctors are learning about alternative approaches, and most will appreciate your sharing the information. There's at least one very good reason to inform your doctors—all your doctors—about everything you are taking, and that's to avoid the possibility of dangerous interactions. People who combine natural remedies such as St. John's wort with conventional drugs without telling their doctor may be putting their health on the line. For your own safety, it's best to use any treatments for depression—whether complementary or conventional—under a doctor's supervision.

WHAT IS COMPLEMENTARY OR ALTERNATIVE MEDICINE?

Natural treatments, including herbs, acupuncture, and relaxation techniques, have been rising in popularity in this country for several decades. One challenge has been what to call this category of treatment. Two frequently used terms are *alternative medicine* and *complementary medicine*. Technically, alternative medicine refers to natural treatments used *instead* of treatments normally offered by a conventional health care provider, while complementary medicine refers to natural treatments used *in addition to* conventional medical care. People often use the terms interchangeably, however.

Even more confusing, an increasing number of conventional health care providers now recommend that their patients try complementary approaches—for example, relaxation techniques for anxiety. Does this mean relaxation techniques should no longer be considered a complementary (or alternative) treatment? Different people have different answers. The majority of people still consider herbs and most supplements complementary treatments—even though, today, bottles of herbs often sit right next to the aspirin and laxatives on pharmacy shelves.

HERBS AND SUPPLEMENTS

St. John's wort, 5-HTP, SAMe, ginkgo, phenylalanine, folic acid, phosphatidylserine—these are only some of the herbs and supplements that naturally oriented practitioners recommend for depression. If you tried all of them, you'd be spending hundreds of dollars a month on treatments, some of which might help, and some of which might do nothing for you. In addition, you could be setting yourself up for some possible negative interactions. The following information can aid you in making a decision about what might work best for you, although, as with antidepressants, people respond differently to different herbs and supplements. Please note that the safety information on the herbs and supplements cited here is incomplete. Before deciding to try one of these natural treatments, talk it over with your doctor. For more information, you may also want to pursue some of the further reading suggested in appendix B.

St. John's Wort

A brilliant yellow flower that likes sun-drenched slopes (see figure 4.1), St. John's wort has become a standard treatment for depression in Germany. Its use is increasing in the United States as well. In 1998, the herb accounted for an estimated 10 percent of sales of herbal medicine in this country.[4]

"People who would never consider taking a standard antidepressant will take St. John's wort," says Dr. Steven Bratman, author of *The Natural Pharmacist: Treating Depression*. "They like it because it's an herb, not a drug, and that feels more natural to them. It also may cause fewer side effects than antidepressant drugs—unless you combine it with other medications. Then it can be very risky."

Figure 4.1—*St. John's Wort*

According to Dr. Bratman, research has found that St. John's wort may be as effective as standard antidepressants for mild to moderate depression. "One study found it was even more effective than Prozac in people with mild or moderate depression," he says.[5] "But when they tested it for severe depression, it didn't work nearly as well as the antidepressant imipramine." In fact, one recent study of the herb in people with severe major depression found it worked no better than a placebo.[6] Dr. Bratman advises people with severe depression to see a doctor.

Just as with standard antidepressants, not everyone seems to benefit from St. John's wort, even after excluding people with more severe de-pression. As with standard antidepressant drugs, full effects take time to develop, usually about 4 to 6 weeks.

Although many good-quality studies have found St. John's wort effective, most of them tested the herb for two months or less. Cur-rently, researchers at North Carolina's Duke University are completing a long-term study comparing St. John's wort to both a placebo and a standard antidepressant. Many doctors are eagerly awaiting the results.

St. John's wort has become a standard treatment for depression in Germany. In the United States, in 1998, the herb accounted for an esti-mated 10 percent of sales of herbal medicine.

Side effects with St. John's wort tend to be mild, and may be less frequent than with conventional antidepressants. "In published stud-ies, the people who reported side effects mostly said they had mild stomach upset or rashes," Dr. Bratman says. "If you give a lot of peo-ple almost anything, some of them will probably get these reactions. But millions of people have taken St. John's wort in Germany, and there haven't been any reports of serious side effects so far."

Nonetheless, St. John's wort is not completely risk-free. It may cause an increased sensitivity to sunlight in some people, especially in high doses. Like standard antidepressants, it may also occasionally in-duce mania in people with bipolar disorder.

The main safety issue with St. John's wort is that it can interact with some critical medications. The National Institute of Mental Health has issued a public alert noting reports of interactions between St. John's wort and two drugs: Indinavir, which treats HIV; and a drug used to cut the risk of rejecting a transplanted organ. The herb may also interact with some heart medications, chemotherapy drugs, standard antidepressants, the blood thinner warfarin (Coumadin), treatments for schizophrenia and asthma, and possibly even birth control pills. "The bottom line," says Dr. Bratman, "is that if you're taking any medicine that's critical to your health, don't take St. John's wort."

> **Medical Alert**
>
> If you're seriously depressed, don't rely solely on alternative remedies: See a doctor.

It is also not wise to switch from a standard antidepressant to St. John's wort without consulting a doctor. St. John's wort is thought to work by affecting levels of neurotransmitters such as serotonin. Beginning the herb too soon after stopping a drug may raise levels of serotonin dangerously high.

St. John's wort has a long history of use for emotional difficulties. Ongoing research should clarify its role in treating depression today.

5-HTP: A Natural Prozac?

5-HTP sounds like something you add to your gas tank, but it's actually short for a natural chemical called 5-hydroxytryptophan. 5-HTP is one of a series of chemicals your body makes in order to produce serotonin, the same neurotransmitter whose levels are affected by antidepressants like Prozac. Several decades ago researchers began wondering whether giving people 5-HTP might boost the levels of serotonin in their brains and alleviate symptoms of depression. A number of small, preliminary studies suggest that 5-HTP may indeed help, but scientifically speaking, the jury's still out.[7] Longer, better-quality studies would answer many questions, but research on this supplement seems to have lagged in recent years. Nonetheless, European doctors frequently use 5-HTP as a treatment for depression.

Trina Doerfler, a naturopathic physician practicing in Seattle, Washington, finds that 5-HTP helps some of her depressed patients, but not others. She describes one young man whose improvement with 5-HTP has been dramatic. "This man has been suicidal since he was 10. He had tried all of the drugs, all of them, and nothing worked—or they worked for a very short time and then stopped working," she explains. "So he was pretty desperate." With 5-HTP, his symptoms decreased enormously, and seem to have stayed that way. "He's working, he's in a relationship, it's just been quite miraculous for him," says Dr. Doerfler. But this type of response is rare, in her experience. "He's my best case. There are a whole variety of reactions, down to people feeling nothing."

5-HTP generally seems to be safe, with the most common side effects being stomach cramps, nausea, and diarrhea.[8] The FDA, however, has raised concerns about possible contamination of some 5-HTP products, potentially causing the same serious blood disorder that led the FDA to remove the related supplement L-tryptophan from the market in the past.[9] So far the FDA hasn't been concerned enough to stop people from taking 5-HTP. If you decide to take this product, watch for updates in the news.

Don't combine 5-HTP with other antidepressants or prescription pain medications without first checking with your doctor. The level of serotonin in your blood may rise dangerously. 5-HTP may also interact with carbidopa, a medication for Parkinson's disease, causing serious skin disease.[10]

Ginkgo biloba

Better known as a treatment for memory problems, the herb *Ginkgo biloba* may also help reduce symptoms of depression in some people, according to Wayne Jonas, M.D., the former director of the federal government's Office of Alternative Medicine. (The Office of Alternative Medicine has since been renamed the National Center for Complementary and Alternative Medicine.) Dr. Jonas notes that ginkgo is often recommended for elderly people with depression, especially if their depression may be partly due to mini-strokes or other circulatory problems in the brain. "Ginkgo has been shown to be effective in a couple of clinical trials," Dr. Jonas says, referring to research on depression. One of these trials studied older people with memory difficulties and moderately severe depression, who weren't improving with standard antidepressants.[11] Taking ginkgo on top of their antidepressants decreased their depression significantly. Their thinking ability also improved.

> *Ginkgo is often recommended for elderly people with depression, especially if their depression may be partly due to mini-strokes or other circulatory problems in the brain.*

There's even a bit of preliminary evidence that ginkgo may help reduce sexual side effects from antidepressants like Prozac, report psychiatrists Jonathan Davidson, M.D., and Kathryn Connor, M.D., in their book *Herbs for the Mind*.[12]

In general, ginkgo seems to be very safe when taken in recommended dosages, although it sometimes causes stomach upset. But if you're taking blood thinning medication (including regular doses of aspirin) ginkgo may raise your risk of bleeding.

Amino Acids

If you remember your high school science classes, you'll know that amino acids are the building blocks of proteins. The body uses two amino acids—tyrosine and L-phenylalanine—to make the neurotransmitters norepinephrine and dopamine, which may play a role in depression. At this point there's not much scientific evidence that tyrosine helps treat depression, although some people believe in it regardless. There are some small but interesting studies, however, that suggest that certain forms of phenylalanine may be helpful.[13] In one study of 27 people with depression, one group took phenylalanine for 30 days while another took imipramine (a tricyclic antidepressant) for 30 days. The two groups had equal decreases in their symptoms of depression.[14] A longer study might have allowed a better comparison, because imipramine can take more than 30 days to become fully effective. Nonetheless, the results are intriguing. Some naturopaths can put together individualized blends of amino acids based on an analysis of your blood.

If you take drugs for schizophrenia or Parkinson's disease, talk to your doctor before taking amino acids such as phenylalanine, as there may be serious interactions. People with PKU (a rare hereditary disease) should not use phenylalanine at all.

SAMe

SAMe (pronounced sammy) is the friendly-sounding acronym for another popular supplement for depression, S-adenosyl-L-methionine. According to Dr. Bratman, its popularity began in Italy, then spread to the United States, based on several small studies that found it helped with depression.[15]

One of the reasons people choose SAMe is that it's supposed to work more quickly than standard antidepressants. The speed of action, however, may have more to do with how the supplement is administered than with the supplement itself, according to Dr. Bratman. Most of the Italian studies used injected or intravenous forms of the supplement. Taking it by mouth, the way people do in this country, may well lead to slower results. (It's very risky to inject drugs intended for oral use—don't even consider it!)

One problem with SAMe is that it's extremely expensive, at least in the doses that Italian researchers found to be helpful (the equivalent of 1,600 milligrams or more per day in oral doses). "What happened in this country is that the people marketing SAMe began saying you should take 200 milligrams twice a day, which makes it affordable, but that's three or four times too low according to the researchers," says Dr. Bratman. "Nobody in Italy believed it worked

Word-of-Mouth: Is It Reliable?

People often decide to try a treatment because it helped someone they know. Doctors, too, are more likely to recommend a treatment if they've heard good things about it from their patients or other doctors. But is word-of-mouth the best way to determine whether a treatment might help? Dr. Steven Bratman thinks not.

"Very often treatments work just because people believe in them," says Dr. Bratman. "You can take a treatment that does absolutely nothing on its own, but if you expect it to help you, it probably will."

Researchers are well aware of this phenomenon, and have a term for it: the placebo effect. A placebo is a fake drug used in studies that are designed to test a real drug's effectiveness. Researchers typically give half the study participants the real drug being tested, and half of them the placebo, without telling the participants—or their doctors—which people are getting the actual drug. Researchers rate a drug as effective only if it consistently brings more improvement than the placebo. But what's interesting here is how much people can benefit from the placebo. Usually about 30 percent of people taking the placebo report improvement in their symptoms, but some studies report much higher rates.[16] Depression is one condition for which the placebo effect tends to be particularly strong.

Dr. Bratman has repeatedly watched the seeming effectiveness of certain alternative remedies soar among his patients, then wane

for depression at that low dose. Of course, here in this country, everybody was getting better on the lower dose—but a lot (or maybe all) of that was probably from the placebo effect."

Dr. Bratman notes that very few of his patients seemed to benefit from SAMe before it became famous. When it hit the news, all at once his patients seemed to find it much more effective. Yet while

when the treatment loses popularity in the press. "When a treatment first becomes famous, all of a sudden it seems to help a lot of people," he says. But a couple of years later, it doesn't seem to work anymore. Instead, the current hot treatment gets all the results.

Rather than relying on individuals' experiences, Dr. Bratman relies more and more on the results of scientific studies. "If a number of studies consistently find that a treatment works better than placebo, then I'll believe that it's the treatment itself that's working. But otherwise, no matter how many people tell me that a treatment is helping, I'm going to be dubious until I see some hard facts."

Most people still feel better about a treatment if someone they know has used it successfully. But more and more, medical professionals are relying on placebo-controlled studies in determining what treatments to recommend.

"Besides the placebo effect, there's another factor at work," says Dr. Bratman, who's investigated the scientific research on scores of herbs and supplements. "Observers tend to see what they expect to see. If, as a physician, I think a treatment will work, I will tend to evaluate its effect more positively. I have arrived at a point where I don't even believe my own experience of any treatment. I want to see what the studies show."

SAMe was on the upswing in the United States, its popularity declined in Italy. "People in Italy have mostly abandoned SAMe now," he says. "They don't consider it as effective as regular antidepressants, especially in oral forms. There is another problem as well. SAMe is an unstable molecule, and supplements that you buy in the store might not have much active SAMe."

If you do decide to try SAMe, definitely contact your doctor before combining it with other medications, as it may cause interactions.

Folic Acid

Can a simple B vitamin—folic acid—help treat depression? Investigators are researching this possibility. A recent study found that 500 micrograms daily of folic acid boosted the effectiveness of Prozac in women.[17] This exciting piece of research didn't come out of the blue: Previous preliminary studies have found that forms of folic acid enhanced the effectiveness of other drug treatments for depression.[18]

Some studies even suggest that folic acid on its own might help. One preliminary study found that giving a form of folic acid to depressed elderly people boosted the moods of 81 percent of them, even without other treatment for depression.[19] This study was very small and lacked a control group, however, so it's possible that the participants were experiencing the placebo effect.

A recent study found that 500 micrograms daily of folic acid boosted the effectiveness of Prozac in women.

Don't take more than 400 micrograms of folic acid per day, unless you're under a doctor's care. Too much folic acid can mask a deficiency in vitamin B_{12}.

Vitamin B_{12}

Earlier in this century it was common for doctors to inject patients with vitamin B_{12} to boost their energy. These days most conventional doctors give B_{12} only when their patients have a particular type of anemia, *pernicious anemia*, which is most common in the elderly. One study, however, linked B_{12} deficiency to a twofold increase in the risk of depression in older women.[20] Whether B_{12} can help treat depression in the elderly or other people isn't clear. But it makes sense to test for this deficiency, especially if you're 65 or older, and treat it if it's present.

Phosphatidylserine

Like *Ginkgo biloba*, phosphatidylserine is a natural treatment used for memory impairment in the elderly. Phosphatidylserine is a component of the membranes surrounding our cells. In more than one small study, it also helped reduce symptoms of depression in the elderly.[21] More research is needed to know for sure whether or not it works for depression. The price can be prohibitive, however—about $60 or more per month.

Fish Oil for Bipolar Disorder

People used to call fish "brain food," and research has indicated that fish may be a possible preventive for heart disease. Now, an exciting preliminary study suggests that fish oil, which contains omega-3 fatty acids, may help control depression in people with bipolar disorder. Harvard University researcher Andrew Stoll, M.D., and colleagues gave fish oil or an olive oil placebo to people with bipolar disorder along with participants' usual medications. People taking the fish oil had significantly longer periods of remission and fewer symptoms of depression when compared to those taking the placebo.[22]

The idea of taking a natural and healthful product as a mood stabilizer appeals to many people with bipolar disorder. It's a bit too early to tell if the treatment really helps, however. More studies are needed with larger groups of people.

Fish oil has a few drawbacks. Number one, it's not recommended as a stand-alone treatment; people still need to take their usual mood stabilizers. Number two, to get the recommended amount of omega-3 fatty acids, you have to take a lot of fish oil capsules, which can have a distinct, fishy aftertaste and may cause some burping and loose stools. Some health care providers recommend flaxseed oil as a

> *Some exciting new research suggests that fish oil, which contains omega-3 fatty acids, may help control depression in people with bipolar disorder.*

substitute; you don't need as much, and it causes fewer burps. Unfortunately, if our information on fish oil is slim, it's even slimmer for flaxseed oil, which contains a different type of omega-3 fatty acid.

Both fish oil and flaxseed oil seem to be safe. In fact, naturopathic physicians frequently recommend both to the general public as a

Rosalie's Story: Using Natural Remedies

Rosalie, a 45-year-old clinical social worker and psychotherapist, developed major depression two years ago after the death of her father was followed only 3 weeks later by the death of her stepfather. Her depression didn't occur immediately, but as a result of other factors piled onto these. "My father left a big complicated estate. And I have a brother who is brain-damaged who is really rageful, who felt that I was trying to rip him off as executor," says Rosalie. In addition, Rosalie's mother became suicidal. "I was trying to handle my mom, I was dealing with my brother, I was dealing with the estate, which was about 20 hours a week of extra work, and I have a challenging job," says Rosalie. "So I didn't have time to grieve. I didn't have time to miss my dad very much because I was constantly on call for the estate, for my mother, for other people who were grieving my dad, and for my brother," she says. "I really did shoulder this load for a while, for about 9 months." At that point, Rosalie began to have difficulty concentrating and remembering things. "It was like I could not think. I couldn't pay attention very well, and in my line of work, paying attention is what I do," she says.

Unsure what these symptoms indicated, Rosalie went to her primary care doctor. "She asked me a bunch of questions and said, 'You have clinical depression,'" Rosalie remembers. Something in Rosalie loosened at these words. "I just cried and cried and cried," she recalls.

means of improving their overall health. There's even some preliminary information—discussed in the next chapter—that fish or fish oil might benefit people prone to other types of depression. A note of caution, however, if you take blood-thinning medication: Fish oil may slightly increase the risk of bleeding.

Rosalie saw a psychiatrist, who prescribed first one SSRI, then another. Both gave Rosalie intolerable side effects. "The first one made me fall asleep. The second one made me really nervous, and I am not a nervous kind of person. I said, 'I'm going to try something else,'" says Rosalie.

Rosalie did some research and came up with a list of alternative remedies including fish oil and flaxseed; St. John's wort; 5-HTP; and phosphatidylserine. She consulted a naturopathic physician, who approved her choices. In addition, Rosalie began seeing a psychotherapist she'd seen in the past. She exercised relentlessly. She also took a series of vacations. "During those vacations I did very little," she recalls. "I would just cry and cry and cry about my dad." Within 4 months, her depression had largely resolved. "I was feeling pretty good," she says.

Since that time, Rosalie has continued some of her natural treatments while discontinuing others. A naturopath whom Rosalie is now seeing recommended she not combine St. John's wort with 5-HTP. "I am still taking St. John's wort. I'm not taking 5-HTP anymore," says Rosalie. She's also cut out the phosphatidylserine because of its cost. Although she's no longer seeing her psychotherapist, she continues to practice good emotional self-care. "I really try to notice when I need a break, when I need to say no, when I need a vacation," she says.

Rosalie believes her approach has paid off. She notes that she never felt suicidal, and never felt the world was a horrible place, and that she now feels back to her normal self. Of the natural remedies, she says, "I think that they were useful." Still, she believes that clearing out her grief in psychotherapy was the most helpful thing she did.

Other Herbs and Supplements for Depression

Depression has occurred throughout history and across many cultures. Traditional healers have long treated it with a variety of herbs in addition to those named; others include lemon balm, ginseng, basil, and wild oats.[23]

Besides herbs for depression, many people take kava kava for symptoms of anxiety and valerian to help with sleep. There are quite a few scientific studies demonstrating that these two herbs can indeed help with these conditions. Be sure to read up on safety information, first—there are a few situations you'll want to avoid, such as combining kava kava with other sedatives.

Natural Treatments for Premenstrual Depression

According to Susan Thys-Jacobs, M.D., many premenstrual symptoms resemble those of calcium deficiency. In a groundbreaking study, she gave calcium supplements or a placebo to nearly 500 women with ordinary PMS (premenstrual syndrome) for several months. Mood swings, depression, tension, short-temperedness, and crying spells, along with other symptoms such as bloating, all improved more with calcium than with the placebo. It took three menstrual cycles for the full effects to kick in.[24]

Medical Alert

Be sure to tell your health care providers all the treatments you're using, including alternative remedies and over-the-counter and prescription drugs.

Taking 1,200 milligrams of calcium per day (the amount given in the study) may benefit your health in more than one way. Doctors have long recommended calcium to maintain bone strength in women. If you have premenstrual depression, talk to your doctor about trying calcium—it can't hurt.

Vitamin B$_6$ may also help premenstrual depression, according to an analysis of studies on the subject.[25] The evidence, however, isn't nearly as strong as for calcium, and the best dose to take isn't clear. Researchers suggest perhaps 50 to 100 milligrams per day. Taking 200 milligrams daily or more may lead to neurological problems, so it's wise to stick to a lower dose.

Some alternative practitioners treat premenstrual syndrome with natural progesterone; however, most well-designed studies have found that neither natural or synthetic progesterone seems to help.[26] It's also not clear at this point whether magnesium or evening primrose oil, both popular remedies, actually reduce symptoms of premenstrual depression.[27]

HOMEOPATHY

Developed in Germany in the nineteenth century, homeopathy is a system of medicine entirely different in philosophy from standard Western medicine, and from herbal approaches as well. In homeopathy, rather than taking a medicine to suppress symptoms, people take a substance, called a remedy, that in a healthy person produces similar symptoms. This approach is termed *like treats like*. Another unusual feature of homeopathy is that the more dilute the remedy, the stronger it is supposed to be.

Homeopathic remedies designed to treat particular symptoms are available in health food stores. The original or *classical* form of homeopathy follows a different approach, however. According to Dr. Wayne Jonas, "Classical homeopathy is a system of medicine that treats a set of symptoms that is based on the entire person, not just on a particular diagnosis." Practitioners look at the entire person—his or her symptoms, character traits, and so on—and select a single remedy designed to bring that person to optimum wellness.

"At least in classical homeopathy, there's no such thing as treating depression," says Dr. Jonas. Instead, you treat the individual, considering their entire picture of symptoms in choosing a remedy. "If you get a good match between the homeopathic picture and the

Safe Use of Complementary Treatments for Depression

Dr. Wayne Jonas has some suggestions for people interested in using complementary treatments for depression or other health problems. "I think the biggest concern for the consumer is lack of data about safety and efficacy," says Dr. Jonas. He notes that companies and research institutes have invested relatively little money in testing how effective herbs and supplements are in treating disease, compared to the vast sums spent by pharmaceutical companies seeking FDA (Food and Drug Administration) approval for their drugs. Dr. Jonas recommends using complementary treatments—whether herbs, supplements, acupuncture, homeopathy, or other approaches—under the supervision of a primary care provider or other health care professional qualified to diagnose and treat depression. "Depression is a serious illness," he notes. He suggests setting a timeline and some goals with your doctor, including how much you're going to use, for what period of time, and what you expect to happen during that time—"just as you might do for a drug." If the treatment doesn't work, your doctor will be there to suggest other options.

Your doctor may also be able to help protect you against another possible risk: drug-herb interactions. Dr. Jonas notes that it can be difficult for researchers to gather information on drug-herb interactions because there are so many drugs and so many herbs. As more people combine the two, dangerous interactions are surfacing in some cases. "That's been illustrated recently by a couple of case reports in which individuals on anti-retroviral treatment for HIV started taking St. John's wort and it began to reduce their blood levels of those drugs. Consequently, their blood levels of HIV virus increased," says Dr. Jonas. Your doctor can help you to steer clear of combinations known, or suspected, to be risky.

Your doctor can also help you evaluate possible side effects of your herbal treatments. "There are reported adverse effects from herbs," says Dr. Jonas, although he believes this problem is probably not as large as that posed by drug-herb interactions.

What about selecting a particular brand of a product? Many people assume that anything sold on a drugstore or supermarket shelf is safe and accurately labeled. Not necessarily, according to Dr. Jonas. Whole herbs or combination products imported from India or China carry a risk of contamination. "This can be contamination with toxic elements such as arsenic, or contamination with pesticides," says Dr. Jonas. He notes this problem is uncommon with herbs and supplements manufactured by reputable companies in the West. In fact, some of the most reliable standardized products come from Germany, where for some time the government has regulated companies producing natural products.

In addition, Dr. Jonas notes that the label on the container often incorrectly identifies the contents, even in products claiming to contain a standardized percentage of the active ingredient(s). Some research analyzing off-the-shelf St. John's wort preparations has shown that "the content of some of the ingredients varies anywhere from 20 percent of what was on the label all the way up to 140 percent," says Dr. Jonas. Analyses of other herbs such as garlic have shown even wider disparities. "There's been a several hundred-fold difference in the amount of allicin, which is thought to be one of the active ingredients, between garlic products," says Dr. Jonas. He suggests looking for companies that have a reputation for quality manufacture of herbs and supplements and, if they are pharmaceutical companies, drugs.

medication, I have observed very good improvement in moods, including depression."

Dr. Jonas notes that researchers haven't studied classical homeopathy specifically for depression, because it's not used specifically for depression. Depression is just one part of an overall symptom-picture that includes many other features as well.

Medical Alert

Don't take any herb or supplement without medical supervision if you are pregnant, breastfeeding, or have a serious medical problem.

"The current evidence indicates that, overall, homeopathy does seem to work better than placebo," says Dr. Jonas. "The problem is that since it isn't used for single clinical conditions, there aren't enough studies looking at single clinical conditions to say whether it works in that particular condition. However, it seems to work generally for improving people's symptoms across a number of conditions."

Dr. Jonas suggests that homeopathy is a reasonable approach to try for mild to moderate depression, if done under supervision. "Again," he says, "you have to make sure you're under good clinical supervision. Depression is not something to be taken lightly."

RELAXATION TECHNIQUES

Learning to relax deeply is a more popular approach to treating depression than any herb or supplement, according to the Harvard survey mentioned at the start of this chapter. Children and animals know how to relax and do so spontaneously. Adults usually need training, however—a sad statement about our culture.

People who practice regular deep relaxation report an increased ability to handle the stresses of daily life. A dozen or so studies suggest that deep relaxation can help treat depression—although probably only the mildest depressions respond to relaxation therapy alone.[28]

If you're interested in learning some relaxation techniques, there are a host of tapes and books available on progressive relaxation, guided imagery, self-hypnosis, and other methods. A few more innovative techniques are described in the next chapter.

ACUPUNCTURE

Acupuncture is part of the system of medicine first developed in China thousands of years ago and now practiced worldwide by specially trained practitioners. By placing fine needles into specific points in the body, acupuncturists aim to restore natural patterns of energy flow along pathways known as meridians.

"Ultimately everything in Chinese medicine, any kind of pathology, is an imbalance from an ideal state of harmony," states Andrew McIntyre, an acupuncturist and faculty member at Bastyr University in Seattle. Harmony depends on having a good flow of *qi* (pronounced chi), a Chinese term for energy. "An imbalance of qi can happen in any number of ways," explains McIntyre. "Imagine yourself, for example, experiencing stress. You start to hunch up. You start to impede the flow that's only there when you're nice and relaxed. If this goes on long enough, it affects one of the major organ systems." At this point, he notes, you might receive the Chinese diagnosis of *liver-qi stagnation*, roughly corresponding to some Western diagnoses of depression. (Other qi-based diagnoses for types of depression include *spleen and heart deficiency*, or the more poetic *phlegm misting the mind*.)

You may be better off seeking care from a certified acupuncturist with a minimum of 3 years' professional training, rather than an M.D. or D.O. with just a few weekend workshops under his or her belt.

Traditional acupuncturists use an entirely different system of examination from that of Western doctors. Expect to have your tongue examined and your pulse taken in several different locations. The examiner may raise questions unusual in most Western medical histories, such as what time of day you are most alert or most tired.

Serena's Story: Help from Homeopathy

Serena, a 42-year-old customer service representative, had positive feelings about homeopathy. When her son was two, she'd taken him to a homeopath after a series of ear infections failed to respond to penicillin. "That was very successful," she says. Serena's health insurance, however, didn't cover homeopathy for herself. So when she developed depression, she went to a conventional primary care doctor and received a prescription for Zoloft.

Serena didn't like taking Zoloft. She was unhappy with the side effects she experienced, including a decreased sex drive, headaches, and disrupted sleep. In addition, even on Zoloft she continued to have some symptoms of depression. After a year she tried discontinuing Zoloft on her own, but developed new symptoms that scared her. "I became very agitated. I had a very short temper," she recalls. She also experienced increased anxiety attacks, a symptom of her depression. "I immediately put myself back on the Zoloft," she says.

Based on your Eastern-style diagnosis, the acupuncturist places needles in specific points on your body to restore the normal flow of qi. Most acupuncturists will recommend a series of treatments to restore you fully to balance. Generally, you should note improvement within 3 to 5 treatments, although you may need 10 to 12 for full recovery. Practitioners must use sterile needles. In general, acupuncture is quite safe.

Some of the points needled may be somewhat painful, according to McIntyre, "but that varies with the individual and with the point itself." Overall, the session is likely to be extremely relaxing. McIntyre compares the sensations induced by acupuncture to the dreamy state many people experience just before falling asleep. "In acupuncture, we can induce that state and get it to last for 20 minutes. That is

Then Serena's health insurance changed, allowing her to switch from the doctor she'd been seeing to the homeopathic doctor who'd treated her son. "She's a medical doctor—she has a medical degree—but she only practices homeopathy," explains Serena.

Serena's initial meeting with the homeopath lasted two hours. Serena told the doctor she wanted to try discontinuing the Zoloft again. After the evaluation, the doctor recommended a remedy she felt would help Serena. "I stopped taking the Zoloft, and started the homeopathy remedy, thinking it wasn't going to work," says Serena. She recalls thinking, "How can these little white pellets work? They're just not going to work." However, Serena had none of the side effects she'd experienced when she tried discontinuing Zoloft earlier. After several months, her symptoms of depression resolved completely. She sees her homeopath every three months, but hasn't needed the original remedy for some time.

Serena is thrilled she no longer needs to take Zoloft. There's another advantage to homeopathy, she notes: "It's cheaper!"

very, very pleasurable," he notes. "People experience a lot of very deep calm."

Western-style research on the effects of acupuncture on depression is still in its infancy. Several small studies have found acupuncture to help, while a few others have not. It's worth noting that acupuncture poses some unusual challenges to Western research. For example, developing a believable placebo is difficult, since people are likely to notice whether or not needles are inserted. Nonetheless, creative researchers have found ways to produce more-or-less objective means to test acupuncture's effectiveness, by inserting needles into presumably inactive points, for example.

You may be better off seeking care from a certified acupuncturist with a minimum of 3 years' professional training, rather than an M.D.

or D.O. (doctor of osteopathy) with just a few weekend workshops under his or her belt. Acupuncture is a complex form of medicine and requires extensive training.

MASSAGE

Just a generation ago, many Americans associated massage with escort services and other seamy activities. Since then massage has established itself as a bona-fide health care intervention, albeit a far more pleasant one than most. That massage can have healing properties is no surprise to many people around the world. Massage has been part of traditional healing and medical care in many cultures since time immemorial.

One group of researchers studied the effects of massage in a group of hospitalized children and teens, half of whom suffered from depression. The researchers arranged for the young people to get daily 30-minute back massages for 5 days, then compared their levels of depression with similar children who watched a relaxing video instead. Massage lowered levels of depression significantly.[29] Massage can also help ease depression in new mothers.

Five days of daily back massages significantly lowered the depression levels of children and teens hospitalized for depression.

One thing that massage offers is very basic: touch. In many species, including humans, touch is necessary for an infant to thrive—or even survive. As we grow older, our need for touch diminishes. Many adults lead healthy lives with only an occasional hug. But others find that frequent, affectionate, nonsexual touching enriches their lives and leads to feelings of well-being.

Touch is one way that humans show intimacy and love. When we're depressed and feeling as if we don't deserve love or even, sometimes, membership in the human race, a hug, a pat on the back, or an arm around the shoulder can remind us that we do belong, that we are acceptable, and even lovable, despite our imperfections. Some people have friends or partners who feel comfortable providing this kind of loving touch. Others keep cats or dogs because they, too, provide affectionate physical contact. But even if we're living in a no-pets apartment isolated from family and friends, we don't need to go untouched. Massage provides a safe outlet in a professional setting.

Massage is not the only hands-on therapy available. It belongs to a group of modalities collectively known as bodywork, including Rolfing, Tragerwork, Hellerwork, Feldenkrais training, Alexander Technique, shiatsu, and more. Philosophies, techniques, and, sometimes, goals differ. You may enjoy experimenting. Be sure to discuss any medical problems with the bodywork practitioner before you begin.

YOGA

A discipline of mind, body, and breath originating in India, yoga's original purpose was spiritual enlightenment. Westerners often practice yoga as a means of limbering the body and reducing stress. Students of hatha yoga, the most popular form, learn specific poses called *asanas* with picturesque names such as cat-cow, triangle pose, or cobra pose. Maintaining the correct posture in most asanas requires intense concentration. Many people find the combination of physical effort, mental focus, and deep breathing very calming, and each class ends with a period of deep relaxation.

Although it's possible to learn some basic asanas from a book or tape, a teacher is invaluable in teaching the nuances of the poses. Currently, yoga's popularity is soaring and classes are widely available.

Few researchers have studied yoga's effects on depression. If you're interested, it may be worth experimenting. A good teacher will help you modify poses to suit your body if you have specific injuries or are generally out of shape.

MEDITATION

Meditation of one kind or another is common to many religions and cultures. Many people find it profoundly restful, while others find it absolutely intolerable.

Darlene's Story: Healing the Mind, Body, and Spirit

Darlene, a 36-year-old research scientist, used a combination of yoga, meditation, and nutrition to recover from major depression five years ago. She sought care from a naturopathic physician who specialized in the traditional healing practices of India, a system of mind-body medicine known as Ayurveda. "Ayurvedic medicine integrates healing modalities that help the client be more aware of the mind-body-spirit connection," says Darlene. "It doesn't necessarily just focus on the body."

The doctor asked Darlene to alter her diet according to Ayurvedic principles to achieve a balanced state. "She recommended I eat a specific group of foods to help bring me into balance. She also had me drink a daily protein drink to increase my protein levels," says Darlene. In addition, the doctor suggested Darlene meditate twice a day. "The doctor taught me how to meditate in her office," recalls Darlene. "It was very simple: focusing on my breath going in and out."

One of the practices that Darlene found especially helpful was yoga. Just before she began seeing the doctor, Darlene enrolled in an intensive yoga class—90 minutes a day, 5 days a week. "It was very physical," says Darlene. "It was really nice to focus on helping my body to feel better. At the same time it had elements of integrating mind and body." Each class ended with a session of deep relaxation. "The doctor totally supported my doing yoga," says Darlene.

Darlene began to feel better after several months, and within 9 months felt back to normal—and was celebrating her first pregnancy.

In one form of the discipline, sometimes called single-pointed consciousness, meditators seek to concentrate their attention on a specific point: either a word (such as *om, peace, one*) silently repeated over and over; or a sensation, such as the feeling of the breath moving in and out of the nostrils. Beginning meditators often get frustrated because their attention continually slips away from the focus. Yet the point of the exercise is simply to notice when the mind wanders, and to remind yourself once again to think about whatever you've chosen to think about: breathing in, breathing out, breathing in, breathing out, for example.

For 77 percent of study participants, those who had had at least 3 previous bouts of depression, mindfulness-based cognitive therapy cut the rate of relapse in half.

In another form called mindfulness meditation, people take note of any thoughts, physical sensations, and feelings that arise during meditation, and then consciously let them go. With time and practice, meditators learn not to focus so much on the content of each wayward impulse or thought.

A group of researchers in the United Kingdom and Canada, headed by John Teasdale, studied a variation on mindfulness meditation among people who'd previously had at least two bouts of major depression.[30] They wanted to see if it would help prevent further recurrences. They called their form of meditation "mindfulness-based cognitive therapy" (MBCT), since they included a few aspects of cognitive-behavioral therapy, such as the messages "thoughts are not facts," and "I am not my thoughts." Overall, the purpose of their approach was to teach people to become more aware of thoughts and feelings and to see these as neutral "mental events" rather than necessarily true reflections of reality or of themselves.

Everyone in this study received treatment as usual for mental health difficulties. In addition, people in the meditation group received an 8-week training program in MBCT. Researchers followed participants for a year after the training, comparing rates of relapse and recurrence between the groups. What they found was interesting. For 77 percent of participants who had had at least 3 previous bouts of depression, MBCT cut the rate of relapse in half. For the remaining 23 percent with only two previous episodes of depression, MBCT didn't affect the rate of relapse at all. The researchers theorized that perhaps those people with more frequent recurrences had more ingrained patterns of negative thinking associated with their depressions, and therefore benefited more from learning how to respond differently to their thoughts.

The study's designers cautioned that they based their approach to meditation specifically for people who weren't currently depressed. They felt that people who were acutely depressed might have a difficult time learning the technique, which requires concentration. In addition, they felt that the intensity of negative thinking that many depressed people experience could also cause problems.

OTHER TREATMENTS FOR DEPRESSION

Taking a pill—whether an herb, supplement, or standard antidepressant—may be helpful for relieving symptoms, but it's unlikely to be *fun*. Some of the complementary treatments available, however, can be very pleasurable in themselves, regardless of any other healing properties they may possess.

Surrounding yourself with pleasant scents in aromatherapy, expressing your feelings physically in dance and movement therapy, or experiencing uplifting melodies in music therapy can help some people regain their sense of pleasure in life. Alone, each is probably not sufficient to treat depression, but as adjuncts to antidepressants or psychotherapy, you may find them intrinsically rewarding. Unfortunately, researchers have devoted little attention to most of these techniques.

SUMMARY

A remarkable percentage of people with depression has tried alternative and complementary treatments. The most popular treatments include relaxation techniques, spiritual healing, herbs and supplements, and homeopathy. Other approaches include yoga, meditation, massage, acupuncture, aromatherapy, and music and dance therapy. Despite the popularity of alternative and complementary medicine, research funding—and research itself—is often slim. Important questions remain even for St. John's wort, despite numerous studies comparing it to placebo and to standard antidepressants. If you're interested in trying alternative approaches for depression, it's safest to have a doctor or other qualified health professional overseeing your care. Always let your doctors know what treatments you are using.

Several of the approaches described in this chapter—including yoga, relaxation techniques, and meditation—focus on interactions between body, mind, and spirit. The next chapter provides additional information on such physical, mental, and spiritual approaches to depression.

CHAPTER 5

Body, Mind,
and Spirit

⌒∽

*As I become more self-aware, I feel like I'm collecting tools
in a tool chest of ways to take care of myself. I'm also
becoming more and more responsible for being the one to
pick up those tools, without needing to be reminded.*

—DARLENE, A RESEARCH SCIENTIST WHO'S RECOVERED
FROM MAJOR DEPRESSION

BODY, MIND, AND spirit—depression affects them all. Depression can alter our sleep, appetites, and activity levels, dull our mental faculties, and submerge the spark of our spirit in a wash of self-absorption and pain.

But our body, mind, and spirit are not only the objects of depression's damage; they can also be routes by which we heal. By attending to our body, mind, and spirit, we may be able to diminish depression's power. Adequate exercise, nutrition, sleep, and exposure to daylight can revitalize our bodies. Reducing stress, talking to others, and learning to quiet or challenge our depressing thoughts can help heal our minds. Religious or spiritual beliefs and practices and pure honest fun can nourish our souls. As a result of these activities and pursuits, depression may loosen its grip.

None of these approaches in itself constitutes treatment for depression. Appropriate treatment requires the skilled assistance of a doctor or mental health care professional; first for diagnosis, then for planning and monitoring care. Nonetheless, the practices described in this chapter can make up an important part of your overall plan for coping with the disorder. Some of these practices may help resolve depression. The same or other practices may work well to prevent its return. Research suggests that exercise is a particularly strong tool—and may even be enough to treat depression in some people. But don't make that determination by yourself. See a doctor—and then begin your program of physical, mental, and spiritual wellness.

THE BODY

Nature designed our bodies to flourish in an environment very different from the one in which we live today. Optimum health requires vigorous exercise; fresh, wholesome food; and sound sleep during the hours of darkness. Our bodies' needs stem from millions of years of genetic adaptations. Finding ways to support our genetic requirements within our modern environment can help restore natural vigor and boost our spirits.

Francis Mondimore, M.D., a psychiatrist on the faculty of the Johns Hopkins University School of Medicine, notes that people can benefit by "all the boring old stuff that your health education teacher told you in high school"—including nutrition, exercise, and plenty of sleep. Tedious as these healthy habits sound, they can help restore your enjoyment of life.

Exercise

In the Stone Age, few people sat around all day. If they didn't move, they didn't eat. Our bodies are built for movement. Is it any wonder that research has found that exercise may combat depression?

According to two exciting studies from Duke University Medical Center, it's possible that aerobic exercise could be as effective as antidepressants in treating mild or moderate major depression.

Several years ago, James Blumenthal, Ph.D., a clinical psychologist on the faculty of the Duke University Medical Center, set out to test whether exercise could effectively treat major depression among older adults.[1] Why this age group? Steve Herman, another Duke psychologist who worked on the study, explains that older people often can't tolerate antidepressants, they often have drug interactions, and chronic illnesses frequently interfere with antidepressant treatment. "If there can be an alternative to medications for people later in life, that would be particularly beneficial," says Dr. Herman. The researchers hoped to show that exercise was equal to antidepressant medications in treating major depression in this age group. And, says Dr. Herman, "That's what we did."

> *A*erobic exercise may be as effective as antidepressants in treating mild or moderate major depression.

The 156 participants ranged in age from 50 to 77. Researchers divided them into three groups, treating one group with aerobic group exercise, one group with Zoloft, and one group with both Zoloft and exercise. Exercisers met three times per week, putting in 10 minutes of warm-up, 30 minutes of aerobic jogging or walking, and 5 minutes of cool-down each session. After 4 months, researchers retested participants' levels of depression. "We were able to determine that approximately the same percentage in each group benefited," says Dr. Herman. About two-thirds of the people in each group were no longer considered depressed at the study's end (see figure 5.1). These numbers are based on an assumption that people who dropped out of the study were still depressed. When the groups were compared, there were slight differences in the percentage of people in each group who recovered after 16 weeks of treatment. However, from a mathematical perspective, these differences are insignificant.

Dr. Herman points out that although other studies of exercise and depression exist, theirs, to his knowledge, is the first to study

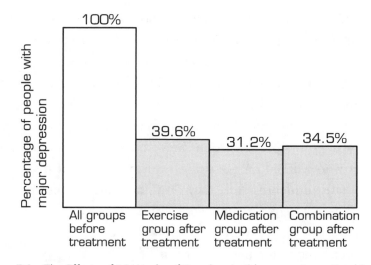

Figure 5.1—*The Effects of 16 Weeks of Exercise, Antidepressants, or Combined Treatment on Older People with Major Depression*

Source: Based on a study by James Blumenthal, Ph.D., and associates.[2]

people who were actually diagnosed with major depression according to the *DSM*. "The exercise really proved effective. It was very exciting," he says.

One surprise was that the combination of exercise and drug treatment was no more effective than either treatment alone, according to Dr. Herman. Follow-up interviews 6 months after the study's end underscored this result.[3] "We found that the folks that maintained their freedom from depression the best were those who just received exercise," says Dr. Herman. The researchers are doing another study to see if home exercise provides the same antidepressant effects as exercise in a group.

Dr. Herman is careful to say that their research doesn't constitute absolute proof about the effectiveness of exercise. For one thing, study volunteers were highly motivated, having signed up for a study of exercise in treating depression. "We're just not sure whether you would get the same results if you took people who just walked into a doctor's office and said 'I'm depressed,'" he explains. "But at least we were able to show that for middle-aged and older folks who are inclined to do the exercising, if they followed through with it, they would have a very excellent chance of getting better."

The Duke study found mental health benefits with aerobic exercise, but several older studies suggest that other types of exercise may also improve mood. One study found that weightlifting worked as well as running at reducing depression among women.[4] Another study found that yoga lifted moods in male and female college students as much as swimming did.[5] A third study found that aerobic dancing diminished depression a bit more than the less-aerobic racquetball in moderately depressed women.[6]

Keep in mind that none of these early studies examined people with depression diagnosed according to the *DSM*. Also, in each of the studies, social factors—being with a group of people doing pleasant activities—might have caused at least some of the improvement. Yet overall, the evidence suggests that people are likely to benefit from doing something—*anything*—physical. As one researcher wrote, "The available evidence suggests that any type of exercise alleviates depression."[7]

What do you like to do? Rollerblade, swing-dance, walk the malls, garden, hike? *Do* it. If you lack motivation to exercise alone, join a friend or a class. Here are a few tips on maintaining an exercise program: choose an activity you actually *like* (at least when you're

---

Rosalie's Story: Walking Away from Depression

Rosalie, a 45-year-old psychotherapist, used exercise extensively during a bout of major depression. "I got aerobic every day," she says. "Sometimes when I could not get myself out there, I asked my husband to 'walk the wife.' I'd say, 'Could you take the wife for a walk?' And he would." Rosalie believes the exercise helped her recover. She has continued her daily exercise as a means to prevent recurrences.

not feeling depressed); ink it into your schedule; and give yourself a reward—even just a verbal pat on your own back—each time you exercise.

If you'd like to try exercise for depression, be sure to get a physical examination (especially if you're over 40 or have been sedentary). To prevent injuries, get proper instruction on the activity before starting, begin each session with a warm-up, end each session with a cool-down, and build up the amount you exercise over time. If you're having a hard time sleeping, schedule your exercise during the day or early evening, so you have several hours to wind down before bed.

Diet

We know that our mood can affect our diet. For some people—especially those with winter depression—nothing says "comfort" as clearly as a bowl of ice cream or a hunk of bread. On the opposite end of the spectrum, major depression can ravage the appetite, sometimes causing significant weight loss.

If our mood can affect our diet, is the opposite true as well? Can our diet affect our mood? Some theorists say yes.

Diet is a complex phenomenon. After air and water, food is most essential to our survival. A well-balanced diet can prolong life and prevent or slow disease. Food has its social and psychological sides as well. Feeding others, and being fed, has profound symbolic, even spiritual, importance. How our food looks, how it's served, how it tastes and smells can be as crucial to our appetite as the precise combination of nutrients on our plate. Even time of day is important: How many people would revolt at hamburgers and salad at breakfast, yet relish them at dinner?

During depression, people often pay little attention to the social, nutritional, and sensual aspects of food. Food becomes mere physical or psychological fuel—a way to stave off hunger or reduce tension. Taking time to select food with care, to serve it attractively, to notice its taste and aroma, can nourish our souls as well as our bodies. A good meal can tell us that, yes, our needs and desires *do* matter—because *we* matter.

In addition, there's evidence that certain foods and substances can worsen problems with depression, while others can alleviate such problems. The most obvious offenders are caffeine and alcohol. Increasing evidence suggests that certain vitamins, minerals, and even fats can help lift mood.

You may want to try some of the nutritional suggestions in this chapter. But don't make it a do-or-die proposition. There's an old British saying, "A little of what you fancy does you good." A better diet is a goal to strive for. Don't make occasional dietary lapses reasons to attack yourself for failure.

> *Certain foods and substances can worsen problems with depression. The most obvious offenders are caffeine and alcohol.*

Caffeine

One of the chief culprits in sleep disturbance, caffeine is found in coffee drinks, black tea, cola, chocolate, and a few noncola soft drinks. Green tea and decaffeinated coffee contain small amounts of caffeine. If you're troubled by anxiety or sleep difficulties, "Avoid too much in the way of caffeine—coffee, tea, chocolate, and caffeinated beverages," suggests Dr. Mondimore.

Caffeine causes your body to pump adrenaline into your bloodstream. Studies have found that even among good sleepers, caffeine can lighten sleep, creating more restlessness during the night. Caffeine may also contribute to mood swings during the day. Caffeine is popular because it boosts energy levels. Several hours later, however, energy—and mood—can plummet.

Some people metabolize caffeine more slowly than others. If you're a slow metabolizer, up to 50 percent of the caffeine you imbibe may remain in your bloodstream more than 7 hours later.[8] For such people, eliminating caffeine entirely may work best. If you're a heavy coffee drinker, cut back gradually, however, or you will risk several days of caffeine-withdrawal headaches.

Alcohol

Alcohol can help some people relax and temporarily feel less depressed, but it's technically a depressant. It interferes with thinking, judgment, and behavior. Large amounts kill brain cells. If you're depressed, your brain is already not functioning optimally. "People with mood disorders should drink alcohol very, very sparingly, if at all," says Dr. Mondimore.

Alcohol is also a major culprit in sleep disruption. As a sedative, it initially helps people fall asleep. The problem arises several hours later, as its effects wear off. The resulting restlessness and shakiness causes many people to wake up in the wee hours, or have bad dreams. Sleep specialists advise avoiding alcohol for at least several hours before bed.

Finally, alcohol can interfere with the action of antidepressant drugs, according to A. John Rush, M.D., professor of psychiatry at the University of Texas. If you're on an antidepressant, it's important to clarify with your doctor whether it's all right to drink and how much.

Vitamins and Minerals

If you're depressed, you may have lower-than-normal levels of certain B vitamins. No one is quite sure if this is cause or effect—or even necessarily true. (Not every study of depressed individuals found these deficiencies.) The sometimes-implicated vitamins are B_2, B_6, B_{12}, and folic acid. You'll find B_6 in foods such as beans, nuts, seeds, bananas, and avocados; B_2 and folic acid in dark leafy greens; and B_{12} (as well as B_2) in meat, eggs, and dairy foods. Those who shun all meat, dairy, fish, and eggs may develop B_{12} deficiency unless they take a supplement.

Eating foods rich in B vitamins is a reasonable form of self-care, and a multivitamin containing the recommended daily intake can't hurt either. Too much B_6, however, can cause neurological problems. Don't take more than 50 milligrams of B_6 daily without checking with your doctor, and limit folic acid to 400 micrograms daily unless your doctor has ruled out a B_{12} deficiency. High doses of folic acid can mask a deficiency in B_{12}.

Calcium is another nutrient you may want to ensure you take in adequate quantities, not necessarily because it will help your mood (although it could if you have premenstrual depression; see chapter 4, page 128), but because depression may increase your requirements. One study found decreased bone mineral density in women with a history of major depression, compared to other women.[9] The researchers didn't try giving calcium supplements to depressed women to see if it helped strengthen their bones; nonetheless, it makes sense to take at least the minimum daily recommended amount. The daily requirement for calcium is 1,000 milligrams for both men and women ages 19 to 50, and rises to 1,200 milligrams for older people—yet few people get nearly this much calcium each day. Low-fat dairy products, dark green leafy vegetables, tofu, and calcium-fortified orange juice are good sources. Some physicians recommend taking calcium in combination with magnesium for best results, making sure you meet the recommended daily requirement of both.

People with iron deficiency may also have low energy and depression. But iron is not something to take in large quantities unless you know you are deficient. Too much iron can be harmful. It's best to have your levels of iron—and possibly B_{12} and folic acid—checked when you first see the doctor for depression.

Fats and the Brain

In our society, we tend to label all fats with one word: *bad*. Nonetheless, scientists have demonstrated that some fats—the essential fatty acids—are vital to good health. These include the omega-3 fatty acids, present in fish, walnuts, and canola and flaxseed oils; and the omega-6 fatty acids, present in vegetable oils, lean meats, and eggs. In contrast, researchers have implicated saturated fats and the fatty substance cholesterol in our epidemic rates of heart disease. Both cholesterol and saturated fats appear in such appealing foods as well-marbled steak, cheese, and ice cream.

Interesting research suggests that the amount and proportion of different kinds of dietary fats may affect the activity of neurotransmitters such as serotonin, and thus have a potential impact on depression. Since fats make up a large part of the membranes surrounding brain cells, it makes sense that they may play a role in our moods.

Much of the discussion on fats and depression centers on the omega-3 fatty acids, with three research points in particular supporting their positive role. First, these fats appear in large amounts in brain cell membranes.[10] Second, "There is some information that people who are depressed have lower amounts of omega-3 fatty acids in the blood," says Douglas Taren, Ph.D., associate professor of public health at the University of Arizona. Third, long-term studies have found that people who eat large amounts of fish rich in omega-3 fatty acids have lower rates of depression and suicide. "At this point there is no conclusive evidence that increasing omega-3s will prevent depression, but we are at the point where people are starting to study it more," says Dr. Taren.

> *Long-term studies have found that people who eat large amounts of fish rich in omega-3 fatty acids have lower rates of depression and suicide.*

In Finland, Dr. Antii Tanskanen found that people who ate fish more than once each week had a smaller risk of depression than people who ate fish less often.[11] A 17-year study in Japan found that people eating a large amount of fish rich in omega-3 fatty acids had 19 percent fewer suicides than people eating less fish.[12] Other studies came to similar conclusions.[13] There is also some evidence that fish oil supplements may be particularly beneficial for people with bipolar disorder. Harvard researcher Andrew Stoll, M.D., theorizes that the omega-3 fatty acids in fish may help stabilize moods by dampening some signals from nerve cells.[14]

Fish particularly rich in omega-3 fatty acids include salmon, herring, cod, and sardines. "All fish have omega-3 fatty acids as a proportion of their fat," explains Dr. Taren. "Cold-water fish like salmon and cod tend to have more omega-3 fatty acids because they have more fat."

If you're not a fish fan, you can find omega-3 fatty acids in other sources. "There are some products out there now that are fortified with omega-3 fatty acids," says Dr. Taren, "and people may want to look at those products. There are some egg products, for example, that are high in omega-3 fatty acids. It's also possible to take fatty acid supplements." He recommends that those interested in supplements discuss them with their doctor before taking them.

Besides omega-3 fatty acids, some researchers have suggested that cholesterol—despite its negative reputation—may play a protective role against depression. The research on cholesterol is confusing, however. Some studies appear to show that people on low-cholesterol diets, or taking certain types of cholesterol-lowering drugs, may have higher rates of depression and suicide.[15] (The cholesterol-lowering "statin" drugs do not seem to have this effect, says Jan Fawcett, chairman of the psychiatry department at Rush–Presbyterian–St. Luke's Medical Center in Chicago.) Other research has found that people who have attempted or completed suicide sometimes have lower amounts of cholesterol in their blood. Multiple studies also show the opposite result, however, in the case of both depression and suicide. The exact role of cholesterol is—to say the least—unclear.

Some researchers think that cholesterol may be a false lead.[16] The real issue, they believe, may be that low-cholesterol diets tend also to be relatively low in omega-3 fatty acids. "Some of the older drugs that were used to decrease cholesterol levels decreased the amount of fat that was absorbed; for example, decreasing the amount of omega-3 fatty acids that was absorbed," says Dr. Taren. It may be that it's the omega-3 fatty acids, not cholesterol, that are key.

A Balanced Diet

Good nutrition requires more than specific vitamins and minerals. It requires adequate intake of protein, carbohydrate, and fats. Most modern nutritionists suggest we eat large amounts of carbohydrates (grains, fruits, and vegetables), moderate amounts of protein, and sparing amounts of fats, oils, and sweeteners.

Some people's diets are surprisingly short of protein. Inadequate protein may be a problem for people taking antidepressants, writes Georgetown University psychiatrist Robert Hedaya in his book *The Antidepressant Survival Program*.[17] In his experience, if you are on antidepressants, eating some protein whenever you eat carbohydrate-rich foods can help stabilize your moods and prevent food cravings.

Not all experts would agree with Dr. Hedaya's nutritional program, which includes smaller portions of carbohydrates than many nutritionists recommend. Making sure you have adequate daily protein, however, is simple nutritional sense.

> **Medical Alert**
>
> If you take several different medications and supplements, talk to your doctor or pharmacist about how to schedule them during the day. Sometimes one medication or supplement will interfere with absorption of others.

Exposure to Daylight

Our dispositions might be sunnier if we had more access to daylight, especially in the winter. Although most people don't have full-blown seasonal affective disorder, "There are a lot of people who each winter have a tougher time waking up, sleep more, gain weight, and are a little more lethargic," says Dr. David Avery, professor of psychiatry at the University of Washington. "They don't really fulfill the criteria for major depression. They have a more mild condition, sometimes called subsyndromal seasonal affective disorder, or winter blues."

According to Dr. Avery, surveys conducted in Maryland and Copenhagen found that symptoms of so-called seasonality occur on a continuum in the general population. Researchers assigned people

---

Cynthia's Story: Increasing Light Exposure

At age 59, Cynthia began feeling "really low," she says. She saw a psychiatrist at her HMO who suggested, among other things, that she get more light, although the doctor didn't believe that Cynthia had true seasonal affective disorder. Cynthia, who worked at home, began going out for 20 to 30 minutes daily without sunglasses. "I used to wear really dark glasses," she says. "Now I don't anymore."

Cynthia found the increased light exposure made a tremendous difference in her mood. "When I went outside, it was like layers coming off," she says. She has a lightbox and uses it when she knows she won't be able to get out, sitting beside it and reading. "I don't have to look at it much," she says. "I just look up at it once in a while."

"Using the lightbox or getting out makes a huge difference in my mood," states Cynthia.

---

scores ranging from 0 to 24, based on their degree of seasonal symptoms. "Some people had clear SAD scores, say scores greater than 12," says Dr. Avery. But many had scores of 11, 10, 9, and 8. "It turns out that people who had no seasonality at all are in the minority," he says.

What does this mean? For most of us, it means that the amount of daylight we receive affects our mood. If we want to feel better, especially in winter, one thing we can do is go outside more during the day. Even on a cloudy day, outdoor light is about 100 times brighter than indoor light, notes Dr. Avery. There is also the option of light therapy (see chapter 3, page 105).

Sleep

Just as depression can alter the appetite, so, too, can it disrupt our sleep habits. Usually, depression makes sleep briefer and more difficult. Awakening very early in the morning is particularly common. "For people who are depressed, what they think of as a good night's sleep is what most people would consider a terrible night's sleep," says Dr. Mondimore.

While insomnia is more common, some depressed people sleep too much. In some cases, says Dr. Avery, too much sleep can worsen depression. Finding the right sleep balance is important. "Try to go back to the sleep duration that you had when you were feeling good," he says. "Too much sleep may be bad, too little sleep may be bad. There's probably an optimum amount that's appropriate for a given person."

> **Medical Alert**
>
> Use over-the-counter sleep aids for no more than 2 weeks before consulting your doctor.

Of the two difficulties, oversleeping is probably easier to avoid than insomnia. It's easy enough to set an alarm clock, although getting yourself out of bed requires more motivation. Ending insomnia, on the other hand, can require major alterations in lifestyle.

Dr. Avery emphasizes the importance of a regular sleeping schedule and a dark environment at night. "Our ancestors evolved over millions and millions of years in an environment in which they had very regular light-dark signals," he explains. "The days were very bright, relative to ours, and the nights very dark, relative to ours. Our bodies are designed to deal with that kind of environment, a very regular environment. And now, since the advent of the electric light, we have had the freedom to create light cues at any time we wish."

During the day, the rooms we spend time in may be too dim for good mental health. This is especially true for people with seasonal affective disorder but, as noted above, people for whom seasonality is not an issue at all are in the minority. At night, our rooms may be too bright: "About 10 to 100 times brighter than the moon," says Dr. Avery. Unfortunately, the result of our control over light is often sleep disturbance.

"The light we get in the evening may be perceived by some of us as sunlight. It may be powerful enough to send a signal that the sun is still up," he explains. "It may be tough, therefore, for some people to get to sleep. And some of us go into a bright kitchen or bright bathroom late in the evening, and turn on these bright lights, and then we can't sleep." He recommends that people "keep the evenings relatively dark, and not turn on lights in the middle of the night."

One way to darken bedrooms is to invest in thicker, wider draperies or blinds. Sleep masks, available in travel stores, can also help.

Tips for Improving Sleep

If you are having trouble falling or staying asleep, the following suggestions might help:

1. Establish regular hours for going to sleep and waking up, 7 days a week if possible.

2. Leave time to wind down and relax before bed. "That becomes especially difficult for people who work odd shifts," says Dr. Mondimore. "Often they want to get off from work, come home and go right to bed, and they don't allow themselves the decompression time that everybody needs."

3. Cut out caffeine and other stimulants.

4. Don't smoke just before bed; smoking acts as a stimulant.

5. Avoid alcohol, one of the worst disrupters of sleep.

6. Reserve your bed for sleeping (or sleeping and sex, say some experts). Don't eat, watch television, or read in bed. Dr. Mondimore recommends that you "not do anything except try to go to sleep in bed, so you begin to associate the bed with going to sleep."

7. Turn the clock away from the bed. "When people can see the clock from the bed, if they wake up at 2 in the morning, they'll look over, say, 'Oh my god, it's 2 o'clock in the morning, that means I only have 6 more hours to sleep,'" says Dr. Mondimore. The ensuing anxiety adds to wakefulness.

8. Get regular exercise.

9. Try using a lightbox or going outside in the morning. Even if it doesn't improve your mood, "It does frequently have a kind of an energizing effect," says Dr. Mondimore—which can help people groggy from poor sleep. "I tell people that in the morning, if the weather's right, to make themselves get up, go outside, and take a walk."

10. Avoid medications that interfere with sleep. Some antidepressants or other drugs, including common over-the-counter cold remedies, can interfere with sleep. Decongestants, common in cold treatments, can act as stimulants, for example. Your doctor may be able to suggest alternative medications that pose less of a problem, or even enhance slumber.

11. Reduce the noise in your bedroom. Installing double-paned windows can help muffle sound, as can utilizing a source of so-called white noise, such as an air-conditioner or fan.

12. Determine what works best for you to do when sleep won't come. Some sleep specialists suggest getting out of bed after 20 or 30 minutes if you can't sleep, and staying up until you become sleepy. Other experts suggest staying in bed. "I've heard people say either works for them," says Dr. Mondimore. "I can imagine that if you get up and turn on a light, that is an awakening stimulus. I would tend to say not to do that."

13. List your worries. Take 20 minutes well before going to bed to write down all your worries, along with possible solutions, and leave the list in another room. If you choose to try this approach, make sure you leave yourself time to relax between making the list and going to bed, cautions Dr. Mondimore.

14. Use progressive muscle relaxation, meditation, visualization, or other relaxation techniques while lying in bed. These can help people fall asleep, especially if practiced nightly for more than 2 weeks. Even simple deep breathing for 10 minutes or so can help. Some religions have specific bedtime prayers. For example, many

observant Jews make it a point before falling asleep to forgive anyone who harmed them, whether intentionally or not.

15. Try Grandma's remedy: a bath and a cup of warm milk before bed. Sometimes the oldest approaches work the best.

THE MIND

Depression has a number of negative effects on the mind. It interferes with our ability to hope. It increases our tendency to criticize ourselves and others. It makes it harder for us to concentrate, to remember, to make decisions. Stress and anxiety further disrupt mental functioning.

Given how depression impairs the mind, can we use the mind to counteract depression?

For many people, the answer is yes. It's possible to learn mental techniques for decreasing stress; to learn to recognize, and challenge, some of the thinking that is symptomatic of depression; and to use a journal or another technique to gain better self-understanding. Once depression begins to lift, people can use their problem-solving abilities to tackle larger issues that might otherwise contribute to recurrences.

Decreasing Stress

One of the best ways for a depressed person to reduce mental stress is to talk to others, says psychologist Ken Goodrick, Ph.D., associate professor of family and community medicine at Houston's Baylor College of Medicine and author of *Energy, Peace, Purpose: A Step-by-Step Guide to Optimal Living.*[18] Sharing your feelings can decrease the sense of loneliness, a common symptom of depression. Classic research suggests that having a "confiding relationship"—someone you regularly tell your troubles to—may make women less vulnerable to depression. Obviously, it's best if the person you talk to refrains from making critical remarks.

Another stress reduction technique Dr. Goodrick suggests is free writing. "Start by sitting quietly with a pad and pen in your lap," says Dr. Goodrick. "Let your mind drift wherever it wants to go. Whenever you become aware of the subject of your thoughts, write it down." If you do this for 10 minutes, you may discover some interesting patterns. You can also try journaling, writing down your thoughts and feelings on a regular, perhaps daily, basis. Writing and then rereading your entries can help you identify problems that you can then decide how to resolve. "Journaling is most helpful when you discuss the writing later with support people," says Dr. Goodrick.

Other techniques can help some people stop worrying about their problems and focus on the here and now. Dr. Goodrick suggests going to a place where you can see trees, grass, and other plants, and noticing how many different shades of green you see; or closing your eyes and noticing all the sounds you hear. But you don't need to go somewhere special to relax. "Just sitting down and noticing how your body feels can be very relaxing," he says. To reduce stress, Dr. Goodrick recommends doing this or another relaxation technique several times during the day. "Think about the sensation of contact with your chair, air against your skin, or the sound of your own heartbeat." he says. Occasionally, this kind of practice can make people feel tenser or more depressed because they're unable to get their minds off their troubles. In that case, try a different approach, such as physical exercise.

The Importance of Reducing Stress During Recovery

"I think there are two phases to getting better from depression," says Dr. Mondimore. The initial phase, during which the mood is returning pretty much to normal, may last several months. Then there is a recuperation phase, during which people build back up everything they let fall away while they were depressed. This can take 6 months or even a year, says Dr. Mondimore.

Tips for Reducing Anxiety

1. If you notice yourself worrying, stop and take a deep breath, or imagine the face of a loved one.

2. Break big tasks into little ones, and approach them step-by-step.

3. Allow extra time to get places and complete tasks.

4. Allow yourself to be imperfect. Remember, mistakes are the reason that pencils have erasers.

5. Use relaxation tapes, meditation, yoga, or other mind-body techniques regularly.

6. If something—a project, a problem, a relationship—seems too hard to handle, get help.

7. Try to find time, every day, to do something you want to do, not a task for somebody else.

In their eagerness to resume normal life, people may take on too much during their recuperation, says Dr. Mondimore. "I think people get into a lot of stress by getting in over their heads with taking on too many responsibilities, accepting too many invitations, and so forth. I encourage people to go very slowly as they reintegrate into the real world again, as far as what kinds of responsibilities they take on. People need to be aware of the health risks of trying to do too much too soon."

Dr. Mondimore gives the example of a senior manager of a big corporation who is recuperating from a mood disorder. What if, he asks, the manager is offered a job that pays more, but requires a lot more responsibility? Accepting the position might cause a relapse of depression. "You have to think about the health implications of taking the job," says Dr. Mondimore.

Your doctor or psychotherapist may be able to help you evaluate the potential stress of taking on major responsibilities as you recover from depression. Dr. Mondimore emphasizes the need to "realize how severe an illness it can be, and how long it can take to really get completely better."

Recognizing and Challenging Depressing Thoughts

One of the principles of cognitive-behavioral therapy is that our thoughts affect our mood. This type of therapy teaches people to observe their thoughts, to notice how these thoughts make them feel, and to determine whether their depressing thoughts are useful or true. (See chapter 3, page 100.)

It is easiest to learn such specific approaches from a psychotherapist, says Leslie Sokol, a psychologist at the Beck Institute in Bala Cynwyd, Pennsylvania. "It's very hard to learn tools from reading a book."

A 1997 analysis of several studies concluded, however, that some people do benefit significantly from certain self-help books on cognitive-behavioral therapy.[19] The analysis looked at six small studies comparing people who used specific books for treating depression (an approach termed bibliotherapy) with a control group of people who either had no treatment or had short-term psychotherapy. Overall, reading books such as David Burns' *Feeling Good: The New Mood Therapy* and Peter Lewinsohn's *Control Your Depression* helped. "Seventy-nine percent of control people had a worse outcome than the average member of the group receiving bibliotherapy," wrote experts who reviewed the results.[20]

Before you head for your bookstore, be aware that the researcher noted several caveats. First, it's important to get a diagnosis before commencing. If you have bipolar disorder, severe depression, suicidal thoughts, or addiction problems, treating yourself "by the book" is not a good idea. Second, if you're depressed, you may have a hard time completing the book—and may feel even worse about yourself as a result. Third, in these studies, a therapist met with participants at the outset and checked in with them by phone periodically after that. This is a far cry from complete self-treatment. Finally, these studies were small, and the levels of depression among the participants varied. It is possible that larger studies of more seriously depressed people would show different results.

Still, if you're a bookish sort of person, a self-help book based on principles of cognitive-behavioral therapy may be a useful complement to other forms of treatment. Be aware that the benefit of using these books depends partly on your interest, motivation, and personality; partly on the severity of your depression; and partly on the quality of the book you use. If you're depressed, talk to a doctor before trying such self-help approaches. If you've recovered from a depression, you may find such a book makes it easier to stave off a recurrence.

Handling Bigger Issues

When we're depressed, it's usually best to set small goals for ourselves. It's often hard enough to get lunch on the table, let alone tackle long-standing problems. But big, hard-to-manage issues, or an overload of smaller ones, can create stress that may lead to or worsen depression. At some point, it's important to deal with chronic issues, tensions, and problems, says Dr. Mondimore, "Because we know they are associated with worsening of mood problems, and with mood problems being more difficult to treat."

> *It's important to deal with chronic issues, tensions, and problems because they are associated with worsening of mood problems, and with mood problems being more difficult to treat.*

As a general preventive to depression, Dr. Mondimore suggests something he calls "mood hygiene." One aspect of mood hygiene is not procrastinating. "People get into a lot of stress by procrastinating," he says. Another major component of mood hygiene involves identifying chronic sources of tension and problems, such as "debt that you worry about all the time, problems with your landlord that don't seem to be getting better, relationship problems." Dr. Mondimore suggests people look at each of these issues and determine "What do I need to do to make this go away?" And then don't be afraid to do it, he says.

THE SPIRIT

Whatever their personal orientation to spirituality may be, doctors and other health care providers rarely discuss this subject in a medical setting. This situation may be changing as conventional medicine begins to acknowledge the role that religion and spirituality can play in improving health.

"Almost by definition, spiritual issues are beyond the realm of science," says Dr. Mondimore. "That being said, there have been a number of studies that show that a more active spiritual life seems to have a beneficial effect on a whole variety of illnesses."

Harold Koenig, M.D., professor of psychiatry and medicine at Duke University Medical School, specializes in studying the effects of religion on health. In his research, he has found that religion can help both prevent and resolve depression in medically ill older adults.[21]

Dr. Koenig's research focuses specifically on religion rather than on spirituality, because he finds religion easier to define for research purposes. "I consider religion to be the major religious traditions such as Christianity, Judaism, Islam, Buddhism, and Hinduism," he says. "Religion involves being part of a group with similar beliefs. It also means that the group has to be stable over time." In contrast, he says, "Spirituality is such a broad concept that it's hard to measure and hard to define." The vast majority of Dr. Koenig's research subjects are Christian, reflecting the population in his region.

Dr. Koenig notes two ways in which religion seems beneficial in depression: both the social aspects of religion and religious beliefs themselves exert healing effects.

Regarding the social aspects, Dr. Koenig notes that volunteering, attending services, and participating in prayer groups or religious study groups all seem to help. According to Dr. Koenig, the most helpful of these activities seems to be volunteering. "Volunteering in the religious setting is particularly important because, first of all, it provides a wonderfully close group of volunteers," he says. "They support each other more than just other members, say, of a church. The volunteers have a similar mission and they end up being very supportive toward each other." Also, the act of volunteering in any setting may be of value. "Volunteering helps people get their minds off their own problems and on to somebody else's. Rather than obsess about their problems, they oftentimes will compare themselves to the people they are helping, who are in much worse shape than they are," explains Dr. Koenig. "So all of that works together and helps to reduce depression."

Both the social aspects of religion and religious beliefs themselves exert healing effects on depression.

Besides the social aspects of religious activities, Dr. Koenig found the most benefit from what he termed the "cognitive aspects of religion," that is, the particular religious thoughts or beliefs held by participants. "How deeply are they committed to their religious faith? How much is it a part of their whole life and integrated in their life?" The deeper their commitment to their religion, the stronger the protection against depression, Dr. Koenig believes.

Deep-rooted religious or spiritual beliefs are not always protective against depression, however. Sometimes, depression interferes with religious beliefs or practices. During her major depression, Genevieve, a devout Christian, "felt pretty far away from God. It wasn't like I had my usual prayer relationship." She wonders, though, whether prayer, her own or that of others, didn't help speed her recovery. One night, after months of devastating depression, she says, "I was reading out loud from the Psalms. I read one that said, 'How long, O God, forever?' and I thought, 'How long was this depression going to last?'" The next day she noticed a distinct lightening of her mood. This marked the beginning of her emergence from depression.

Although there's no single, generally accepted definition of spirituality, people often associate it with a sense of something greater than the self. "Learning to see life as a whole, instead of the hole that people are currently in," is how social worker Barbara Rohde puts it.

Some people are interested in spiritual beliefs and practices, but uncomfortable with the religion of their childhood, or other traditional religious institutions. For some of these, meditation can be "a door to spiritual awareness," says Michael Speca, who studied

---

Religious Beliefs That Can Help in Depression

"If you think about what the main tenets of the Western religions are," says Dr. Mondimore, "they have to do with a kind of ultimate optimism, having trust in a benevolent force." He notes that these are comforting concepts.

According to Dr. Koenig, some of the specific religious thoughts and beliefs that may be helpful for people with depression include:

God is with me.

God loves me.

I can turn a problem over to God and God will take care of it. I don't have to worry as much about it.

I'm sick, but I'm still useful.

My life still has meaning even though I can't go to work because of my disability. My life has meaning and purpose because God created me.

Just because I'm disabled doesn't mean I'm worthless and of no use to anyone.

My disability can be a gift; it can be used to help me become more compassionate towards those with these kinds of problems, and maybe even reach out to them and offer support.

the effects of mindfulness meditation on the mood states of cancer patients.

Dr. Speca makes it clear that mindfulness meditation, as used in a health care setting, is not in itself a spiritual practice. "It's really the teaching of our own capacity for awareness and insight," he says. "It doesn't have explicit spiritual aims." Nonetheless, he says, people who practice it often begin to pay more attention to spiritual aspects of living. During mindfulness meditation, he says, "You see how wonderful, how vivid, how precious each moment is. I think it can play a valuable role in enhancing spiritual awareness."

Notably, not only Hinduism and Buddhism, but also the other major religions each has its own meditative traditions and practices: "centering prayer" in Christianity, and mystical practices in Judaism and Islam.

Music, art, and poetry are other avenues that many people, whether as observers or participants, find spiritually uplifting. There's an ancient example in the Bible of the healing power of music: When King Saul was stricken by melancholy, young David soothed his spirits by playing on a lyre. In more recent times, current research suggests that music therapy can help ease depression in the elderly.[22]

Fun

There's another aspect to our spirits, and that's our sense of joy, rapture, or ecstasy—or even simple fun. One of the hallmark symptoms of depression is lack of enjoyment of things that people previously found pleasurable (a symptom clinically known as *anhedonia*). But does that mean you should stop doing the things that used to give you pleasure? Far from it, say many experts.

"People who are depressed have cut themselves off from pleasant things. They're no longer doing the things that they used to find very pleasant. When they start doing them again, they wind the depression up faster," says Larry Beutler, Ph.D., editor of the *Journal of Clinical Psychology*, noting that research backs up this conclusion.

Peggy's Story: Making a Spiritual Connection

"I was very depressed, but I also knew that one of the things I was dealing with was a spiritual hunger," says Peggy, a woman in her sixties. "I'd been so busy in life, just raising the kids and doing all of that, that I hadn't really ever spent much time thinking about spirituality. I knew that I had a need for something, which I suspected was a spiritual life, a spiritual dimension to the life I was leading. I started going to a church, returning to the religion I was raised in as a child. I found a wonderful congregation that I felt a lot of support and involvement with. I can work with them and do volunteering for them. It's been great." She adds, "My therapist is very supportive."

What are the activities you used to enjoy? Sailing, shopping, gardening, basketball, singing, painting? You might make a list, then pick one or two to try. It's a good idea to start small and increase your participation as you find you can tolerate it. You may not feel as wonderful as you normally would while you're taking part, but with depression you're unlikely to feel wonderful doing anything. If the alternative is lying in bed feeling just as bad, why not at least try? As your treatment progresses, the amount of enjoyment you feel is likely to increase.

Sometimes treatment can make the activity more fun than ever. Psychologist Paul Rohde, Ph.D., senior scientist at the Oregon Research Institute, notes the case of a teenage boy treated with cognitive-behavioral therapy for major depression. Before treatment, the teenager didn't take pleasure in doing things with his dad because they spent the entire time bickering. But with therapy, the youngster learned to respond differently to his father. Now doing exactly the same things—playing games, going to movies, being outdoors together, engaging in sports—gives him a great deal more pleasure than before. Fun has become even more fun.

PREVENTING FUTURE DEPRESSION

Once people recover from depression, the last thing they want is to experience it again. Yet recurrences are extremely common. They are not inevitable, however. Research has found that specific treatments and approaches may help fend off a repeat attack.

One of the most important things you can do is to continue your treatment for the recommended period of time, which may range from months to years in the case of taking antidepressants. If you have bipolar disorder, you may need long-term treatment with mood stabilizers, at least until other forms of effective treatment are discovered.

Drugs are not the only answer to preventing depression's return. Cognitive-behavioral therapy and interpersonal therapy can help, too. Lifestyle measures may also be important. Researchers at Duke University found some evidence that, among older adults, exercising may help protect against relapse.[23]

> *Your own experiences with depression can help you learn what makes you feel better or worse. If you attend to these experiences, you may be able to come up with a list of practices that reliably—or at least occasionally—boost your mood.*

Published research aside, your own experiences with depression can help you learn what makes you feel better or worse. If you attend to these experiences, you may be able to come up with a list of practices that reliably—or at least occasionally—boost your mood. Then you can intentionally integrate these practices into your life on a daily or as-needed basis. You can also learn what is likely to trigger your depression—an intimidating new assignment at work, for instance—and pay special attention to self-care during those times.

Mental health educator Mary Ellen Copeland, M.S., M.A., author of *Winning Against Relapse*, has developed a systematic approach

John's Story: Preventing Recurrences

John, a 48-year-old teacher, had recurrent bouts of depression for many years. "My life was extremely diminished," he says of his early experience. "It was not a good life." In recent years he's turned things around with a combination of approaches—a major one of them being medication. Although initially he balked at taking medication long-term, he has overcome his qualms. "I do it because it seems to work," he says.

"It's like being sick—you take medicine. As long as my body needs this medicine, then I'm going to take it, and I'm not going to worry about what other people think or say. I take the view that it helps me get back to my normal me, where I should be. It's fine."

John also learned, through psychotherapy, to monitor his thoughts, watching for negative thinking. "When I start having

toward preventing relapses or new episodes of depression. "I was working with a group of people in Northern Vermont in 1977," she says, "teaching them recovery skills and strategies—various things that people can do to help themselves get better, and things that they can do to maintain their wellness. At the end, the group concurred that all this stuff is really great, but they didn't really know how to organize it into their lives. So we spent some time working together developing what has become known as the Wellness Recovery Action Plan, or WRAP." Copeland, who has had a number of incapacitating depressions in her own life, notes that she designed a WRAP for herself.

For information on how to obtain a copy of the WRAP, see Copeland's Web site at *www.mentalhealthrecovery.com*. Briefly summarized, the steps of the WRAP go like this:

1. Get a binder with several dividers.

2. Identify and write down the things that you can use to relieve your symptoms. These might include talking to a supportive person,

thoughts that I'm a bad person, I say, 'I'm not going there.' I'm just going to keep a positive outlook." He rarely has such thoughts these days. "If I do, I don't give them any weighting. I say they're not really true." He's found this to be a key tool in preventing recurrences.

John also controls incipient depression through lifestyle factors. "I can recognize when I start getting depressed and make small adjustments to my life. I try to eat a little bit better. I also found that if I was depressed it was way better if I did any kind of physical activity. I used to play basketball and that would help a lot."

John is very aware of the changes in his mental state over the past few years. "In the winter, I would normally spin into a gray, horrible depression that lasted for months and months and months. I don't go there anymore," he says.

doing some deep breathing exercises, or taking a walk around the block. They could also include taking time out to do something that you really love to do, like painting a picture or going fishing or flying a kite, says Copeland. This list becomes your "Wellness Toolbox."

3. List those things you need to do every day to maintain wellness—for example, eat regularly. The list would differ from person to person. Copeland's own plan includes avoiding caffeine and sugar, drinking six 8-ounce glasses of water a day, and exercising for half an hour a day. "But for somebody who is just beginning to do this kind of work, the only thing on their list might be a half hour of exercise," says Copeland.

4. Identify triggers that might set off your symptoms. "A trigger might be getting a big bill that you didn't expect," says Copeland. "It might be having car trouble. It might be the anniversary date of a trauma or loss."

5. Develop a plan for how you are going to respond so the triggers don't result in depression—for example, painting a picture, taking the bubble bath, or calling a few friends.

6. Identify your early warning signs of depression. These are "Very subtle internal symptoms that are clues that something is about to happen," says Copeland, such as "a weird feeling in the pit of your stomach, not feeling like answering the door, or not buckling the seat belt."

7. Develop a response plan if these early warning signs occur, to prevent worsening of symptoms—for example, seeing your counselor, or taking a day off work to de-stress.

8. Identify signs that your depression is continuing to worsen, to the point "Where things are really bad but you are still in control," says Copeland.

9. Develop a plan for addressing these increasing symptoms. For example, you might plan to call your doctor and follow his or her instructions.

10. Identify those symptoms that would indicate that you were out of control, where, says Copeland, "There is a chance you could end your life." When do you want people to take over for you?

Darlene's Story: Maintaining an Inner Spark

Darlene, a 36-year-old research scientist, recovered from major depression several years ago. Since then she's generally felt well emotionally, but notes that she's had some times when things have seemed less manageable. "What I'll notice is I'll start losing sleep. My mind will be racing. I'll get kind of a hopeless feeling, like nothing I do matters anyway," says Darlene. "Now, when I get those feelings, I'll start doing more yoga again. I'll walk a lot. I may see a counselor. I'll try to get outside, get fresh air, drink lots of water, until I feel back in alignment with who I feel I am. I have, in my character, a spark for living, which is the essence of who I am. So I'll do things to take care of myself until that spark comes to the fore again."

11. Finally, develop a plan telling other people what you want them to do for you if such a severe crisis occurs. You might plan in advance which hospital you wish to be taken to, and who you'd like to water your plants, feed your dog, or visit you in the hospital. Then share the plan with your doctor and supporters before such a severe crisis occurs.

A relapse prevention plan such as the WRAP combines common-sense and feel-good approaches to maintaining wellness with a system for managing increasing levels of symptoms. You can use some parts daily, and others only when needed. Ideally, you would never have to use the final sections at all. Copeland stresses that such a plan works only if developed voluntarily by the person who intends to use it. It can be a powerful tool for maintaining control of your life.

SUMMARY

Physical, mental, and spiritual approaches can all promote healing from depression. Research has found that taking care of your body—particularly through exercise—can help support your mood. Other physical approaches include getting good nutrition, enough sleep, and access to light during the day.

You can also use your mind to promote healing from depression, by reducing stress, challenging your negative thoughts, and communicating your feelings in a journal or by talking with others.

Finally, research suggests that religious and spiritual practices can be of help. Organized religion may provide avenues for social support and promote nurturing beliefs. Other helpful practices can include meditation and those activities that give you a sense of satisfaction and joy.

People who've recovered from depression are often strongly motivated to prevent its recurrence. You can develop your own wellness program by identifying those activities that raise and support your mood, and deciding which to incorporate into your regular schedule, and which to use during high-risk times or when you feel early warning symptoms of depression.

It's possible to take most of these steps on your own. But many people have found that recovering from depression and maintaining emotional health is easier with the support of family and friends. The next chapter discusses how depression can affect relationships with family members, employment, and a sense of community, and how to promote recovery in each of those settings.

CHAPTER 6

Family, Work,
and Community

∽

*In some ways it was like I was a child, rather than an equal,
because I needed somebody to help with decisions. I really
depended on my husband for that. So I felt kind of worthless
as far as a wife. Now, though, the relationship is probably
better than it's ever been before. We are so appreciative of
the fact that I am so well now, and I'm so appreciative
of the fact that he stuck with me through all that.*

—*GENEVIEVE, TALKING ABOUT HER RELATIONSHIP WITH
HER HUSBAND DURING AND AFTER HER DEPRESSION*

W HEN DEPRESSION STRIKES, it doesn't affect only the
person who has the disorder. "It affects marriages; it affects
parental relationships with children," says Michael Yapko, Ph.D., psychologist and author of *Hand-Me-Down Blues: How to Stop Depression
from Spreading in Families*. It also affects the depressed person's friends,
other family members, coworkers, supervisor, and even community.

People with depression may be temporarily unable to manage
their usual responsibilities, leaving others to pick up the pieces. They

may withdraw emotionally, or lash out over minor difficulties, hurting others who do not understand what is going on. As the depression persists, their feelings of helplessness and hopelessness may infect those around them, causing people who were initially helpful to stop trying to help. At its worst, depression has the potential to scar relationships in ways that make recovery more difficult, or even in ways that can outlast the depression itself.

Yet this situation is certainly not inevitable. Although depression makes people feel helpless, those with depression can take steps to minimize the impact of their illness on their jobs, families, and relationships. Sometimes these actions can actually strengthen ties, leaving a more resilient relationship or work situation once the depression lifts.

There are also concrete ways for family members, friends, coworkers, and supervisors to help people recover, and to maintain positive relationships until recovery takes place.

"Depression gets very frustrating for everybody," says Francis Mondimore, M.D., a faculty member in the Department of Psychiatry and Behavioral Sciences at Johns Hopkins University School of Medicine. Yet ultimately, the news is good. Depression is a very treatable disorder. People do get better in time, with treatment. Meanwhile, there are coping methods and techniques that can ease the burden on everyone until full recovery occurs.

COPING WITH DEPRESSION IN THE FAMILY

Depression, like any type of illness, adds stress to family life. In addition to meeting their usual responsibilities, family members may have to take on tasks that the depressed person usually managed—whether bill-paying, walking the dog, or taking the kids to soccer practice. Further, they often expend enormous amounts of energy coping with guilt, frustration, anxiety, confusion, and blame—their own and that of other family members. Frequently, everyone in the family, even very young children, feels responsible for contributing to the person's depression. The depressed person, often already feeling inappropriate guilt as a symptom of the disorder, may feel even guiltier as he or she sees the family struggling. Yet in the throes of depression, the person typically feels powerless and hopeless about making any improvements.

If the family doesn't get help, it can eventually exhaust itself. Family members who once rallied around the depressed person, striving to instill hope, may feel aggrieved as the person continues to feel and act hopeless, apathetic, or powerless. Relatives may resort to blaming the victim—believing the depressed person responsible for the symptoms of the disorder—even if they know on an intellectual level that this is not true. In response, the depressed person may appear to them to resist even more their efforts to help. Guilt and resentment can snowball.

> *Family members who once rallied around the depressed person, striving to instill hope, may feel aggrieved as the person continues to feel and act hopeless, apathetic, or powerless.*

What can you, as a depressed person or a family member, do to help prevent or change such a painful scenario? Experts vary in their specific suggestions, but overall the themes are: educate the family about the disorder and its treatment to facilitate realistic expectations; communicate honestly, while being attentive to others' feelings; protect children from feeling responsible for a parent's depression; and find sources of outside support.

Protecting Intimate Relationships

How can someone with depression protect a marriage or intimate relationship during his or her recovery? "The first place to start is with a self-awareness of how your depression affects other people," says Dr. Yapko. He notes that depression often involves an internal orientation or self-absorption, which can make this step difficult. Treatments that focus solely on the individual, without mention of depression's impact on family members, can worsen this tendency toward self-preoccupation.

Dr. Yapko suggests that people with depression share information with a partner, "Helping this person understand that there is, in fact, a treatment plan; that there is something that they are going to do about it, that they are actually going to actively pursue recovery." In doing so, he says, the depressed person "is demonstrating to their partner that they care." That means, he says "You have to learn how to deal with your depression sooner, rather than later, so that you are not having a negative effect on family." Getting prompt care and following your treatment plan is crucial.

Dr. Yapko also suggests that depressed people evolve an attitude of protectiveness toward others. "You are going to have to learn what to say and what not to say." This doesn't mean you can't talk about your depression, says Dr. Yapko. "It means being able to say, 'Here's what's going on.'"

The unhelpful things to say are those that are mean or hurtful; sometimes people voice these in the belief that they're expressing their feelings honestly. For example, someone might say, "You know I'm suffering and you don't do anything to help me. I think you're an insensitive jerk." People with depression often aren't aware of the effects of such statements on their partners. "You can inform people about what you are dealing with, without it being an ever-present spewing of negativity," says Dr. Yapko. A psychotherapist can help you learn to distinguish helpful statements from those that worsen the situation.

As a further step, people with depression can choose to involve their spouse or family in treatment, says Dr. Yapko. "That's what couples therapy and family therapy are about." He notes three advantages to this approach:

1. It acknowledges that your partner and other family members are a significant part of your life.

2. It tells them that you want to take steps to protect and assist them.

3. It helps them gain a clear perspective on what's occurring, so they are not blaming themselves for your problem.

As a caution: Avoid deciding to divorce when one partner is in the throes of a depression. Depression colors thinking and can make situations appear hopeless when, in fact, there is much reason for hope.

Protecting Children When a Parent Is Depressed

Through her work in Boston's Judge Baker Children's Center, social worker Lynn Focht-Birkerts helps children cope with their parents' depression. "Of course there is a burden for both children and spouses of a depressed parent or mate," she notes, but "that burden or stress doesn't have to lead to a long-term emotional difficulty, or be the root through which depression itself is transmitted."

Focht-Birkerts has a number of suggestions for parents who are depressed, to help their children remain emotionally resilient through this stressful time. "The first thing parents need to do, obviously, is get treatment for their depression, so they can tell their kids the good news that there are many effective treatments available," she says.

The next step is for the parents to gain an understanding of how depression is affecting them. In her work with parents, Focht-Birkerts helps them explore their specific symptoms, and how these symptoms affect their behavior. Two of the symptoms she commonly addresses are withdrawal and irritability. For example, many parents with depression stop coming down to dinner with the family—a sign of withdrawal.

> *The first thing parents need to do is get treatment for their depression, so they can tell their kids the good news that there are many effective treatments available.*
>
> *—LYNN FOCHT-BIRKERTS*

Once the parents understand the reason for their own behavior, they can explain it to their children. They might describe depression and its symptoms, explain that they're going through a tough time right now, and tell their children that they are not coming down for dinner—or are being especially irritable—because of the depression. This helps children understand what is going on, "so it doesn't remain an unspoken silent pall over family life," says Focht-Birkerts.

She also teaches parents some of the things that children need in order to develop into confident individuals. These include active relationships with children their own age and activities outside the house. She helps parents find ways to encourage their children to "get involved with their peers, and stay involved with things that they are passionate about."

Overall, Focht-Birkerts emphasizes three things that depressed parents can do for their children:

1. Be truthful with your children about what's going on.

2. Help them push through with their own lives despite the difficulties you are going through.

3. Have the faith that you can continue to parent.

"Most often there are effective things parents can do even though they are very depressed," Focht-Birkerts concludes.

Telling Your Child About Your Depression

Children commonly believe that they are responsible for their parent's depression, says Dr. Yapko. They may think, "If I was a good enough daughter, or if I was a good enough son, then Dad, or Mom, wouldn't be feeling this way." It's important for parents to tell their children that the children are not responsible for the parent's depression.

Dr. Yapko suggests that a depressed parent might want to talk to their school-age child this way: "I'm having difficulties with handling my feelings or handling these pressures, and so I'm not feeling as good as I usually do. I'm going through a tough time right now, but the important thing for you to know is that I love you and I will stay connected to you." He suggests the parent reassure the child that they will still go places and do things together.

Besides what you say to the child, what you do to resolve your depression is very important, says Dr. Yapko, since children learn styles of coping from their parents. "You want to model that you do the appropriate things, whether it's seeing your physician and inquiring about the appropriateness of medication, or seeing a psychologist and inquiring about the appropriateness of psychotherapy." He suggests you tell your child some of the things you are doing to manage your depression. In that way, you are demonstrating to your child that when you face hard times in your life—as everybody does—you're not going to roll over and give up.

> *B*y managing your depression, you are demonstrating to your child that when you face hard times in your life— as everybody does— you're not going to roll over and give up.

Talking to Your Children After You've Recovered

Lynn Focht-Birkerts is researching how talking about a parent's depression can help children come to terms with the experience, even years after the parent has recovered. In family meetings, she encourages children to describe what a parent's depression was like for them, including their reactions to a parent's withdrawal or irritability. Focht-Birkerts acknowledges that setting up such a family meeting may be a frightening idea for parents. "It takes a lot of courage," she says. But it can be helpful to both children and parents to express and understand what the children found most difficult during the depression.

If the parent's depression recurs, the parent will have a better idea how to protect the children if they've discussed their experiences during a family meeting. And children will have a better understanding of their own feelings and behavior during the experience.

Judith's Story: Honesty and Education

Judith Snyder, a motivational speaker and parent educator, has been coping successfully with her bipolar disorder for many years. She has worked hard to maintain positive relations with her husband and three children despite her mood swings. "It's probably what I'm proudest of," she says. After she received her diagnosis and understood the cause of her mood swings, her focus was on educating her children about her illness. "When we finally did learn what the behaviors were, we told the kids. When they became teenagers, we had our regular arguments, and my son would say to me, 'You're going on and on again, Mom. You've got to stop.'" She is proud that her children learned to point out her negative behavior when it became obnoxious. "My husband taught them how to do it, and it works really well."

She also arranged for family therapy, something she acknowledges that not every family will want to do. In making the arrangements, she made it clear to her children that it was because of her own difficulties, not theirs. Judith's daughter brought a notebook to the first session with a list of 12 questions she wanted to ask. Judith and her husband had told the children that was the reason why they were going—so they could ask about whatever they needed to know. "We dealt with it openly," says Judith.

For parents who are interested in such a family meeting, Focht-Birkerts suggests finding a facilitator such as a therapist. She also believes, however, that it is something families can reasonably do on their own.

How Family Members and Friends Can Help

If a family member or friend is depressed, the most important thing you can do is persuade that person to get professional help. This can be

She also attributes some of her success with her children to who she is. "I have an extremely affectionate personality, so my children got a lot of affection." She notes that she herself was not raised with much warmth, but instead got a lot of "negative verbiage" from her mother. Judith was determined not to do the same with her children.

Judith became a parent educator, learning—and teaching others— to substitute constructive communication for critical remarks. "Instead of saying, 'You're going to get a spanking,' I'd say, 'We both need a break; you need to sit, and I'm leaving the room.'" Seven years ago, she put her expertise into a book entitled *I Told You a Million Times: Building Self-Esteem in Young Children Through Discipline.*

Judith believes that honesty and education are helpful in protecting children from the effects of a parent's depression. "The most important thing, though, is the expression of love," she says. She notes that when depression causes a parent to be irritable, it's all the more important to balance it with love. "In a nutshell, you have to really make sure you are expressing the love that you have for every individual child in your family, for who they are and their individual qualities."

challenging—and sometimes even impossible. "You can't make someone go for treatment who doesn't want it," says Dr. Yapko. He notes that two common attributes of depression are passivity and hopelessness, both of which can interfere with the person's seeking treatment.

Friends and family can remind someone with depression that treatment is highly effective, and that they care. "You can certainly state in a variety of ways that you are empathetic to the person's suffering," Dr. Yapko says. "The husband or wife of a depressed person might say, 'I can see how much pain you are in. It pains me because I care about you. This isn't what I want for you and it isn't what I want for me. Maybe we should go talk to somebody about this. Would you be willing to go for a physical and see what the doctor says?' If the spouse agrees, Dr. Yapko suggests calling ahead to the doctor's office and forewarning the doctor that you suspect depression. Otherwise, he notes, it is statistically "highly likely" that your spouse will report specific symptoms such as sleep disturbance or fatigue, rather than depression. "If the physician doesn't pick up on it, which we now know happens a lot, the person ends up going undiagnosed and untreated."

Medical Alert

Don't ignore friends' or family members' comments about suicide. Report them immediately to the person's doctor or therapist.

Once someone begins treatment, says Dr. Mondimore, "The best thing that families can do is learn about the illness, learn what realistic expectations of treatment are, and then do two things. One is to be a coach and a supporter for the person being treated. Be the one that looks forward to how things are going to be better. People really do lose that ability with depression. They look at the world through foggy distorted lenses and it's hard to see anything in the future." As coaches, family members can remind their depressed relative that their condition is an illness, a treatable illness, and say, "People do get better; you'll get better, too." It is also important to keep reminding them that sometimes it takes a long time to get better and it may require several trials of different medications, so "we need to hang in there and keep persevering."

The second thing that Dr. Mondimore encourages family members to do is be part of the treatment, even so far as going to appointments with the depressed person. A family member can be an extra set of eyes and ears for the doctor. "Frequently, in depression, the patient is the last one to notice that things are getting better because the mood often is the last thing to change," he says. Early signs of improvement may be subtle, such as slight changes in energy level or body language or the demonstration of a little more interest in things.

Family members are often the first to notice these slight improvements. "Any number of times when I've asked the patient, 'Do you think it's working?' I get the answer, 'Well, no, I don't think so, things seem to be about the same,'" says Dr. Mondimore. "But when I ask the husband, wife, mom, dad, whoever, they say, 'Oh, yes, things are definitely different—she asked to help with the dishes for the first time in weeks; she cooked a meal; Dad wanted to come along to the soccer game.'"

Helping Children and Teens with Their Depression

Children and teens can suffer fallout from a parent's depression, but they can also suffer from their own depression. "One of the big risk factors for depression is a family history of depression," says Paul Rohde, Ph.D., a psychologist who's worked extensively with teens in Oregon. "If a parent has been depressed, it's not 100 percent guaranteed that their teenager is going to become depressed, but it does increase the likelihood."

If a family suspects depression in a teen, one of the most important things they can do is ask about it, says Dr. Rohde. "A lot of parents don't know the extent of sadness and depression in their teenagers," he notes. "They may suspect, but sometimes they're afraid to open up that topic." Dr. Rohde encourages parents to know the symptoms of depression, and if they have any questions about their child, to ask the child. Parents may be aware of appetite changes, but they may not know that even though the child goes to his room at 10 or 11 o'clock at night, he doesn't fall asleep until 2 or 3 in the morning. Dr. Rohde especially encourages parents to ask about suicide, if they have any concerns about it. Parents sometimes refrain from asking for fear that the question itself will suggest the idea of suicide to a child who may not have thought of it before. "You're not going to put ideas into kids' minds," says Dr. Rohde.

One of the best things you can do for a teen who may be depressed is to describe your own experience with depression, says Dr.

Rohde. "If as a parent you've been depressed, talk to your kids about that. Explain that depression happens, that it's one of the most common psychological problems, but it's also one of the most treatable." You can tell your child: the bad news is that depression is common; the good news is that there are effective treatments both for teenage and adult depression.

> *It can be helpful for children with depression to hear that it is a constellation of problems or symptoms that other people—maybe even their own father or mother—have experienced.*

"Depression affects not only the way we feel, but it affects the way we think," says Dr. Rohde. "One of the ways it affects our thinking is that we believe that no one's experienced this before, or no one has suffered as much as we have." It can be helpful for children to hear that this is a constellation of problems or symptoms that other people—maybe even their own father or mother—have experienced.

If you determine that your child may be depressed, "Of course you want to get them in for help," says Dr. Rohde. "Talk to your physician. Or try to get them to a therapist."

The Value of Listening

"The best thing that anybody can do for anybody who is depressed or having any kind of psychological problem is just listen," says educator Mary Ellen Copeland, author of *Living Without Depression & Manic Depression* and *Winning Against Relapse*. "You can even say to them, 'Look, I've got half an hour (or however much time you have) and I can just listen to you.' Then listen without interrupting, without judging, without saying 'That's not true,' without telling them your own story. Just listen and let them know that you are paying attention by saying things like, 'I'm here for you, I really care what's happening.' Just small comments like that, but not anything more than that."

Being listened to in this way can help the depressed person make decisions about what actions to take, notes Copeland. "At first they may just be rambling, and then after a while they figure out what they need to do for themselves," she says. "Usually a person is all stuck inside," she says. "It's scary releasing it, but very freeing."

Besides listening, she suggests using the technique of modeling to help a family member engage in positive experiences. "If your spouse is really depressed, you can watch a funny video and maybe your spouse will join you. Do nice things for yourself, and keep activity going on that might interest your spouse. Some of it won't and some of it will."

How Much Should You Encourage a Depressed Person to Do?

"I have generally told people that it's important that they do as many normal things as possible," says Dr. Mondimore. "That they push themselves to do whatever they can manage to do. Because once they've done it, they often feel better, and have some sense of accomplishment."

Dr. Mondimore acknowledges, however, that knowing how much to encourage a depressed person to do isn't always obvious. "It's a fine line that one has to figure out how to walk. On the one hand, you don't want to push someone too hard, ask someone to do something they're really not up to, or give that person something else to feel bad about. That's the risk. But on the other hand, if you can help the person with depression to maintain some kind of schedule and range of activities, that's going to be helpful." He notes that with depression, "People's lives can just kind of fall away after a while. They lose interest in things, they stop doing this, they stop going to that, and after a while they have basically nothing going on in their lives. So I encourage

> *You don't want to push someone too hard, ask someone to do something they're really not up to, or give that person something else to feel bad about. But, if you can help the person with depression to maintain some kind of schedule and range of activities, that's going to be helpful.*
>
> —FRANCIS MONDIMORE, M.D.

Claire's Story: A Teen's Experience

Depression struck Claire in the middle of seventh grade. Now 14, she remembers last year's depression vividly. She describes it as dark and lonely. "I'm usually a very bouncy person," she says, "and I usually love school. I just started not being interested in it. Nothing made any sense to me, and I was thinking, 'What's the point?' I was always down. At times I started crying for no reason. I knew something was up, but I didn't feel like anybody cared enough for me to sit down with them and tell them."

Claire's friends were among the first to notice her difficulties. "They asked me, like, 'Claire, what's wrong? Are you okay?' And I would just shrug it off. I would say, 'I'm fine.' They told me later that they were extremely worried about me. They didn't know what to do. They knew I wasn't being myself."

Eventually, Claire reached out to a leader in her church, who referred her to her school counselor. The school called Claire's mother, who left work immediately to meet Claire and talk about it. She then took Claire to the doctor for antidepressants, and to a psychotherapist for counseling.

people, as far as going to work, going to school, socialization, and so forth, to do as much as they possibly can."

The Value of Support Groups

Support groups can be invaluable for both depressed people and their family members. Such groups provide a forum for members to express their feelings, share coping strategies, and learn more about depression. Some groups sponsor speakers or have Web sites with substantial amounts of educational material.

Support groups are particularly helpful for parents of children with depression and people with chronic or recurrent mood dis-

Claire credits family and friends for much of her recovery. One person who helped was a relative she saw at Thanksgiving. "It just so happens that my step-grandfather has depression, and so I started a conversation with him about it. It was pretty neat to talk to him about it. Just to know that somebody I know is on antidepressants was comforting for some reason," she says.

Claire's advice to family and friends of people with depression is first, "Have an open ear. Be willing to listen to them." And second, "Keep an eye out for them. Don't watch their every move, but be a little more protective than you've been." Also, she suggests friends and family research depression to get a better idea of what is going on inside the person experiencing it.

Claire learned three main lessons from her experience with depression:

1. There is a way out.

2. You can get help.

3. People do actually care.

orders. But they can help anyone who feels isolated, burned-out, or embarrassed at having to cope with depression—whether it's their own depression or someone else's.

Fred, who has bipolar disorder, has been attending support group meetings for about 10 years. Fred learned about the support group, a local chapter of the NDMDA (National Depressive and Manic-Depressive Association), from a pamphlet in his psychiatrist's office. "It's very good to see the faces and hear the stories that are like mine," he says. "You know you're not alone."

Rebecca, in contrast, went to only three meetings of a support group. There she established connections with a couple of other members. Now, instead of regularly attending meetings, she keeps in touch with these individuals by e-mail.

Like Fred's group, many support groups for depression are actually local chapters of national organizations. Often, these organizations also push for legislation, public education, or social changes to improve the lives or social standing of people with mood disorders. A major goal of such organizations is to reduce the stigma of depression and bipolar disorder.

See appendix A for a list of national support and advocacy groups for depression. You may be able to find a local support group by calling them or contacting them via their Web sites.

COPING WITH DEPRESSION IN THE WORKPLACE

Depression can damage not only our family life, but our work life as well. As depression interferes with our memory, our thinking ability, and our sense of confidence, we may find ourselves stymied by tasks that we'd ordinarily snap our fingers at.

Barbara E. Rohde, a clinical social worker with expertise in business management, has a number of practical suggestions for people coping with depression in the workplace. She bases her suggestions on the recognition that recovery from depression takes time, even after the person has begun treatment. "I think the first thing is that the person needs to understand that they are recovering from a major illness," she says. She compares the recovery period to the stock market, with its many fluctuations.

One of the hardest decisions people have to make is whether or not to tell their supervisors. "You may not need to say anything," says Rohde. "But if your work is suffering significantly, then it's perhaps better to let your supervisor know so that you can negotiate some restructuring of your job." She suggests that before deciding whether—and how much—to tell supervisors, people evaluate their standing in the company, the corporate culture, their relationships with their supervisors, and their job security. "You may want to get advice either from the EAP (Employee Assistance Program, see page 194) counselor, or from the personnel department if you feel that that information will be kept confidential, and you can find someone there who's trustworthy," says Rohde.

It may not be in the company's interest to fire someone, even in the face of a major drop in productivity, notes Rohde. "Then the manager has to go through the time-consuming task of interviewing and training a replacement. It's costly to the company, costly to the manager, and costly to the employee. So really, I think it's a win-win situation to work with employees to try to help them during this time—assuming they agree to get some kind of treatment—and hang in there with them for a few months. This is a highly treatable illness."

There's another reason companies may be willing to accommodate people with depression, and that's the Americans with Disabilities Act (ADA). According to Linda Sturdivant, president of the International Employee Assistance Professionals Association, "What the act says is that an employer cannot discriminate against folks who are covered by ADA. One of the illnesses or diseases covered is depression. So you cannot penalize someone, as far as a hiring decision or a promotion decision, based on the knowledge that that person has that type of psychiatric disability."

One of the hardest workplace decisions people with depression have to make is whether or not to tell their supervisors.

The ADA protects people with depression in another way as well. "If a person comes forward and wants to claim protection under ADA, then the employer has to offer some reasonable accommodation," says Sturdivant. For example, she says, "Maybe the person's on an antidepressant that makes it really difficult for them to wake up in the morning. So an employer might think about changing that person's work shift to an hour later."

Recent Interpretations of Disability Under the ADA

Since 1999, the Supreme Court has made it somewhat more difficult for people to prove disability under the Americans with Disabilities Act (ADA). The issue? Whether disability is to be measured in its treated or untreated state. Prior to 1999, courts generally assessed the level of a person's disability based on how they functioned without treatment. In many cases, having a diagnosis of significant depression was enough to qualify as disabled, regardless of the effectiveness of treatment. In several recent cases, however, the Supreme Court has decided that a person's level of impairment needs to be determined when their condition is being treated. People must now show that their depression substantially limits a major life activity even during treatment.[1]

Companies need not accommodate all such requests, however. "If it has a pretty dramatic negative impact on the workplace, they're not bound by that standard of reasonable accommodation," notes Sturdivant. For example, if the depressed employee is a nurse in a hospital, patient care might be compromised if the employer changed the nurse's work schedule to accommodate her disability. Still, if you're depressed, it may be helpful to learn what your legal rights are before talking with your employer.

Handling Your Depression at Work

Barbara Rohde suggests the following strategies for employees recovering from a major depression:

- Understand that you are recovering from a major illness, and that this takes time. Expect some ups and downs, and relax your expectations of yourself.

- Reevaluate your current strengths and weaknesses on the job. Depression tends to make you focus on your weaknesses, so it's very important to focus on your strengths.

- If you're suffering from anxiety as well as depression, break your work down into smaller segments and focus on one small piece at a time, rather than feeling overwhelmed by the entire project. Over time, you may see that you can successfully complete some tasks and build toward finishing a project.

- Since depression can impair your memory, take good notes. List all tasks and assignments on a central calendar. You may want to keep lists of where you have put important documents. Memory impairment will fade as your depression lifts.

- Ask for help from coworkers, subordinates, and outside friends for tasks that are temporarily difficult. You don't necessarily have to reveal why you need the extra support.

- Assess your value to the organization. (A coworker may be able to provide a reality check.) If it's high, and your work performance is suffering significantly during your depression, you may wish to talk to your supervisor about your depression.

- If undecided whether to tell your supervisor, consider consulting your company's Employee Assistance Program, if one exists, or your personnel department. First find out if the information will be kept confidential.

- By talking to your supervisor, you may be able to negotiate temporary changes in your schedule or responsibilities that will help you cope during your recovery.

Suggestions for Supervisors

What if you're supervising someone you suspect is going through depression? "I realize that there is always a tension between the needs of the employee for a humane work environment and the needs of employers for increased productivity and profitability," says Barbara Rohde. She offers the following pointers to employers and supervisors:

- Recognize that depression doesn't always show up as just a sad, despondent mood. Irritability, anxiety, or a precipitous decline in work performance can also be symptoms.

- Recognize that although depression is highly treatable, treatment may take weeks to months to work. Be patient.

- Think of an employee with depression as you would an employee who has any other kind of medical condition, such as high blood pressure, for example.

- Consult with your EAP administrator or personnel specialist to learn what your particular company policies are regarding depression. Are you allowed to refer an employee to an EAP or discuss counseling?

- Talk to the employee about the parts of the job that are causing difficulties. Provide clear feedback, focusing on the employee's strengths, if possible.

Employee Assistance Programs

An Employee Assistance Program, or EAP, is a worksite-based resource that some companies provide. Part of an EAP's role is to help employees cope with personal problems, including mood disorders, that may be affecting their functioning on the job. Such organizations maintain confidential records, says Linda Sturdivant. "We tell employees that we can maintain confidentiality except where state and federal statues dictate," she says. The exceptions to confidentiality include suspected child abuse or situations in which individuals have a clear intent, a plan, and the means to hurt themselves or someone else.

EAPs provide a number of different services to people with depression, including mental health assessment, short-term therapy,

- Allow the employee greater input in scheduling work. Many people with depression think more clearly in the afternoons.

- If possible, allow part-time telecommuting or flex time, on a temporary basis, to help the employee handle doctor's appointments or juggle work, home, and family responsibilities. Depression can increase the stress of managing home life as well as work life.

- If possible, help the employee restructure his or her job, or move the employee to a special project or team where he or she can be supported by others.

- Before deciding to let someone go, consider the costs of finding and training a replacement. Usually, it's cheaper to wait for treatment to take effect.

Suggestions for Coworkers

If you suspect a coworker is depressed, "I think it's very important to be as supportive as possible," says Barbara Rohde. What else you

and referrals for ongoing psychotherapy and medication. Employees can contact the EAP on their own (a self-referral) or may be referred by a supervisor because of problems such as decreased productivity, tardiness, or absenteeism. In the latter situation, "After we assess the individual, we may find out that the person is depressed, and the performance problem is just a symptom of the depression," says Sturdivant.

"Some companies take a proactive stance as far as helping employees who have depression," she notes. "Lots of companies are aware of the cost of depression in the workplace. Some have pretty darn sophisticated programs to try to get help for their employees."

do depends on the nature of your relationship. "If you feel that you know someone fairly well and can broach the subject, I encourage you to tell the person that you've noticed that he or she doesn't seem to be feeling well, and to ask if there's anything you can do to help in day-to-day tasks." If your coworker feels comfortable talking about his or her difficulties, you might suggest consulting the EAP if the company has one, or offer to find a referral to a doctor or psychotherapist. Always take seriously anything people say that suggests they may harm themselves or others. In that case, insist that they call a health care professional right away, or call for help yourself.

Changing Jobs During Depression

A deep depression is rarely the best time to be making major decisions, including whether or not to change jobs. Depression interferes with our ability to appraise our skills and deficits objectively. We may find ourselves ready to give up on a career when such a move is far from necessary.

> *Depression interferes with our ability to appraise our skills and deficits objectively. We may find ourselves ready to give up on a career when such a move is far from necessary.*

John, a teacher, received a critical evaluation from his supervisor one quarter when he was suffering from depression. "I thought I shouldn't be a teacher anymore, I should try something else," he said. He went so far as to consult a vocational counselor. Luckily, she picked up on his mood state and referred him for treatment. John ended up continuing a generally satisfying career.

Sometimes a high-pressure job may contribute to depression. Nonetheless, it's usually best to wait until the worst of the depression has lifted before making a major change, advises Barbara Rohde. "When they're in the recovery phase, I encourage people to keep their life as stable as possible.

Tread water, work with your existing employer, do whatever you can to keep yourself afloat." Once you are stabilized in treatment, which may be several months later, then you can look at your life picture and begin to reevaluate, says Rohde. She notes that life stress can often precipitate major depression. "It's very important to know that once you've had one incident of depression, that depression tends to beget more depression. If you stay in a very stressful environment, you are really inviting trouble."

COPING WITH DEPRESSION IN THE COMMUNITY

"If you're depressed, you're not alone," says Dr. Paul Rohde. "You may think you are, but this is a common problem, so you're not the only one dealing with it. You just may not know who else is struggling with depression in your school or your family or your community."

Historically, depression and other mental disorders have carried a stigma. In the past—and unfortunately, the present as well—some people have viewed such difficulties with distrust, embarrassment, stereotyping, anger, fear, bias, or avoidance.[2] The negative repercussions of stigmatization are many. Stigma interferes with people's willingness to share information about their depression, increasing feelings of isolation. Stigma makes some people reluctant to obtain a diagnosis and treatment. It can also lead to persistent feelings of shame.

> *F*ar too many people erroneously believe that depression stems from laziness, weakness, or lack of willpower—beliefs that only make it harder for people to recover.

Some of the roots of stigma lie in ignorance. Far too many people erroneously believe that depression stems from laziness, weakness, or lack of willpower—beliefs that only make it harder for people to

Support for College Students

If depression is interfering with your ability to manage your college coursework, you may be able to find help through your school's student counseling services. But there's another, less obvious resource for students with diagnosed depression or bipolar disorder. That's your college's Disability Services Office, sometimes called Disabled Student Services or Educational Access Center. Federal law requires that colleges maintain programs allowing students with disabilities equal access to education. If a qualified health care provider documents that you are disabled by depression, you may be eligible for such assistance.

Rebecca found help at such a center when her depression, combined with a recent car accident, made it difficult for her to keep up with her college courses one semester. "I ended up missing the end of the quarter and having incompletes, and it snowballed," she says.

recover. Others stigmatize people with depression as "crazy," a word that can conjure horrifying images.

One of the best things that people can do to reduce stigma is to share information, both accurate information about depression and, if they feel so inclined, information about their own experiences with the disorder. This is not to say that people should feel obliged to inform everyone they meet about their mental health—just as they wouldn't tell everyone about other health details. You have the right to decide whom to tell, which may be no one except your doctor and your immediate family. You may also choose to wait until you are fully recovered before talking.

Nonetheless, the more that people, particularly public figures, acknowledge their experiences with depression, the more the stigma decreases. When, in 1998, *60 Minutes* host Mike Wallace talked about

She went to a counselor at the college and described her concerns. The counselor helped her talk to her professors, but also suggested she contact the Educational Access Center. Rebecca was surprised. She'd assumed the center helped only students who were blind or in wheelchairs. Her counselor told her that the general category of disabilities includes mental disabilities as well.

Depending on the situation, disability services may help depressed students arrange extra time to take tests or complete assignments, or arrange note-takers if they have difficulty concentrating in class. Rebecca received help in maintaining her financial aid packet, despite having to cut back on the number of credits she was taking. She was very pleased with the assistance, and the fact that the nature of her disability was confidential. Unfortunately, "I think very few people take advantage of programs like this," she says.

his own depression on television, he delivered a major blow to the stigma surrounding the disorder.

SUMMARY

Depression occurs, not in a vacuum, but in the context of our families, our jobs, and our communities. It can pose challenges to relationships in each of these contexts. Yet within each setting, opportunities exist to protect our relationships and promote recovery. Making the best use of these opportunities requires action on the part of both the person with depression and others.

Within the family setting, a number of approaches can help strengthen relationships, promote healing, and reduce the burden of depression on everyone, including children. Good communication

Penelope's Story: Overcoming Stigma

Penelope was 31 when she suffered her one-and-only episode of depression. Apart from crying jags, her main symptom was fear that she was "going to lose her mind, go berserk, and do all kinds of horrible things," she recalls 50 years later. "I would sit there and think that the only thing in my future was a bare room and a bed where I could hide away from the world. That's what I wanted; I was so scared." Penelope sought care from a psychiatrist, a kind man. "In our conversations, he discovered that from my childhood I had some very screwed-up ideas about mental illness. So every time I went there, almost from the very beginning, he had books from the library there for me to read. And they were all on mental health, mostly about depression." The books opened Penelope's eyes to the realities of mental illness. She learned that her stereotypes about "craziness" had little to do with depression and other common mental health problems. Penelope went on to full recovery, and eventually served on the board of a mental health center.

plays a central role. In the workplace, managing depression—whether your own or a colleague's—requires balancing the organization's need for productivity with the individual's need for support. Organizations may find that accommodating reasonable requests results in a positive outcome for everyone. On a local or national level, advocacy organizations are helping to combat depression, by offering education and support on the disorder and related topics—including suicide, the subject of the next chapter.

CHAPTER 7

Suicide Prevention

⧴

*There is a church leader—I've been in her youth
group since I was in the sixth grade—and she can
tell when things are up. She was there for me last summer
when I tried to kill myself and I know that I can go to
her with anything, and she will not judge me.*

—CLAIRE, A TEENAGER WHO TRIED TO KILL HERSELF A YEAR AGO

MORE THAN 30,000 people die each year in the United States
from suicide: an average of one person every 17 minutes.
Each suicide means a life gone, with all that implies: years lost that
might have been spent in creativity, at play, at work, in solitude, and
with others. Researchers estimate that each person who dies by suicide leaves at least six other people intimately affected by the loss.
Aftereffects of each suicide ripple out even further, touching school-
mates, acquaintances, colleagues, the community, the nation.

"Suicide is much more common than most people are aware of,"
says Jan Fawcett, M.D., chairman of the department of psychiatry at
Rush-Presbyterian-St. Luke's Medical Center and Rush Medical
College, and a leading authority on suicide. "It's the eighth most common cause of death in the country (see table 3). It's more common

Table 3.   The 10 Leading Causes of Death in the United States in 1998

Rank	Cause of Death	Rate per 100,000 People	Deaths
1	Diseases of the heart	268.2	724,859
2	Malignant neoplasms	200.3	541,532
3	Cerebrovascular diseases	58.6	158,448
4	Chronic obstructive pulmonary diseases	41.7	112,584
5	Accidents	36.2	97,835
6	Pneumonia and influenza	34.0	91,871
7	Diabetes mellitus	24.0	64,751
8	Suicide	11.3	30,575
9	Nephritis, nephrosis	9.7	26,182
10	Chronic liver disease and cirrhosis	9.3	25,192
—	All other causes (residual)	171.5	463,427

Source: Adapted from "Deaths: Final Data for 1998," *National Vital Statistics Reports* (July 24, 2000)[1]

and has a higher incidence in males over 65, and is still very common in young people." In 1998, the most recent year for which reliable statistics exist, suicide was the third leading cause of death in people between 15 and 24 years old. In this age group, only accidents and homicides caused more deaths.

Faced with these grim statistics, in May 2001, the United States surgeon general, David Satcher, unveiled a national campaign to prevent suicide. Calling on communities, public and private agencies, clinicians, researchers, and others, the National Strategy for Suicide Prevention aims to increase awareness of the problem, reduce stigma, develop and implement suicide prevention programs, improve access to mental health care, and promote research on suicide and its prevention, among other goals.

People often believe that suicide is inevitable. In fact, says Dr. Fawcett, "Suicide is a preventable outcome." Between 90 and 95 percent of people who die by suicide have a mental illness. According to Dr. Fawcett, "If a person is treated for their illness, the risk of suicide can be decreased."

A recent survey by the National Mental Health Association found that as many as 4 percent of American adults may have contemplated suicide.[2] With the power of the surgeon general's office focused on this issue, perhaps our country can succeed in slowing the tide of deaths.

WHO IS AT RISK?

Among the myths about suicide, says Madelyn Gould, Ph.D., professor of psychiatry and public health at Columbia University, "is that everyone is at risk for suicide; that suicide is a mysterious act by an otherwise healthy person; that suicide is the result of one factor, whether it's a breakup with a girlfriend or a fight with a parent or getting into trouble. Suicide is never the result of just one thing. It's complex." Yeates Conwell, M.D., professor of psychiatry at the University of Rochester, agrees. "Suicide cannot be and should not be understood as something that's caused by any one thing in any individual," he says. "It's got to be a number of things coming together at a particular point in time that make an individual's life not worth living to them."

What are some of the factors that may lead to suicide? Experts agree that the most important is psychiatric disease. "Suicide is the outcome of a mental illness," says Douglas Jacobs, M.D., faculty member at Harvard Medical School and the founder and executive director of the National Depression Screening Day, "usually depression, schizophrenia, alcoholism, or severe personality disorder, and usually in combination." People who die by suicide commonly have two or more disorders, for example depression and substance abuse, or schizophrenia and substance abuse, or depression and a personality disorder.

Risk Factors for Suicide

- Depression
- Male gender
- Previous suicide attempt(s)
- Abuse of alcohol or other substances
- Being widowed or divorced
- Social isolation
- Financial problems
- Recent loss or other stressful event: romantic breakup, physical illness
- Inability to experience pleasure
- Hopelessness
- Psychosis
- Panic attacks
- Severe anxiety
- Impulsiveness or aggressive tendencies
- Family history of suicide
- Age over 60
- Easy access to lethal drugs, poisons, or guns

By and large, says Leonardo Tondo, M.D., a psychiatrist at McLean Hospital and Harvard University, "Suicide is related to depression." He includes under this term major depression, the depressed phase of bipolar disorder, and more minor depression stemming from some precipitating factor, such as romantic problems, physical illnesses, or financial difficulties. "A depressive state is probably related to 80 to 90 percent of suicides," he says. Others quote a lower figure, based on a narrower definition of depression. Dr. Jacobs states that between 40 and 70 percent of people who commit suicide are believed to have some type of mood disorder.

Although depression is a key risk factor for suicide, that doesn't mean that everyone who is depressed is at high risk for taking his or her life. While over 30,000 Americans die by suicide each year, 18 million suffer from depression, estimates Dr. Jacobs. Assuming that half of all those who die by suicide suffer from a major mood disorder, that means that approximately 99.92 percent of people with mood disorders do not commit suicide each year.[3] "In any given year the overwhelming majority of persons with depression do not commit suicide," says Dr. Jacobs. These numbers are what make suicide a very difficult topic to study: It's such a rare event.

Over a lifetime, the risk of suicide among people with depression rises, but perhaps not as much as previous studies suggested. "The lifetime risk of suicide in people with depression traditionally has been quoted as 15 percent," says Dr. Jacobs, "although there have been some new studies which suggest that it is lower than that."

Young people who die by suicide share many risk factors with suicide victims in general, such as being depressed, being male, and having made prior suicide attempts. For young people, however, substance abuse may play a larger role, says Dr. Tondo. In addition, young people's risk rises with early marriage, unwanted pregnancy, absence of parental support, a history of abuse, school problems, lack of social acceptance, readily-available firearms, unemployment, or a homosexual or bisexual orientation.[4] In the face of some of these

A Few Facts About Suicide

- More U.S. residents kill themselves than die from homicide.

- Between 6 and 15 percent of people with bipolar disorder die from suicide.

- Suicide causes twice as many deaths as HIV/AIDS.

- More teenagers and young adults die from suicide than from cancer, heart disease, AIDS, birth defects, stroke, pneumonia, influenza, and chronic lung disease combined.

- Nearly three-quarters of elderly people who died from suicide saw a doctor within the previous month.

stressful circumstances, young people's ability to solve problems may diminish. When confronted with a major loss—whether emotional, social, physical, or financial—their overtaxed coping systems may fail them utterly, and they may opt for death.

Suicide and Gender

"Suicide is predominantly a male problem," says Dr. Jacobs. "Eighty percent of suicides are male, with the exception of bipolar disorder, where it's fifty-fifty." This doesn't mean that women don't contemplate or attempt suicide; in fact, suicide attempts are more common in women than in men. Women, however, use highly lethal means less often than men do. Rather than using a gun, they are more likely to use drugs or poisons, for which there is a greater possibility of intervention before death occurs.

As men and women age, the gap between their suicide rates widens. Dr. Jacobs notes that suicide in the elderly is much more common in men. "The suicide rate for men over 75 is greater than 37 per

100,000 where the suicide rate for women over 75 is approximately 5 per 100,000," he says. Although the rates of suicide rise as men age, the reverse occurs for women. The suicide rate for 40-year-old women is higher than the suicide rate for 75-year-old women, he notes.

In the last few decades, the gap between men and women in rates of completed suicide has increased. In the United States from 1970 to 1998, annual suicide rates rose from 16.2 to 18.7 per 100,000 men, but decreased from 6.8 to 4.5 per 100,000 women.[5] Researchers postulate that women may be more inclined to seek help than men, and that this help-seeking may account for women's decreasing rates of suicide. Effective help is now more readily available.

Suicide Risk in the Elderly

Many people regard suicide as a problem of adolescence and, indeed, it is one of the most common causes of death in this age group. Nonetheless, the group at highest risk for suicide is elderly widowed men, particularly those living in isolated or rural settings.

According to Dr. Conwell, risk factors for suicide in people over 65 resemble those of younger people. "Psychiatric illnesses are a very possible risk factor for suicide in older adults just as they are at younger ages; in particular, clinical depression," he says. Among elderly people who kill themselves, however, this depression is less likely to be recurrent or long-standing. In most cases, he says, "This is a first episode of depression occurring later in life," perhaps in response to bereavement, loss of independent functioning, and health problems.

> *Another risk factor for both depression and suicide in the elderly is social isolation.*

Another risk factor for both depression and suicide in the elderly is social isolation. "I think there is a significant association between suicide risk and living alone, and not having the kinds of social interaction and social support on a day-to-day basis that others might have," says Dr. Conwell. "Older people have probably more reasons to become socially isolated."

They may be physically ill and functionally impaired, and can't get out to drive or walk or participate in activities. They aren't employed, so they don't have that as a social outlet. Death or illnesses of friends or family reduces their social circle. Also, he notes, depression can lead people to withdraw and isolate themselves.

"Physical health problems represent risk factors for suicide in all ages," says Dr. Conwell. Certain health problems that occur with age may be particularly likely to lead to depression—for example, some kinds of stroke.

Substance abuse and psychotic illness are not as common risk factors for suicide among the elderly compared to younger adults, according to Dr. Conwell. Personality characteristics of some older people may put them at higher risk, however. These personality traits may "Lead people perhaps to be somewhat more rigid in the way they approach life, more constricted, less active, less flexible. These are folks who may, as they age, encounter significant stressors and life changes, and be more vulnerable to depression because they don't cope as well," Conwell says.

Fred's Story: Turning Away from Suicide

"I attempted suicide twice," says Fred, who survived a severe depression. "Once I tried to cut my wrists, and then another time I tried to run out into traffic. I got out to the edge of the freeway and I didn't do it. I remember I cut myself on the little barbed wire fence out there, and I came back in, and I saw the blood on my leg, and I thought, *God, the blood looked so good.* It was my own blood. I thought, *It means you're alive, and things will get better.*" He was right. More than a decade later, Fred is in a long-term relationship, has a stable job he enjoys, and gets much pleasure from his life.

Among elderly who are not at risk, "It may be that, in addition to social support and interaction, spirituality and engagement in faith communities may offer some protective influence," says Dr. Conwell.

Suicide and Ethnicity

Suicide occurs more commonly in some ethnic groups than others. Generally, white Americans kill themselves at about double the rate of nonwhites. (See table 4.) Nonetheless, certain nonwhite communities and age groups are at particular risk. For example, many Native American and Alaskan Native communities experience extremely high rates of suicide. In the 16 years preceding 1996, the rate of suicide among 15- to 19-year-old African American males more than doubled. Increasing use of firearms accounted for nearly all of this increase.[6]

Protective Factors

Just as some factors increase the risk of suicide, others decrease its likelihood. Generally, researchers have spent less time studying protective factors than they have risk factors.

Dr. Fawcett believes that feeling responsible for another's well-being can help deter suicide. "We have evidence that the rate of suicide is less in people who have children under 18 in the home for whom they feel responsible," says Dr. Fawcett. "It's a statistical difference. So it does have a deterring effect to have that kind of responsibility. I know, clinically, that some people who have been in very great pain and very depressed seem to keep themselves alive even because of a pet, feeling responsible for a pet."

Although less-studied, religion may also decrease suicide's frequency. "I think religion certainly plays a strong role in deterring suicide if it's practiced religion, if it's something that the individual actually practices and participates in, not just a religious affiliation, or a sort of routine observance of religious affiliation," says Dr. Fawcett.

Table 4. Suicide by Race and Sex: Nation, Elderly, Young (1998 Data)

GROUP	ALL AGES COMBINED (NATION)		ELDERLY (65+ YEARS)		YOUTH (15–24 YEARS)	
	Number of Suicides	Rate of Suicide per 100,000 People	Number of Elderly Suicides	Elderly Suicide Rate per 100,000 People	Number of Youth Suicides	Youth Suicide Rate per 100,000 People
Nation	30,575	11.3	5,803	16.9	4,135	11.1
Men	24,538	18.6	4,847	34.1	3,532	18.5
Women	6,037	4.4	956	4.7	603	3.3
Whites	27,648	12.4	5,542	18.1	3,434	11.6
Nonwhites	2,927	6.2	261	6.9	701	9.2
Blacks	1,977	5.7	150	5.3	488	8.6
White Men	22,174	20.3	4,640	36.6	2,934	19.3
White Women	5,474	4.8	902	5.0	500	3.5
Nonwhite Men	2,364	10.5	207	13.7	598	15.6
Nonwhite Women	563	2.3	54	2.4	103	2.7

Source: Adapted from *1998 Official Final Statistics: U.S.A. Suicide,* prepared for the American Association of Suicidology by John L. McIntosh, Ph.D.[7]

"It depends on how severely ill the patient is. In most patients, it plays quite a role in deterring suicidal behavior."

In his 1999 *Call to Action on Suicide*, the surgeon general lists the following protective factors:

- Effective and appropriate clinical care for mental, physical, and substance abuse disorders

- Easy access to a variety of clinical interventions and support for seeking help

- Restricted access to highly lethal methods of suicide

- Family and community support

- Support from ongoing medical and mental health care relationships

- Learned skills in problem solving, conflict resolution, and nonviolent handling of disputes

- Cultural and religious beliefs that discourage suicide and support self-preservation instincts[8]

High-Risk Times for Suicide

People with depression or bipolar disorder are at higher risk for suicide at certain times in the course of their illness. Statistically speaking, says Dr. Jacobs, one of the highest risk times is following a discharge from a hospital. He notes, however, that "The overwhelming number of people who get discharged from hospitals don't commit suicide." Another high risk time in depression is early on, before diagnosis or treatment of the illness. Suicide risk also mounts during stressful life events, such as after a major loss.

Kay Redfield Jamison, Ph.D., professor of psychiatry at Johns Hopkins University School of Medicine, writes in her book *Night Falls Fast: Understanding Suicide*, "Disconcertingly, one of the highest risk periods for suicide is when patients are actually recovering from depression."[9] As depression begins to ebb, energy returns, and people may

David's Story: Life-Saving Therapy

In his late forties, David, a stockbroker, separated from his wife. He grew so depressed afterwards that he contemplated suicide. "I was ready to cash it in. I was thinking about different ways I could do it," he says. He went so far as to instruct a friend how to handle his belongings "if anything happened to him."

Luckily, David shared his feelings with his therapist. "She talked to me about my children. She said that to have a father who committed suicide would be very hard for my children. That in itself helped me to not go in that direction," says David.

Instead, David continued with therapy and an antidepressant, and gradually his depression lessened and resolved. Today, he is extremely appreciative of the help he received while depressed. "My therapist really guided me," he says. "I credit her with saving my life."

find themselves capable of carrying out suicide plans they may have only fantasized about earlier. In addition, the peaks and valleys of early recovery may dishearten people who expected speedy, clear-cut gains.

Researchers have linked certain times of the year with suicide rates, although this connection may be fading. In the United States, May has historically been the month with the highest number of suicides, while December has had the lowest.

THE VARIED PATTERNS OF SUICIDE

Although it's possible to find common patterns in the way in which people die by suicide, it's important not to overgeneralize. While one person may pull the trigger on a rash impulse, others may plan their deaths purposefully and secretively over a period of weeks or months. Not every suicide is impulsive, says Dr. Fawcett. "People can have constant suicidal preoccupations, or they can suddenly impulsively get these feelings. Usually, the thought comes and goes, becoming more intense each time, but it is highly variable from individual to individual."

A great many people do kill themselves impulsively. Alcohol, drugs, and easy access to guns or other lethal means raise the risk of impulsive suicide. People who are by nature impulsive or aggressive may be more likely to kill themselves on a sudden urge.

Nonetheless, as J. John Mann, M.D., professor of psychiatry at Columbia University, writes, "In many cases of what seems to be an impulsive suicide, what is impulsive is only the choice of a moment for carrying out an action that has been carefully planned."[10]

> *A great many people do kill themselves impulsively. Alcohol, drugs, and easy access to guns or other lethal means raise the risk of impulsive suicide.*

The means by which people kill themselves also vary. In the United States in 1998, the majority of deaths from suicide (57 percent) resulted from gunshot wounds, reflecting both easy access to guns, and the high lethality of this method. About 19 percent of deaths resulted from hanging, strangulation, or suffocation, while slightly more than 16 percent resulted from poisons. Far fewer people died from jumping, cutting or piercing, drowning, burns, or other means.

Suicide Attempts

Besides those who die by suicide, a much larger number of people attempt it. An estimated 25 attempts occur for each death from suicide, although this number varies substantially depending on the age group. Regrettably, researchers sometimes call nonfatal suicide attempts "failed suicide." In reality, those who survive are not failures, but successes.

The seriousness of the intent to die varies from person to person. Most people who attempt suicide have some degree of indecision, and some may even count on being rescued. Others are far more determined. Among the elderly, fully one-fourth who attempt suicide die from it, indicating a high degree of determination as well as the use of very lethal means. Teenagers, in contrast, may make 100 to 200 attempts for every death by suicide, reflecting both a higher degree of ambivalence, and less access to or information about ways to die.

> **Medical Alert**
>
> The risk of suicide increases in the early stages of treatment for depression as energy levels rise.

People who attempt suicide and survive share many risk factors with those who die from suicide. People who survive suicide attempts, however, are more likely to be female and younger than 30 years old. Many have relationship difficulties or live alone.

Very often, nonfatal suicide attempts reflect a thread common to suicide itself: ambivalence. Those attempting suicide frequently want both to live and to die. People with a high degree of ambivalence about dying may choose a method less likely to cause death, or may alert others after they have taken the pills or slashed their wrists, allowing the possibility of rescue. Other times, people's intent to die is strong, but they unknowingly use a method that is not particularly lethal.

"All self-destructive behavior should be taken seriously, should be evaluated by a health professional, and should be attended to," says Dr. Jacobs. "Whether it's scratching of the wrists, taking a few aspirin, or what we call aborted suicide attempts, in which people have a plan and do something such as get a gun, sit in a car in a garage, buy a rope, or go to a bridge, but nothing happens—all of these need to be taken seriously." While doctors may assume that taking a few aspirin indicates a less serious intent to die, it's possible that the person who took them believed them to be highly lethal. "People should ask the person what their intent was," says Dr. Jacobs.

On occasion, surviving a suicide attempt is a matter of luck and timing: the unexpected passerby, the gun that misfires. Once something delays a suicide attempt, the impulse may fade. Nonetheless, each attempted suicide raises the risk of future attempts, one of which may be fatal.

Suicide: In Defense of Identity

Dr. Tondo believes that suicide is often a response to a profound threat to an individual's sense of identity. "I think that that's a common denominator in most age groups," he says. In the elderly, he says, "There are some social issues like the loss of a role in society after retirement and the loss of a spouse. If you identify yourself with your work, with your relationships, with your success, and at some point all these go away, then you will feel not only the actual loss, but also the loss of your identity related to that particular situation."

Identity can be an issue in other age groups as well. "Adolescents look for an identity, strive to belong to something, like a group," he says. "Sometimes they try to reach their own identity through dependence on a drug or from a high-risk behavior such as driving under the influence, driving very fast, or engaging in extreme sports. All these are behaviors with a very high risk for suicide."

> *All self-destructive behavior should be taken seriously, should be evaluated by a health professional, and should be attended to.*
>
> —DOUGLAS JACOBS, M.D.

Depression, too, can cause a loss of a sense of identity, says Dr. Tondo. "The reason depression is probably the most important risk factor for suicide is that, with depression, people feel a loss of identity. When you feel depressed, you feel that your role in society is completely useless." For a depressed person, the loss of the ability to function can lead to a sense of being an outcast. "He cannot really work as he did before, he cannot function and produce as he used to," says Dr. Tondo. As a result, the person may end up "feeling that he doesn't belong to his group anymore." Adds Dr. Tondo, "But all this is true also for physical illnesses, when a person loses physical integrity and may think of suicide, even assisted suicide."

We are at greater risk, says Dr. Tondo, when "our identity has been invested almost completely in just one aspect of our lives." As a protective measure, he suggests investing energy in different aspects of life: work, other interests, relationships, not only with others but with ourselves—"being able to be introspective and to understand better and deeper what is going on in our life." For a person facing retirement, he says, "It will be important to find something other than work, not just an interest, but something that would be important to them, and that may function as a purpose in life."

> *The reason depression is probably the most important risk factor for suicide is that, with depression, people feel a loss of identity. When you feel depressed, you feel that your role in society is completely useless.*
>
> — *LEONARDO TONDO, M.D.*

Signs of Impending Suicide

About 80 percent of the time, people who go on to kill themselves reveal their intent in some way.[11] "People who decide to write a will, who speak of death all the time, or who make an important, unnecessary, and improper gift to friends" may be revealing their intent to die, says Dr. Tondo. An avid fisherman who gives away all his fishing paraphernalia, or a young woman who finds a new home for her beloved cat, may be sending a signal that they are thinking of death. Other ominous signs can include researching and preparing suicide plans, and clarifying life insurance coverage for family members. Certain statements may also provide a clue that someone is thinking of taking his or her life: for example, "I may not be here much longer," "The world would be better off without me," or "Pretty soon, you won't have to worry about me anymore."

If you observe such actions or statements, ask directly if the person is thinking of suicide. Don't expect to necessarily get an honest answer, however. When asked directly about suicidal thoughts, people who go on to commit suicide may or may not admit to them. "Many people who die from suicide deny their intent to do it to people just shortly before they do it," says Dr. Fawcett. "So if people say they are thinking about it, it's important not to ignore."

When suicide follows a denial of suicidal thoughts, this may mean different things, says Dr. Fawcett. "Either they are just not telling the truth because they want to be able to do it, or it means that they don't really feel that way at the time, but shortly afterwards they do get these impulses. It varies very highly from patient to patient." Don't necessarily believe someone who says that he or she is no longer suicidal, cautions Dr. Fawcett, "Especially, if you still see the behavior that goes with it, which is often some withdrawal and just wanting to be left alone. Denials don't always mean they are not going to do it."

SUICIDE PREVENTION

Preventing suicide is a multilayered task. The National Strategy for Suicide Prevention includes plans to involve health care providers, educators, faith communities, law- and policy-makers, reporters, correctional workers, attorneys, researchers, and the public at large, as well as other specific groups. The strategy targets 11 goals, ranging from reducing access to lethal means to supporting research and decreasing the stigma associated with mental health care treatment.

> On an individual level, preventing suicide often means getting an appropriate diagnosis for depression, and finding treatment that works.

On an individual level, preventing suicide often means getting an appropriate diagnosis for depression, and finding treatment that works. Once you've found effective treatment, it's important to stick with it until you're well, and to resume it early if depression recurs. "Relapse prevention is the best prevention for suicide," says Francis Mondimore, M.D., a faculty member at the Johns Hopkins University School of Medicine.

Treatment for Suicidal Thoughts

Assuming you don't need immediate medical attention as a result of a suicide attempt, the first task of a health care provider is to listen to your feelings, and help you feel less alone. As you talk, he or she will probably ask some blunt questions: Are you thinking about hurting yourself? How are you thinking about doing it? Do you have ready access to the means to take your life? Have you made any attempts on your life before this? He or she will try to understand what has led you to feeling so desperate at this point.

Part of the doctor's job is to perform a suicide risk assessment: determining the factors increasing your risk of suicide, as well as those things likely to help you stay alive. Depression or another mental disorder may be part of the picture. If it is, the doctor will want to make a diagnosis and help you find treatment. Yet depression, by itself, is

---

If You Are Having Suicidal Thoughts

Help for people contemplating suicide is widely available. If you are considering suicide, it's imperative to get help. Talk to your doctor, therapist, school psychologist, or another health care provider. If you don't feel up to making an appointment immediately, call 1-800-SUICIDE or your local crisis clinic or community mental health center for emergency assistance. (Check the front of your phone book for listings.) At the very least, ask a friend, teacher, religious leader, or family member to help you. They can help by listening to you, and assisting you in getting to a health care professional.

Suicide is a permanent solution to a temporary problem. Before taking this enormous and irrevocable step, you owe it to yourself to try another option. Most suicidal people are unaware of all their options. That's where others can provide help.

not the whole story. "People are not just illnesses," says Dr. Jacobs. "People are individuals, they have a life history, and they have things that matter to them." When these things are threatened—whether a relationship, a job, or something else, says Dr. Jacobs, "that has to be taken into context."

The doctor may also ask about the factors that make you want to live. "It's important for people to ask not just why you wanted to kill yourself, which is one part of the equation, but why didn't you? What kept you alive? A goal of a therapist is to try to understand what are the pillars keeping this person up," says Dr. Jacobs.

Finally, the doctor's job is to help you find resources that will help you stay alive until your problems seem more manageable. These may include medications, psychotherapy, or, if your risk of suicide seems particularly high, hospitalization. They may also include helping you keep your surroundings safe by, for example, eliminating guns from the home or arranging for friends or family to stay with you until the threat of suicide has lessened.

For the doctor to help you, he or she must know you are considering suicide. "We believe that less than half of people with clinically significant depressive symptoms are recognized," says Dr. Conwell, "and of those who are recognized, less than half receive treatment." Do not assume that the doctor can read your mind. If you are thinking of suicide, let the doctor know.

Suicide Prevention in the Elderly

As discussed previously, the risk of suicide in elderly men is extraordinarily high, and one out of four suicide attempts in people aged 65 or older is fatal. "When there is an older person in a suicidal state, one needs to be very aggressive about getting that person help," says Dr. Conwell. "It is a serious situation at any point in life, but the numbers suggest that more younger people are going to survive that state than are older people."

Preventing Suicide in People with Schizophrenia or Borderline Personality Disorder

An estimated 90 to 95 percent of suicides are linked with mental disorders. In many cases, people who die by suicide have a combination of disorders: depression as well as schizophrenia, a personality disorder, or other mental conditions. Research indicates that two relatively new treatments may help reduce suicide in two groups: those with schizophrenia, and those with borderline personality disorder (a chronic condition characterized by strong fears of abandonment and highly impulsive behavior). An antipsychotic medication known as clozapine appears to reduce suicidal behavior in people with schizophrenia. Likewise, a form of cognitive-behavioral psychotherapy called dialectical behavior therapy may decrease suicidal behavior in people with borderline personality disorder. If you or a loved one has depression as well as one of these conditions, talk to your doctor to see whether one of these treatments might be helpful.

One of the saddest statements about suicide prevention in the elderly is this: At least 70 percent of elderly suicide victims see a primary care provider in the month before taking their lives. Not only that, but typically these suicide victims were in their first episode of depression, and had never even tried treatment for depression. "This isn't to say that there aren't lots of people being treated effectively and suicides averted by primary care practice," says Dr. Conwell. "But there are some who fall through the cracks who have access to care, to diagnosis and treatment that could be lifesaving."

Why do primary care providers so often fail to detect suicidal depression in the elderly? From the doctor's perspective, says Dr. Conwell, "You've got the mind-set of dealing with lots of complicating medical conditions in one individual. Those physical problems often present with symptoms that overlap with depression, like sleep disturbance, loss of appetite, low energy, and so on." The doctor may ascribe these symptoms to the medical problem, rather than thinking of depression. "Then you've also got the fact that older people are less likely to talk about their feeling states," he says.

In addition, bias may play a role. "Perhaps, to some extent, you have an ageist assumption that it's normal to feel depressed or suicidal when you are old and sick." These biases can affect not only doctors, but also family members and elderly people themselves. "I think we all share these values that are inculcated by our general culture and advertising about the value of youth and beauty," says Dr. Conwell. "So I think older people often don't recognize or appreciate that the way they are feeling is not the way they should be feeling, and that can contribute to hopelessness."

Who can best forestall suicide in the elderly? Dr. Conwell suggests three groups of people. "One is, of course, family members—assuming there is a recognition that depressive symptoms are not a normal part of aging, that they are a risk for suicide, and that they are, by and large, treatable." If family members are on the lookout for signs of depression, including subtle changes in mental functioning, they may be well-positioned to identify a relative in need of further evaluation.

Primary doctors form the second group, says Dr. Conwell, and the third is other systems in the community with which older people come into regular contact. He cites a mental health center in Washington State that put together an innovative program, training people in the community, such as meter readers, postal workers, pharmacists, and bank tellers, to recognize when somebody might be functioning poorly or might be depressed. The trained individual then links that person with more comprehensive evaluation and treatment services, Dr. Conwell notes.

Older people may be able to reduce their risk of either suicide or depression, says Dr. Conwell, "By keeping involved, keeping engaged, seeking out other people, and trying to avoid social isolation even in the face of physical and health problems. Even more important is a kind of education," he says. "The older person needs to understand that, while depression is common, it is not normal for older people in particular to be depressed or suicidal. And second, effective treatments are available through counseling, medications, or some combination of the two, or in the most extreme cases, electroconvulsive therapy. All of these can be lifesaving and get people back to feeling as good as they would hope to feel."

> *The older person needs to understand that, while depression is common, it is not normal for older people in particular to be depressed or suicidal.*
>
> —YEATES CONWELL, M.D.

Suicide Prevention in Children and Teens

As noted earlier, the annual rate of suicide among young people in the United States aged 15 to 24 has more than tripled since 1950. A young person commits suicide approximately every 2 hours.[12] Between 2,000 and 2,500 adolescents under the age of 20 die by suicide annually.[13] Many, many more attempt it. For every death by suicide in the 15 to 24 age group, there are an estimated 100 to 200 attempts.

While overall death rates among teenagers are relatively low, "What will kill a teenager is accidental injury, homicide, or suicide," says Alan Unis, M.D., associate professor of psychiatry at the University of Washington.

In younger children, suicide is considerably less common. Statistics from 1998 show only 324 suicides in the entire United States among children under 15 years of age.[14] The rate of suicide in children aged 10 to 14, however, doubled from 1980 to 1996.[15] Contrary to some beliefs, school-age children do have an understanding of death and suicide, according to one study.[16] The reasons for lower rates among school-age children may have less to do with lack of comprehension than with inexperience in carrying out complex undertakings on their own, including plans to take their own lives. Additionally, serious mental illness such as major depression, schizophrenia, or bipolar disorder is much less common in this age group, and rates of substance abuse are also lower.

David Shaffer, M.D., chief of the child psychiatry division at Columbia University, suggests several avenues for cutting rates of teen suicide.[17] One is to directly screen teenagers for depression and suicidal thoughts by having them fill out confidential questionnaires, with additional screening and referrals for adolescents found to be at higher risk. Dr. Shaffer and colleagues have tested this method in New York City high schools. They were able to identify many teens at high risk for suicide who had not communicated their problems to others, and who were receiving no treatment.

Another approach involves decreasing the risk of suicide contagion (to follow) by altering representations of suicide in the media. In addition, Dr. Shaffer proposes increasing advertising of and staff training at suicide hotlines.

Some traditional school-based suicide prevention programs have been less than effective, studies show. In fact, one study found that some such programs might be counterproductive.[18] The intent of these programs is to encourage teens to refer themselves for help by destigmatizing suicidal thinking. Instead, writes Dr. Shaffer, "Students who were exposed to the programs were significantly less likely than controls to seek help for a serious personal or emotional problem. They were also significantly less likely to encourage a depressed or troubled friend to seek professional help." It's important that school systems systematically evaluate suicide prevention programs before putting them into practice.

> *Some traditional school-based suicide prevention programs have been less than effective, studies show. In fact, one study found that some such programs might be counterproductive.*

The National Mental Health Association suggests that adults take the following steps if they suspect a child or adolescent is suicidal:[19]

1. Ask the child or teen about feelings of depression and thoughts about suicide or death. Listen in a caring and respectful manner.

2. Tell the child or teen you care and want to help.

3. Provide information on local resources, particularly in the child's school.

4. Get help from a mental health care provider who has experience helping depressed children and teens. Alert the child's teachers and parents and recommend professional help for the child.

5. If necessary, break a confidence to save a life if you think the situation warrants it.

Stopping Suicide Contagion

Teens are particularly susceptible to a condition experts call *suicide contagion*. Dr. Madelyn Gould has researched this phenomenon. "There have been numerous studies over the course of decades that have shown that, following some reports of suicides in newspapers and television, there were significant increases in completed suicide," she says. Celebrity suicides, or suicides of peers known to people within a community, may be more likely to provoke copycat deaths.

"If parents know that their youngster has just been exposed to a suicide in their school—a classmate—or in the community, or to a suicide that has been well publicized in the media, then a parent might want to discuss that with their youngster," she says. She believes this is particularly important if the youngster has a depressive disorder or other risk factors for suicide. (See sidebar, "Talking to Your Teen About a Classmate's Suicide," page 226, for Dr. Gould's suggestions on how to broach the topic.)

With careful discussion and support, copycat suicides are not inevitable. When the highly popular musician Kurt Cobain killed himself in 1994, many feared that suicide contagion would lead to a rash of deaths among young people in Seattle, Washington, Cobain's hometown. Instead, Cobain's suicide inspired a surge in suicide calls to the Seattle Crisis Clinic, rather than an increase in suicide.[20] "When Courtney Love [Cobain's widow] came out so negatively about his suicide, how it was a waste, that probably contributed to its having less of an impact," says Dr. Gould. In addition, the media made a concerted effort to report the suicide responsibly.

"Media can have quite a positive role in educating the public," says Dr. Gould, especially "If it doesn't portray suicide as a reasonable way of problem solving, or glamorize, romanticize, or sensationalize it in any way." Instead, media should stress the following points: that suicide is preventable; that it's a consequence of a fatal complication of different types of mental illness; and that local treatment resources are available. By doing this, says Dr. Gould, media can contribute to educating the public rather than inadvertently contributing to suicide contagion.

WHAT FRIENDS AND FAMILY CAN DO

People are much more likely to drop hints about suicidal thinking with friends or family than they are with their doctors. The following are things you can do to help someone who is suicidal:

1. Take comments about suicide seriously. It's good to ask directly if the person is considering suicide. Don't worry about putting ideas in the person's head.

2. Listen to the person's feelings. You don't need to talk much yourself. Be empathetic and nonjudgmental. Encourage the person to talk about what is troubling him or her.

3. Get the person to treatment. Suggesting treatment is not sufficient. "Actually take them, actually walk there with them, and make sure they get there, because when people are hopeless, they often say they are going to go, but then they decide it's not worth it and don't do it," says Dr. Fawcett. You may need to call the person's doctor or

Talking to Your Teen About a Classmate's Suicide

Dr. Madelyn Gould is concerned with suicide contagion, the possibility that one suicide can increase the likelihood of suicides in others who know the person or have heard about the suicide through the media. If your teenager has learned of a classmate's suicide, she suggests having a conversation with your son or daughter in which you ask for and share information, perhaps in the following way:

"You know that Johnny died. Obviously, that's a terrible thing to have happened. How do you feel about it? What has been said at school about that? Are people talking about it? What are they saying to you? Let's say we sit down and talk about what you think may have led to Johnny's death and see how you are feeling about it. Does it make you scared? Has it made you really feel down? I just want you to know that after a friend or a classmate or someone we know kills themselves, it can maybe make you start thinking about

therapist yourself. If he or she doesn't have one, contact a community mental health agency or suicide hotline to find someone who can help.

4. Don't promise to keep secrets. The danger to your loved one's life is more important than confidentiality right now.

5. Stay with the person (or arrange for others to stay) until you have brought him or her to a health professional. "If people can stay with somebody and be supportive when they are worried about them—and not just leave the individual alone—that's an extremely important thing," says Dr. Fawcett.

6. Remove guns, poisons, and other dangerous items from the house where the person is staying, if possible.

7. Don't necessarily change your actions if the person suddenly seems to change his or her mind and denies feeling suicidal. "Just because people say they won't do it, if they are still depressed, if they still show signs of depression and anxiety or being upset, you just can't count on it," says Dr. Fawcett. "You have to stay with these people

suicide more, and if you are, I want to know. And if you are, I also want you to know that talking about it is a good thing. And if there is ever a time where you really feel that your feelings are overwhelming, let's get you help for it because there is help, and there is nothing wrong with getting help when you are feeling overwhelmed by life, or overwhelmed by grief, or really all confused about how he could have killed himself. And although people may be saying that he had everything to live for and there was no reason for his suicide, there is always a reason for someone's suicide. So don't think that he didn't have some problems. We may not know about the problems that he had, but he did have some problems. What's very sad is that he probably could have gotten treatment for those problems. But if you are feeling depressed or you are feeling out of control, we can get help for you."

until they are over their condition. You have to get them help. Point out that you can see they are not themselves, that they don't feel so well, and you are concerned that the suicidal feelings might come back, that they should maybe get help with whatever is causing their distress, that there is help, and that this can be helped."

When you are trying to persuade someone to seek treatment, Dr. Fawcett suggests the following approaches:

1. Make a strong argument that his or her feelings aren't just due to a situational problem, but to a treatable condition.

2. Tell the person that he or she has very little to lose by trying to get treatment.

3. Remind the person that even if he or she doesn't believe treatment will work, there's nothing to lose by trying.

4. Stay with him or her and keep repeating these messages.

"I've had patients tell me that when I told them they could get better, they didn't believe me," says Dr. Fawcett. "But because I seemed to be trying so hard they figured I was either crazy or deluded or really believed it, and so they cooperated with me just to see what would happen. When somebody sees by your persistence that you really mean it, I think that's the most important thing."

When Friends Are There

At 13, Claire twice tried to hurt herself while in the midst of depression. Both attempts occurred after she had been receiving treatment

---

A Suicide Prevention Summary

The following summary, provided by Douglas Jacobs, M.D., and Joelle Reizes of Screening for Mental Health,[21] identifies several signs that may indicate that someone you know is at risk for suicide, and lists some things you can do to help.

Danger Signs of Suicide

Depressed mood. Sadness, loss of pleasure in regular activities, changes in sleep and/or appetite.

Talking about death or suicide. "I won't be around to deal with that." "I should just kill myself."

Hopelessness. "Life would be better off without me." "There is no way out."

Making preparations for leaving. Giving things away, making a will.

All or nothing thinking (tunnel vision). "Either I get this job or it is all over."

for some months. Claire describes her first attempt: "I was in the middle of art, and there was some really sharp wire. So I just took it and I started slashing it on my wrists. I didn't get very far because one of my friends just started yelling at me and telling me to throw the wire away. She told the teacher."

The second time, Claire was at summer camp. "I was going through a really rough time. I don't know what was going on. I was alone in my cabin and I took a razor and started doing that to my wrist." This time, she threw the razor away herself. "My friends walked in just about that time. They picked me up and they started running to the counselor."

Be Aware Of
Previous suicide attempts
Family history of mental illness or suicide
Alcohol abuse (50 percent of suicides involve alcohol use)
Physical illness, particularly chronic illness
Life crises or interpersonal turmoil
Presence of a firearm

Be Ready to ACT
A: *Acknowledge* the signs of suicide and that they are serious.
C: Tell the person you *care* about them and want to help.
T: Take the person to *treatment.*

Do *Not*
Ignore the situation
Think it will all go away on its own
Be sworn to secrecy
Debate moral issues

Remember to *Always*
Seek a professional evaluation

Claire says that two of her friends were especially helpful to her during her depression, the same ones who took her to the camp counselor after she cut her wrist. They each wrote a list of reasons why Claire shouldn't commit suicide. "Those two lists—I still have them," says Claire. She remembers some of the points on the lists: "You've been there for me through so many things, and I really want to be there for you during this time. God loves you and he knows you want to be with him, but it's not time yet. Think of your mom, think of your sister, think of your dad."

Claire no longer has serious thoughts of hurting or killing herself. "Occasionally, I get these little thoughts," she says. "But I'm just like, wait a minute. And I just think about everything that's going on in my life, all the happy things, and I'm just like, that's not cool. I can't believe I thought about that a year ago. I'm still in shock that I actually was thinking and tried." Claire feels her mood is "just like average" now, as long as she continues her treatment. "I think that if I tried going a week without medication and therapy, then I would be depressed," she says. "Right now, I have my ups and downs—like every 14-year-old does."

Claire's friends have taken care of her in several ways. They got her help immediately when she cut her wrist. They showed that they cared by writing her letters. And they continue to support her, as friends.

The Author's Experience: What Friends and Family Cannot Always Do

This is a story of good intentions that failed.

James, my older brother, a brilliant, creative, alternately charming and exasperating man, had battled anxiety and depression since high school. A gifted engineer, talented sculptor and photographer, he suffered from atypical depression, an ultrasensitivity to rejection that left him desolate and afraid when things did not go well. Unbeknownst to me, he'd talked of death since his twenties. Only after he died at 44 did I learn that the threat of suicide had dogged him for so long.

How a Group of Friends Helped Save the Union

"There's tons of evidence that being with a person, being supportive, sticking with them, and not allowing them to be alone in a crisis that could be suicidal can certainly be life-saving," says Jan Fawcett, M.D. He notes one of his favorite stories, about a 32-year-old man who was extremely depressed and agitated. "He had all the risk factors for suicide," says Dr. Fawcett. "He had been depressed in the past, had a history of child abuse, had just been turned down by his fiancée, and had all kinds of pressures." The man's friends provided intense support for him during this time. "They moved in with him and stayed with him for a week," says Dr. Fawcett. "He recovered, and later became our sixteenth president."

Who's to say where our nation would be now had Abraham Lincoln not survived?

In the last months of James's life, he was in crisis, seeing threats to both his job and his marriage. He'd been taking antidepressants for years and was in long-term psychotherapy, but his depression was deepening nonetheless. James had never taken drugs as prescribed—he liked to feel in control of his medications—and he missed at least half of his therapy appointments.

One day, James said something to me during a long-distance call that made me suspect he was at risk for suicide. I began to ask probing questions. He answered readily enough: He was thinking of shooting himself if his wife left him. She hadn't told him she was leaving, but he was afraid she might. And, yes, he had a gun. James begged me not to tell his wife. I really wanted to—I wanted to get from her the name and phone number of James's therapist, so I could talk to the therapist myself. Reluctantly, I agreed not to tell her—on one condition. James needed to promise me he would tell his therapist everything he'd told me, including the fact that he had a gun. James agreed. Later, he told me he'd talked to his therapist.

"And?" I said.

"I'm not going to do it," said James.

After that, I relaxed a bit. Celina and James began couples counseling. Celina told James—and me—that she wasn't planning to end the marriage while James was in crisis. I consulted a local psychologist for advice. I'd done enough, she said. Weeks went by.

Then I got the call.

At first, I believed James hadn't told his therapist about his suicidal feelings at all. Later I learned that James had, in fact, talked to his therapist about suicide, but that he talked about it so often the therapist had disregarded it. What James hadn't shared, apparently, was the acuteness of the urge. Or perhaps the urge wasn't so acute when he'd talked about it.

I learned a hard lesson from James's death. If I find out someone is suicidal, it's best to contact the person's health care provider myself, even if the person tells me not to, even if it makes the person mad. Perhaps the therapist would have been able to persuade James to give up his gun—something beyond my own power. Or perhaps he would have found another way to intervene.

But there's another lesson, in some ways a more challenging one: Even when you do your best to help, sometimes it's not enough.

I know that most everyone related to a person who dies by suicide feels somehow responsible. I understand that blaming myself is inappropriate and damaging. But there are times when I collapse into spells of "if only." If only I had called James's therapist myself. If only the doctor had persuaded him to get rid of the gun. If only James had agreed to go into a hospital. If only James hadn't died.

Guns and Suicide

Most people who kill themselves in the United States use a gun. A firearm is one of the most deadly methods used in suicide attempts.

According to Dr. Madelyn Gould, "One of the significant differences between teenagers who have died by suicide and teenagers who are seriously suicidal, but alive, is the presence of a gun in the victim's home." Those without a gun in the home were much more likely to survive. "At least in the U.S., it is the number one method for completing suicide across the age span," says Dr. Gould. "A significant risk factor for completing suicide is the availability of a firearm."

Researchers have attempted to determine if states that have enacted gun control laws have lower rates of suicide. The results haven't been consistent. Nonetheless, since so much suicide is impulsive in nature, it is critical to remove guns from households where someone is suicidal. Of course, it is possible for people to obtain them again, but by the time they do, the impulse to kill themselves may have passed.

Dr. Francis Mondimore believes that people with mood disorders should never have guns in their home. "Not ever," he says. "No ifs, ands, or buts!"

No-Suicide Contracts

One technique therapists sometimes use with clients who have suicidal feelings is asking the individual to make a no-suicide contract with them. In such a contract, the person promises, orally or in writing, not to attempt suicide without first making an effort to obtain help. Sometimes these contracts help build a relationship between the therapist and the client. Sometimes they may even prevent a death.

The problem with such contracts is they're only as good as the person's intention. Some people have no intention of keeping their word, even as they make the contract. Other times, the pain of the moment becomes too strong, and the contract is forgotten or disregarded.

Dr. Fawcett and colleagues researched the suicides of people who died while in a hospital where they'd been admitted to protect them from self-harm. The researchers found that 26 percent of those who died had no-suicide contracts, says Dr. Fawcett. "That means that a fairly high percentage of patients who actually went on to kill themselves had promised in writing or made some sort of agreement not to do that. I think they are not something you can rely on."

If you fear suicide in a friend or family member, it's far better to inform the person's doctor than to rely on a personal no-suicide contract. Don't be concerned about breaking a confidence. Saving a life is more important than keeping your word at such a time.

Planning Ahead for Crises

If you are prone to severe depressions with suicidal thoughts, one way to protect yourself is to plan ahead for the possibility of crisis. Who would you like to assist you during such a time? Which health professionals do you want to have involved? If hospitalization becomes necessary, where would you like to go? Have you checked that this hospital accepts your insurance? Is there a family member, friend, or health professional you do *not* want involved? The more detailed the plan, the better.

If you are prone to severe depressions with suicidal thoughts, one way to protect yourself is to plan ahead for the possibility of crisis. The more detailed the plan, the better.

If possible, develop the plan and write it down at a time when you are not depressed, when you understand that help is available and hope exists. Then share it with your doctor and others you want to help you. Try not to make it so exclusive that you reduce your chances of being helped: for example, saying that you want *only* one or two particular friends or doctors involved. There's always a chance that these people may be unavailable when crisis hits.

Obviously, not everyone has the foresight or desire to think through such eventualities. The idea of planning for a suicidal crisis may be frightening. You might want to consider such a plan in the same light as a birth plan that many couples develop before the birth of their baby. Such plans include information on the couple's desires if all goes well, and also if a tragedy occurs. Planning for difficulties does not make them more likely to arise. Rather, it allows you to state your preferences at a time when you are cool-headed enough to think them through clearly.

In the event of a severe suicidal crisis, it may also allow you to choose, ahead of time, who you would like to make decisions for you if you are not able to make them for yourself. (You may want to obtain a legal document called a "Durable Power of Attorney," to give such a person legal rights to make decisions on your behalf. Consult an attorney for information on whether this approach is a good one for you.)

Mental health educator Mary Ellen Copeland includes suggestions for crisis planning in her Wellness Recovery Action Plan (WRAP). She encourages people to name those they would like to pay bills, perform childcare, or otherwise support them if they are unable to accomplish these tasks themselves. She suggests you describe yourself as you are when you are well, and also list signs that will indicate to your supporters that they can stop following your plan because you are better. For information on obtaining the Wellness Recovery Action Plan, see the listing for Mental Health Recovery in appendix A.

EFFECTS OF SUICIDE ON FRIENDS AND FAMILY: A DIFFERENT KIND OF GRIEF

Suicide survivors, those left behind when people die by suicide, experience a different kind of grief, says Audra Knieper, a licensed clinical social worker and former crisis intervention counselor at Lady of the Lake Regional Medical Center in Baton Rouge, Louisiana. "Their grief is much more complicated than normal. Grief is difficult to begin with, but with suicide, the biggest question is 'Why? Why did it happen?'"

In addition, most people—not everybody, but the majority—who survive a suicide feel guilty, says Knieper. "They say, 'I should have been there; I should have known; I should have stopped it; I could have done something.'"

Judith's Story: Choosing to Get Help

Judith Snyder, mother of three and part-time parent educator, had an episode of depression so severe that she knew she needed immediate help or she might kill herself. She was with her youngest son, then 9, at a Beanie Baby show an hour from home, when she felt "the bottom dropping out. I was having severe suicidal thoughts." Her first response was to take protective action for her son's sake. She told herself, "I know I've got to get home, I know I've got to do it safely because I've got this little guy in the car." The moment she arrived home, she says, "I called two or three neighbors and said, please, somebody come over right now. They came over and they took the dogs and they took the birds. At that point, my husband pulled up." Judith told him she needed to go to the hospital. "I said I need to go right now, and they took me in." Looking back, she says, "I did do the right thing. It stopped those feelings."

Then there is the shame. Frequently, people don't want to explain to others that their loved one died by suicide. "There's a stigma," says Knieper. "If you have someone in your family who died by suicide, then there is something wrong with your family. It's seen as not being a nice family or a close-knit family or a functioning family. That's not necessarily true." Often, she explains, people who kill themselves had other problems—for example depression or substance abuse. "But it doesn't mean that just because someone killed himself or herself that the family is at fault."

The stigma surrounding suicide may make survivors reluctant to ask for support. "When someone is grieving that loss, they are not only grieving the loss of the person that they loved—they're gone— but they are thinking, 'I can't tell anyone about this, they'll think I'm a bad person, they'll think my loved one was a bad person.'" Such fears make survivors less likely to look for professional help. Survivors may fear "that other people will look at them funny, or blame them for not helping the loved one," says Knieper. In fact, others may not respond in this way, she says. The survivors may misperceive others' reactions.

In addition, some survivors suffer from posttraumatic stress disorder or PTSD. "Oftentimes survivors may have seen the act, may have found the body, may have had last contact with the person," says Knieper. This trauma can add another layer of symptoms: nightmares, difficulty sleeping, and seeing the events over and over in flashbacks. "If the PTSD is not treated fairly quickly," says Knieper, "it can become a chronic problem."

How can friends and family best support suicide survivors? "Basically, be there and let them talk about it," says Knieper. Good things to say include, "Would you like to talk about it?" or "I'm here for you. I can do whatever."—just as you might say to anyone in grief. "You don't even have to say anything," says Knieper, "just be around them. Let them know you love them." If survivors focus on self-blame, she suggests keeping what you say brief, perhaps, "We know that you are not at fault. We are here to help you."

Knieper notes that certain comments can be hurtful for example, remarks such as, "Well, they are better off," or "Well, at least they are out of their pain." Avoid asking for details about the suicide itself, such as the means of death. It's up to the survivor to decide whether he or she wants to share this information.

Besides being present and listening, friends and family can research community resources for the survivor, suggests Knieper. There may be support groups or specific types of individual therapy oriented toward survivors of suicide. Supporters

> *Besides being present and listening, friends and family can research community resources. There may be support groups or specific types of individual therapy oriented toward survivors of suicide.*

should be aware that suicide survivors are at higher risk for committing suicide themselves. "So the friends and family need to be able to be around them, make sure they are not isolating too much. Take them out, connect them with mental health professionals who can help them," she says.

Celina's Story: Surviving a Husband's Suicide

What helped Celina, James's widow, the most was talking to James's therapist after his death. "The best thing that ever happened to me in the grieving process was talking to his therapist. That's when I started understanding it," she says. On the other hand, talking to the marriage counselor she and James had been seeing wasn't particularly helpful. "Actually, I ended up helping her, because she was devastated. I guess she was going through the guilt trip—here she was treating somebody and she was not able to help. That was true for James's friends, too. That's why everybody was crying, because they had so much guilt—what could they have done to have prevented this?"

Celina's friends and family surrounded her with support. "They were there for me all the time. I would just call them up and say whatever, and they were there. I hated to be alone." Prayer and meditation also helped a lot.

"The guilt will always be there," says Celina. "You listen to music and all of a sudden it hits you again and you start crying. But then here comes the healing process again, reminding you that you did your best, or that there was nothing you could have done. It's something that will be with me, I guess, for the rest of my life. I've just accepted it. And that's a key for a survivor—all this unfortunate stuff will not go away. I hope I will gain from it and it will make me a better person."

THE CHANGING RATES OF SUICIDE: GROUNDS FOR HOPE?

National statistics suggest a possible leveling-off of suicide rates in the years between 1990 and 1998 (the most recent year for which accurate statistics exist). "The suicide rate in 1990 was a little over 12 per 100,000, while the suicide rate in 1998 was a little over 11 per 100,000," says Dr. Jacobs. During that time period, the population increased by 20 million, but the total number of suicides decreased.

Not only did the rate of suicide overall level off between 1990 and 1998, but the rates for some specific age groups also, seemingly, stabilized. The change in rates for young people, those aged 15 to 24, is particularly dramatic. Between 1950 and 1980, the suicide rate in this age group tripled, according to Dr. Jacobs. "It continued to go up until 1990, but not as dramatically. Since 1990, the suicide rate has stabilized." (See figure 7.1.)

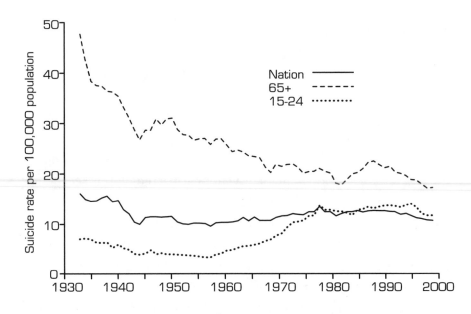

Figure 7.1—*Suicide Rates in the Young, Elderly, and the Nation, USA, 1933–1998*

Source: Adapted from *1998 Official Final Statistics: U.S.A. Suicide,* prepared for the American Association of Suicidology by John L. McIntosh, Ph.D.[22]

Is it possible that certain treatments may be decreasing the rates of suicide? The evidence is clear for one drug only: lithium. Studies repeatedly show that this mood stabilizer significantly lowers the rates of suicide in bipolar disorder. "In our sample population of more than 300 patients," says Dr. Tondo, one of those who researched this topic, "we found a reduction of suicide rates of about 7 times between people during long-term lithium treatment and those without treatment. We have also recently reported a similar reduction in a review of the international literature on this topic."

Statistically, however, people with bipolar disorder make up only a fraction of those who die by suicide. Far more people receive treatment for other types of depression. Have these treatments helped lower suicide rates? "We are actually studying that now," says Dr. Tondo. "But we do not see the same consistent reduction of suicidal behavior with antidepressants as we have seen with lithium." So far, he says, "those other medical interventions do not show the same capacity as lithium to prevent suicide."

> *Action is required—whether it's helping a suicidal friend, volunteering at a crisis clinic, or making sure that you yourself get treatment if you need it.*

We can't conclude that improved treatment was responsible for the decline in suicide between 1990 and 1998, says Dr. Jacobs. "There could be other factors, such as the economy, the divorce rate, a number of social factors. But there has been more access to treatment, further development of psychopharmacology, the acceptance of depression as an illness, and the destigmatization of psychiatry. So, certainly, the figures are supportive that treatment reduces the suicide rate." Still, he advises caution in interpreting the information in this way. "Those are just the statistics," he says. "We do not have a particular study out there that actually confirms that."

Will suicide rates continue to drop? With the recent federal emphasis on suicide prevention, we can certainly hope so. But more than hope is needed. Action is required—whether it's helping a suicidal friend, volunteering at a crisis clinic, or making sure that you yourself get treatment if you need it. Any one act may have little impact on suicide rates in the nation, but, as a Jewish sage wrote about two thousand years ago, "He who saves a single life, it is as if he saved an entire world."[23]

SUMMARY

The eighth leading cause of death in the United States, suicide is a preventable tragedy. Almost always, people who kill themselves suffer from a combination of problems, including depression or another mental illness and a variety of precipitating factors such as a personal loss. Suicide is particularly common among men over the age of 65. Nonfatal suicide attempts are more common among young people, in which group suicide is the third leading cause of death.

If you or someone you know is suicidal, it's imperative to obtain appropriate care. There are many resources available that can help. The support of compassionate doctors, friends, and family can help the individual stay alive until the urge to die passes. Scientists now know that the drug lithium greatly decreases the risk of suicide for people with bipolar disorder. For people with other forms of depression, obtaining care—and the hope it provides—lessens the risk. Tragically, sometimes doctors and others miss signs that someone is suicidal, and other times people die despite the best efforts of others to help. Those who survive the suicide of a loved one may need special care.

Currently the United States Surgeon General's office is urging special attention toward suicide. Scientists are actively researching suicide and its prevention. The final chapter describes some of this research as well as research into other topics related to depression: advances in existing treatments, cutting-edge approaches such as transcranial magnetic stimulation, and basic research that may one day yield still better care.

CHAPTER 8

New Hope
Through Research

❧

They didn't have much medication then
for mental problems. That was in 1951.
So there really wasn't much he could offer me.

—PENELOPE, WHO SUFFERED A ONE-TIME EPISODE
OF DEPRESSION 50 YEARS AGO

ONLY 50 YEARS AGO, when lithium treatment was not yet widespread and antidepressants not yet imagined, people with depression had few choices: psychotherapy (mainly of the Freudian variety), electroconvulsive therapy of the old-fashioned, bone-jarring kind; and institutionalization. Every decade since has seen a major step toward improving care: first, one, then two, then three, and now even more classes of antidepressant drugs; new psychotherapies specifically tested for depression; newer, more humane forms of electroconvulsive therapy; lightboxes for seasonal affective disorder; and modern studies of ancient herbal remedies.

Nor has research on depression and its treatment slowed. Search under "depression" in the National Library of Medicine's database of scientific journals and you'll uncover a list of more than 20,000 studies—and that's just from the past 5 years. Nationally and internationally, researchers are fine-tuning current treatments such as antidepressants and psychotherapies; trying new approaches with older treatments, including enhancements to electroconvulsive therapy and new forms of antidepressant administration; developing new treatments, such as transcranial magnet stimulation, vagus nerve stimulation, new drugs, and new forms of psychotherapy; and doing basic research that may lead to treatments not yet imagined—honing in on genes and the myriad biochemical events that occur when someone is depressed, for example.

Given such an onslaught of research, the likelihood of advances in diagnosis and treatment is high. It's not hard to imagine an era when doctors will fully understand depression's root causes, and treat it quickly and successfully in virtually everyone who seeks care. What may be harder to accomplish is ensuring that people who are depressed *do* receive care. Symptoms of untreated depression will not change: people with the disorder, brought low by indecision, decreased energy, and diminished self-esteem, will still have a hard time persuading themselves to seek help. And unless improvements occur in our health care system, many doctors will still lack time and training to help those who request it.

> *Unless improvements occur in our health care system, many doctors will still lack time and training to help those who request it.*

those who request it. The greatest challenges ahead may lie not in the quality of treatment, but in its availability and use.

FINE-TUNING CURRENT TREATMENTS

Despite the numerous treatments currently available for depression, many people don't recover with the first treatment they try. As each new approach arrives, doctors seek to determine how to use it. Who is best suited to each treatment? Should people use it on its own, or in combination with other treatments? What's the best dose or duration? What might enhance or detract from its effects? Time and experience provide tentative answers to some of these questions, but the best answers come from research.

The National Institute of Mental Health (NIMH) is currently sponsoring several large-scale studies to determine the most effective ways to use standard treatments for major depression, dysthymia, and bipolar disorder, as well as to find the most effective treatments for major depression in teens. Each of these studies involves doctors and participants in clinics and research institutes across the country. Numerous smaller-scale studies funded by other groups are investigating related issues.

Sequenced Treatment Alternatives to Relieve Depression

The NIMH-sponsored study Sequenced Treatment Alternatives to Relieve Depression, or STAR-D, focuses on people with major depression or dysthymia who don't get a satisfactory result from the first antidepressant they try. By studying more than 2,000 people, researchers hope to determine which treatments (including various medications and psychotherapy) are the best "second step." They are investigating which of these second-step treatments are most effective and most well accepted by patients, and comparing rates of side effects and economic costs. Researchers hope that by studying such a large group of people, they will produce clear-cut results that doctors can use to guide their treatment. The 5-year study will end in late 2004.

> *By studying more than 2,000 people, researchers hope to determine which treatments are the best "second step" for those who don't get satisfactory benefit from the first antidepressant they try.*

Systematic Treatment Enhancement Program for Bipolar Disorder

Gary Sachs, M.D., is principal investigator for another large study sponsored by the National Institute of Mental Health. This one is known as the Systematic Treatment Enhancement Program for Bipolar Disorder, or STEP-BD. "We are hoping to learn which treatments really are best for individual patients," says Dr. Sachs. "We will be able to learn whether there are differences between men and women, people in the northwest of the United States versus the southeast. Are there approaches that work better for different racial or ethnic groups?" Such information will help doctors learn how to individualize treatment.

In addition, researchers hope to determine which of several different approaches works best. "There are a number of critical decision points in the course of bipolar illness," says Dr. Sachs. One is how to treat episodes of depression. "Some experts recommend treating with mood stabilizers alone. Others say, very often, that you should give an antidepressant with the mood stabilizer. We are also interested to know the role of psychotherapy at that point. And STEP-BD really will examine those issues." The goal is to gain sufficient information to know how to target individuals' needs. Results will take several more years.

Rif El-Mallakh, M.D., associate professor of psychiatry at the University of Louisville in Kentucky, is one of the researchers involved with the STEP-BD study. "What's exciting about this study," he says, "is that it represents a major investment to create a huge database. This is the first time that NIMH has done that."

Treatment for Adolescents with Depression Study

A third NIMH-funded study goes by the acronym TADS, short for Treatment for Adolescents with Depression Study. Centered in North Carolina's Duke University, its goal is to determine which treatments or combinations of treatments work best for teenagers with major depression.

Paul Rohde, Ph.D., a psychologist and senior scientist at the Oregon Research Institute, is one of the researchers participating in TADS. "There are now up to 15 sites across the country, and we're one of them. All these sites are recruiting teenagers," he says. "We're comparing Prozac versus cognitive-behavioral therapy versus a combination of Prozac plus the cognitive-behavioral therapy." In addition, some participants will receive a pill placebo.

Why the need for this study at this time? "There's no question that the antidepressants work for adults," says Dr. Rohde. "There are dozens or hundreds of studies showing that." He notes that fewer studies have found that SSRIs or other antidepressants are more effective than a pill placebo for teenagers. The few studies of teens so far have found a much smaller effect of these drugs, compared to studies of adults. Says Dr. Rohde of TADS, "It's going to be, we hope, the most important study in establishing whether Prozac is better than a pill placebo, and also what's more effective, the individual psychotherapy or the medication. A really important question to which we don't know the answer is: Is combined therapy better than a single therapy? Therapists think it is, but that's not been proven yet."

Depression Treatment in Children: The Need for Research

Compared to other age groups, children under 12 experience far lower rates of depression. Perhaps in consequence, relatively few studies have investigated which treatments are actually effective for children. Particularly rare are studies comparing a drug treatment to placebo. This circumstance makes it harder for doctors to know the actual effectiveness of medications for this age group.

Research on Improving the Rates of Depression Diagnosis and Treatment

Studies confirm that primary care providers miss many opportunities to treat depression in their patients, identifying only about half of those who come into their offices with depression.[1] According to at least one study, less than 20 percent of individuals with depression or anxiety who see only their primary care providers actually receive appropriate care for their disorder. Periodically, researchers attempt to find practical ways that will help improve this situation.

What actions can clinics and other health care systems take to improve treatment of depression? Research suggests that simple approaches, such as having a nurse specialist call patients regularly to see how they're doing, help people stay with their treatments longer.[3] Besides testing approaches that will improve care, investigators are also trying to find systematic ways to help doctors be more sensitive to the possibility of depression among their patients.

These enormous practical problems deserve more attention by researchers, doctors, people with depression and their families, and the public at large.

NEW APPROACHES WITH OLDER TREATMENTS

Researchers are constantly seeking to improve current treatments for depression—whether drugs, different forms of psychotherapy, or other approaches. Improving effectiveness, decreasing side effects, and applying treatments to a broader range of conditions are some of the goals of research. The following are several examples of new approaches developed from earlier treatment methods.

Advances in Electroconvulsive Therapy

Long considered a treatment of last resort by doctors and patients alike, electroconvulsive therapy (ECT) has made a considerable comeback in recent decades. Current ECT research may lead to still more advances.

"ECT has undergone a profound revolution in the last 20 years," says Harold Sackeim, Ph.D., chief of the biological psychiatry department at New York State Psychiatric Institute. ECT, as noted in chapter 3, reduces depression by sending an electric current through the scalp into the brain, causing a seizure. "The basic assumptions of how ECT works and how best to administer it have been proven wrong, and largely through a series of studies done here at Columbia," says Dr. Sackeim. "What that work established is that depending on where electrodes are placed on the scalp, and the current that is applied, one can have virtually no one getting better, or 70 percent of patients getting better."

> *Improving effectiveness, decreasing side effects, and applying treatments to a broader range of conditions are some of the goals of research.*

One example of the revolution, says Dr. Sackeim, is the end of a 40-year debate on the merits of one-sided or two-sided ECT; that is, administering ECT with electrodes on both sides of the scalp or on the right side only. For years, the standard approach has been two-sided ECT, which works well at relieving depression but commonly causes difficulties with memory. Doctors agreed that administering ECT to the right side alone caused much less memory impairment. Many suspected that right-sided treatment didn't work as well as two-sided ECT in treating depression, however.

"Last year that debate seemed to be resolved," says Dr. Sackeim. A series of studies at Columbia University found that the key was giving enough current to generate a brain seizure in that particular individual. When enough current was given, right-sided ECT was as effective as bilateral. "It is not only equal to bilateral ECT in efficacy, but it causes less cognitive side effects, and less long-term memory loss in particular," says Dr. Sackeim.

Another recent study from Columbia addresses a different problem: relapse. "ECT is a very unusual treatment in psychiatry," says

Dr. Sackeim. "It is the only treatment that we stop once it works." Typically, people undergo a successful series of ECT treatments, then stop abruptly. The result? If no medication is given to people with nonbipolar depression, as many as 84 percent have a relapse within 6 months, Dr. Sackeim's research shows.[4] Dr. Sackeim and colleagues found that giving people with nonbipolar depression a combination of lithium and the antidepressant nortriptyline after they completed a series of ECT cut the relapse rate by more than half. Researchers used these drugs rather than the more commonly prescribed SSRIs because most people who use ECT do so because SSRIs haven't worked.

Dr. Sackeim suggests it may be possible to cut the relapse rate even more. "Eight of 9 patients who relapsed on nortriptyline and lithium did so in the first 5 weeks," he notes. "What happens with ECT is, you give it 3 times a week, you stop it abruptly when the patient is well, you put them on medications, and they are unprotected for 4 to 6 weeks"—the amount of time antidepressants need to take effect. "So you have two alternatives," he says. "One is to taper ECT during that 4 to 6 week period rather than stopping it abruptly, so that you provide some protection until the drug can kick in. The other thing that you can do is start the medication much earlier," beginning it during the weeks the person is receiving ECT. Dr. Sackeim plans to research the second alternative.

In yet another study, researchers at Columbia are experimenting with reducing the duration of the electric pulses given during ECT, resulting in a much smaller total dose of electricity. "Patients wake up much quicker, they are oriented quicker, and they have much less memory loss," says Dr. Sackeim. "We think that that's a further advancement that is going to occur in the field, as these data get confirmed."

Antidepressants Through the Skin

Scientists are constantly experimenting with new methods of delivering medications. Currently under study is the delivery of selegiline, an antidepressant in the MAOI family, via a patch worn on the skin.

When people take drugs orally, the level of drug in the bloodstream rises and falls, depending on when the person last took a pill. A patch allows for more stable blood levels, possibly increasing the drug's effectiveness.

One study of 177 people found that the selegiline patch reduced symptoms of major depression more than a placebo. Unfortunately, about one-third of the people using it got a rash around the patch; this was double the rate among people using a dummy patch.[5]

Perhaps one day patches will be as common a way to take antidepressants as they are to stop smoking.

Enhancements of Psychotherapy

"There are research advances in psychotherapy," says David Dunner, codirector of the University of Washington's Center for Anxiety and Depression. Some of these advances involve refinement of approaches already shown to be effective, as discussed below. Larry Beutler, Ph.D., editor of the *Journal of Clinical Psychology*, and colleagues have undertaken another approach: using research to develop a systematic way for therapists to individualize psychotherapy for different types of people with depression.

Dr. Beutler's work has involved several stages. First, he and his colleagues compared the effectiveness of different types of psychotherapy, "Looking at different kinds of patients, all depressed," says Dr. Beutler. Next, they analyzed the characteristics of each specific type of therapy to determine which aspects led to their different effects. "That's what our recent work is about," he says. Finally, they combined the features of different types of therapy—such as focusing on insight or on behavior change—into a single new type of therapy.

"The therapy that we have now, that we call 'prescriptive therapy,' is one that takes pieces of cognitive therapy, pieces of analytic therapy, and pieces of interpersonal therapy to make a unique package for each individual patient," he explains. He and his colleagues developed guidelines so that therapists can decide what ingredients to put into each package, based on four different characteristics in the people they are treating for depression. These characteristics include the level of severity or impairment in daily activities, the person's coping style, his or her degree of rebelliousness against authority, and the degree of initial distress.

> *The therapy that we have now, that we call "prescriptive therapy," is one that takes pieces of cognitive therapy, pieces of analytic therapy, and pieces of interpersonal therapy to make a unique package for each individual patient.*
>
> —LARRY BEUTLER, PH.D.

For example, Dr. Beutler describes the dimension of coping style. "That's the way they deal with stress," he explains. "Do they tend to act out, and get angry, blame other people, or do they tend to pull away, get reclusive, blame themselves, and feel guilty? If they tend to act out and be impulsive and angry, then we tend to use more behaviorally oriented procedures. If they tend to become introspective, we tend to use more analytic, insight-oriented procedures, and some aspects of cognitive procedures."

Other characteristics would lead the therapist to make other types of decisions. "We put all those things together," Dr. Beutler says. "So any given therapy package may have some cognitive things in it, some interpersonal things in it, and some other aspects to it, depending on the characteristics of the patient."

Advances in Cognitive-Behavioral Therapy

Leslie Sokol, Ph.D., education coordinator of the Beck Institute in Bala Cynwyd, Pennsylvania, describes some of the ways in which cognitive therapy has developed over the years. "The model itself has not changed," she says. "Our ability to understand people based on the model has improved." For example, cognitive therapists now look more systematically at the underlying assumptions that give rise to people's negative thinking. One assumption is, "I should be perfect or others will reject me." People may develop certain behavioral strategies based on this assumption, says Dr. Sokol, such as "Trying to be perfect, overpreparing for a test, or acquiescing all the time, never saying no." She notes that for cognitive therapists, "The ability to identify assumptions and to recognize strategies has improved."

In addition, cognitive therapy has branched out. "It was a model originally developed to treat depression," says Dr. Sokol. "The model has been expanded to treat every psychiatric disorder on the books." For example, psychotherapists are using a form of cognitive therapy in the treatment of schizophrenia.

DEVELOPING NEW TREATMENTS FOR DEPRESSION

The discovery of insulin, early in the twentieth century, has saved the lives of countless individuals with diabetes. Researchers bent on developing new treatments for depression may be striving to do the same. Sometimes their efforts involve laboratory research: identifying biochemicals that may be key in depression, and using this information to formulate new experimental drugs. Other times, researchers take a drug or procedure that's approved for a different medical problem, and try using it to treat depression. On still other occasions, researchers creatively tweak a successful treatment into something quite different—for example, replacing a lightbox with a lamp that mimics the rising of the sun.

> *Cognitive therapists now look more systematically at the underlying assumptions that give rise to people's negative thinking.*

The Brain in Depression

To grasp the essence of some of the research on new treatments, it's not necessary to have a neuroscientist's understanding of the brain. But it's helpful to know a few basics of brain anatomy (see figure 8.1). Here is a brief overview of key areas of the brain that researchers think may be involved in depression.

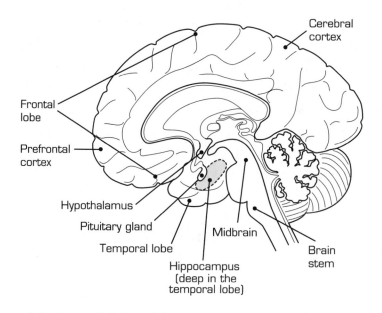

Figure 8.1—*Anatomical View of the Brain*

Encased in its bony skull, the brain contains about a hundred billion nerve cells that communicate with each other and with other nerves that originate in the spinal column. The extent of this communication is virtually unimaginable: Our minds aren't quite able to comprehend the vast complexities of our brains.

The largest portion of the brain is the *cerebrum*, the cauliflower-like forward section where we interpret information coming in from our senses, initiate voluntary movements, and think. Scientists describe the cerebrum as having two halves: the right and left hemispheres. (Because many nerves cross from right to left, or vice versa, at the neck, the right hemisphere typically controls the left half of the body, and the left hemisphere the right.) A coating of gray matter, called the *cerebral cortex*, covers the cerebrum. This is where the cerebral brain cell bodies lie, containing the cell nuclei, DNA, and so on. Underneath, the white matter holds nerve fibers that transmit messages between these cell bodies and other nerve centers in the brain and spinal cord.

Two areas of the cerebral cortex are worth special mention. The *hippocampus*, located in the cerebrum's temporal lobe, processes and sorts memories, moving them from short-term brain files to long-term storage. (The hippocampus takes its name from the Greek word for sea monster, which anatomists believed it resembled.) Without the hippocampus, new long-term memories cannot form. The *prefrontal cortex*, at the front of the cerebrum, controls concentration, planning, and problem solving. The prefrontal cortex, says David Avery, M.D., professor of psychiatry at the University of Washington, "Is the part of the brain that makes us human."

Other key areas lie in the *brain stem*, the part of the brain that connects the cerebrum to the spinal cord. In this portion lies the *hypothalamus*, the part of the brain involved in appetite, libido, and sleep. The hypothalamus sends chemical messages in the form of hormones to the *pituitary gland*, which in turn sends hormones to other glands throughout the body, including the adrenal glands.

Finally, brain stem structures, the hippocampus, an organ called the *amygdala*, and other parts of the brain, together form the *limbic system*, sometimes called the "emotional brain" (see figure 8.2). The limbic system creates feelings of anger, fear, pleasure, and sadness.

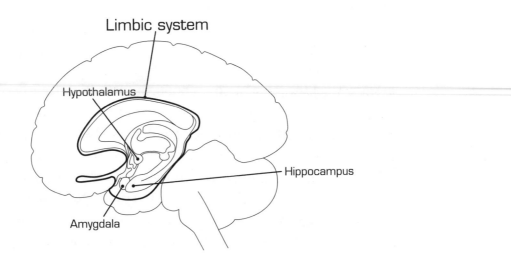

Figure 8.2—*Limbic System*

This chapter describes experimental treatments targeting one or more of these areas: parts of the cerebrum; the limbic system; and the hypothalamus, pituitary, and adrenal glands.

Pictures of the Brain: Imaging Studies in Depression

Imagine two computerized pictures of a brain appearing side by side. In one, dark blue and purple predominate. In the other, vivid yellow and orange light up areas around the periphery. What's going on?

These are PET (positron emission tomography) scans of the same brain. Researchers took the first when the person was depressed, and the second after recovery. The brightly lit-up areas in the second scan represent brain cells that are burning more glucose, indicating more nerve activity. The dimmer blue areas in the first scan indicate less nerve action. Many of the lit-up areas in the second scan are in the prefrontal cortex, that part of the brain that controls planning and other complex thinking. In the first scan, this area appears bluish and dark.

A few decades ago, such pictures would have seemed miraculous. Today, researchers view them as an exciting tool allowing greater understanding of brain functioning.

Says Dr. El-Mallakh, "If you look at those imaging studies, what you find is that there are specific parts of the brain, during depression, that are less active than either normal controls, or less active than they are when the same person is not depressed. It's relatively consistent. And it's consistent even across different types of depression."

Evidence from these PET scans has focused scientists' attention on the role of the prefrontal cortex in depression. "PET studies have found that depressed folks have low activity in the frontal lobes, the left prefrontal cortex," says Dr. Avery. "It is also interesting that individuals who have strokes in the left prefrontal cortex are much more likely to have depression compared to individuals who have strokes in their right prefrontal cortex. So there's this possibility that there are left-right differences with regard to the prefrontal cortex."

To Dr. Avery, it makes sense that the prefrontal cortex plays a role in depression, given what scientists understand about its functions in general. "The prefrontal cortex is important for complex cognition—such as planning for the future and executive function in memory—that is, trying to keep multiple tasks in mind at the same time. In order to do that, you need good frontal lobe functioning. Sometimes depressed folks have low activity in that area, and they also have difficulty performing tasks," he says. Decreased frontal lobe functioning might explain poor concentration, and perhaps even hopelessness. "Part of the prefrontal cortex's function is thinking about the future, planning," he explains. "If that part isn't working well, the future may seem fairly dim and bleak."

> *Part of the prefrontal cortex's function is thinking about the future, planning. If that part isn't working well, the future may seem fairly dim and bleak.*
>
> —DAVID AVERY, M.D.

Researchers have found that PET scans can change dramatically with medication and other treatments, including cognitive-behavioral therapy. In addition to PET scans, advanced forms of MRIs (magnetic resonance imaging) also provide detailed pictures of the brain in action.

New Medications

Not every drug under development meets with success. Frequently, initial optimism turns around as studies find flaws: toxicity, major side effects, or simple lack of effectiveness. Despite all sorts of evidence suggesting a particular substance *should* work, actual studies on animals or humans frequently find that it doesn't. The FDA requires that drug companies provide evidence that drugs work more effectively than placebos in clinical trials, and meet standards of safety as well. No matter how promising a treatment may sound in theory, until it meets with FDA approval, there's absolutely no guarantee it will ever become available for general use.

That being said, here are some brief descriptions of treatments in various stages of development, several of them representing novel approaches to treating depression.

New Antidepressants

For a few years, it seemed that every time you turned around, a new antidepressant had appeared on pharmacy shelves. Says Dr. Dunner, "Although the rate of new medications being introduced in this country for depression has slacked off a bit, we're still looking at one in the pipeline every couple of years that works in different ways than what we have, and that can offer some hope for people who have depression."

One such drug is reboxitine, currently available as an antidepressant outside the United States. Reboxitine inhibits the reuptake of the neurotransmitter norepinephrine. "It may be out, we hope, toward the end of this year," says Michael Gitlin, M.D., director of UCLA's Mood Disorders Clinic. "That's the only one that is going to be out within the next year or so," he predicts.

Stress-Blockers

While antianxiety drugs such as Valium and Xanax have long been available, doctors rarely prescribe them for depression without a co-existing anxiety disorder. Nonetheless, depression researchers have uncovered a number of fascinating links between depression and stress, links that suggest innovative approaches to the treatment of depression. Understanding these treatments requires a little background on the physiology of stress.

"One of the theories of depression is that you're in a high degree of stress," says John Ratey, M.D., associate clinical professor of psychiatry at Harvard Medical School and author of *A User's Guide to the Brain.* "A mechanical way of thinking about that is it means you have a lot of stress hormone, cortisol, circulating." Cortisol is produced by the adrenal gland, and is one of a group of steroid hormones known as *glucocorticoids*.

Most nondepressed people, faced with danger, have a short-term rise in their cortisol levels, preparing their body to fight or flee. In response to this rise in cortisol and other hormones such as epinephrine, their pupils dilate, enabling them to see better in the dark; their heart speeds up; and blood surges into their muscles, enabling them to respond physically. Once the danger subsides, levels of these hormones should drop.

In depression, things often work differently, however. "With depression, what happens is that this response becomes disorganized," says Alan Unis, M.D., associate professor of psychiatry at the University of Washington. "What we've seen in individuals with depression is chronically elevated cortisol," as if the people were always responding to danger. When such individuals face

> *In depression, the stress response becomes disorganized, with chronically elevated cortisol, as if the person is always responding to danger.*

an acute stress, says Dr. Unis, their rise in cortisol is also abnormal. "It's not as high, it's not as brisk, and it doesn't return to baseline as quickly."

As with most of the body's responses, cortisol doesn't act on its own. It ultimately takes its direction from another hormone called *corticotropin releasing factor* or CRF, which is secreted by the hypothalamus. CRF triggers a rise in an intermediary hormone called *ACTH*, which in turn promotes a rise in cortisol. (CRF also acts as a neurotransmitter in the brain.)

One researcher, Charles Nemeroff, M.D., Ph.D., chairman of the department of psychiatry at Emory University School of Medicine, has focused a good deal of research on the substance at the top of the heap: CRF. He has found that CRF is often chronically elevated in depression, and suspects that this overproduction of CRF may be what lays the ground for depression, at least in some individuals.[6]

Several drug companies are now attempting to develop a compound that blocks CRF receptors. Says Dr. Unis, "The hope is that by turning off that chronic stress response for a period of time, the body can recover and get back into the normal physiologic state."

Is blocking CRF the only way to turn off the stress response? Some researchers think not. They are exploring ways to block glucocorticoids such as cortisol. "From my perspective, they are doing the same thing," says Dr. Unis, "only hitting the system at a different level. One is hitting it at the level of the hypothalamus, and the other is hitting it at the level of the adrenal gland itself."

> *The hope is that by turning off that chronic stress response for a period of time, the body can recover and get back into the normal physiologic state.*
>
> —ALAN UNIS, M.D.

If any of these stress-blockers succeed, their mode of action would be quite different from that of any current antidepressant.

Substance P Antagonists

First described in 1931, the mysterious-sounding *substance P* is a messenger molecule present in the brain and intestinal tract. It plays a role in the perception of unpleasant stimuli, including pain. Researchers at one drug company, Merck Pharmaceuticals, developed a compound that interferes with substance P's functioning. In one short-term study, this substance P *antagonist* appeared to combat depression symptoms as effectively as the antidepressant Paxil. Disappointingly, another study found the drug was no more effective than a placebo. (In this study, as sometimes happens, Paxil didn't work any better than the placebo either, leaving the results open to question.) Reportedly, Merck is now testing another stronger drug that also combats substance P.[7]

New Psychotherapies

Investigators are currently studying several promising types of psychotherapy specifically designed for bipolar disorder. One such treatment is called *interpersonal and social rhythm therapy*, designed to help people maintain regular patterns of daily activities such as sleeping, eating, exercise, and emotional stimulation. Researchers developed this therapy based on evidence that shifts in daily schedules, particularly sleep deprivation, can bring on symptoms in people with bipolar disorder. Although early results are promising, more research is needed to confirm how much it helps.

Other New Approaches

A handful of devices show promise in helping people with treatment-resistant depression and seasonal affective disorder. These devices—ranging from a pacemaker-like device for stimulating a nerve, to magnetic stimulation applied to the scalp, to something as simple as a specially wired bedside lamp—are inspiring research here and abroad.

It's too soon to know how helpful these approaches will be. As A. John Rush, M.D., professor of psychiatry at the University of Texas, says of one approach he's testing, "It's exciting if it works. If it doesn't work, it's not exciting." Nonetheless, preliminary research on these approaches has been successful enough to justify additional—often costly—studies.

Transcranial Magnetic Stimulation

Technically, it's not fair to call transcranial magnetic stimulation *new;* it was first patented as a depression treatment in 1903.[8] Only recently have scientists seriously studied its effects, however. In the past several years, the number of studies of the technique has burgeoned. In 1997, 192 such studies hit scientific journals. In contrast, only one journal published a study on this technique in 1985.[9]

In the current forms of transcranial magnetic stimulation (TMS), technicians place an insulated wire coil near the person's head, then pass an electric current through the wire, generating a pulsating magnetic field. The magnetic field, in turn, produces an electrical current in the brain. Researchers can aim this electrical current very specifically. "For example," says Dr. Avery, "one can stimulate the motor cortex—

A Sampling of Research on Depression

Listed below are some of the topics researchers are currently investigating that have bearing on depression. These form just a tiny fraction of all the depression-related topics under study:

- Researchers are investigating the neurotransmitters serotonin, norepinephrine, and CRF in people with suicidal behavior. Autopsies have revealed that these neurotransmitters often aren't working normally in people who die by suicide. The goal is to improve suicide prevention.

- Studies are linking depression to increased rates of death from heart disease and stroke. Could treating depression help prevent death from these causes? Future research may find out.

- Depression often increases people's sensitivity to pain. Learning more about the connections between pain and depression might lead to new treatments for both.

- How exactly do antidepressants work? In hundreds of studies, scientists continue to investigate the intricacies of their effects on neurotransmitters, receptor sites, second messengers (chemicals inside nerve cells), and human beings overall.

- What are the links between the immune system and depression? Can a healthy immune system help prevent depression?

the part of the brain that controls motor activity—through transcranial magnetic stimulation, and the thumb on the other side of the body twitches." In fact, for about 15 years, neurologists have been using this exact procedure to check nerve functioning in certain patients.

The modern research approach to TMS uses information from imaging studies of the brain, studies that are transforming the ways that scientists view depression (see "Pictures of the Brain: Imaging Studies in Depression," page 256). Those studies, says Dr. El-Mallakh,

Can depression affect the level of immunity? Researchers are investigating links between the immune system and brain functioning in animals and on a molecular level.

- What's the safest way to treat postpartum depression? Researchers are investigating the effects of omega-3 fatty acids on mother and baby. Other researchers are testing various forms of psychotherapy, including group forms of interpersonal therapy.

- Exactly how does lithium work so well in treating bipolar disorder? Researchers are still attempting to pin down its precise chemical effects.

- Do anticonvulsants work as well as lithium in preventing mania and depression? Many researchers are investigating the use of different anticonvulsants as mood stabilizers.

- What are the best ways to treat depression in the elderly? Studies are examining the effectiveness and safety of antidepressants alone, psychotherapy alone, and the combination.

- If you're interested in participating in NIMH-funded research on depression, check their Web site: www.nimh.nih.gov.

showed researchers that certain parts of the brain tend to be less active during depression. "People then said, is there any way I can go in there and, leaving the rest of the brain alone, specifically increase the activity in this part of the brain that I know is less active in people who have depression? The answer is yes, there is," he says. "By directing the magnetic field through the specific brain structure that you want, you can stimulate one part of the brain without stimulating other parts of the brain."

Generally, modern TMS researchers focus on the prefrontal cortex, the part of the brain involved in complex thinking, judgment, and planning for the future. Says Dr. Avery, "About 8 years ago, investigators began to stimulate the left prefrontal cortex and found antidepressant effects."

In its mode of action, TMS is somewhat like the older electroconvulsive therapy (ECT). Both techniques seem to work by creating an electrical current in the brain. However, TMS relies on a magnetic pulse to create an electrical current in the cortex, rather than applying an electrical current as in ECT. The magnetic field generated by TMS penetrates the human skull far better than the electrical current generated by ECT. Further, in ECT, the electrical current produces an uncontrolled seizure, affecting much of the brain, while the magnetic stimulation of TMS is localized and produces no seizure. Due to the seizure, ECT necessitates brief general anesthesia to prevent potential injuries. In contrast, people receiving TMS are awake and unsedated.

In ECT, the electrical current produces an uncontrolled seizure, affecting much of the brain, while the magnetic stimulation of TMS is localized and produces no seizure.

The advantage of TMS is the ability to precisely target specific brain areas only. "When you stimulate the left prefrontal cortex, you're directly stimulating that area of the brain," says Dr. Avery. "You're not stimulating the memory centers, which are more in the temporal lobes where the hippocampus is, for example. So our group and other groups have found no evidence of any kind of memory disturbance when TMS is administered to the left prefrontal cortex." With ECT, on the other hand, "The stimulus becomes spread over the whole brain. The entire brain has a seizure." Temporary memory impairment with ECT is common.

So far, TMS may sound like a better choice. There's yet another difference, however, and it's an important one: ECT is one of the most effective treatments for depression known. TMS, though promising, has yet to show the same high degree of effectiveness. For now, it remains experimental.

Researchers still have much to learn about TMS; for example, the best shape of the coil, the best frequency of current, and the ideal number and duration of treatments. "In our protocol," says Dr. Avery, "we have 15 sessions of magnetic stimulation, and each session takes about a half-hour." Other studies treat for greater or lesser periods of time.

So far, not everyone seems to benefit from TMS. In fact, some studies have found no improvement whatsoever. Results of most studies, however, show that TMS reduces symptoms of depression in a percentage of people. Often these are people who have tried multiple antidepressants without success.

TMS seems to have very few side effects. People receiving it need no anesthesia; in fact, many sit and read during the treatments. A few experience headaches. Says Dr. Avery, "There is a risk, although it's a very uncommon risk, of having a seizure." (Most seizures occurred a number of years ago, before researchers learned all they now know about TMS.) Nonetheless, TMS is unlikely to replace antidepressants, says Dr. Avery, for the simple reason of cost. Due to the slight chance of seizures, a physician needs to administer the treatment, which makes TMS a bit on the expensive side. Another factor is convenience. "It's very difficult to beat the convenience and relatively low cost of medication," he says.

The best use of TMS may be as an alternative treatment for people not helped by antidepressants—assuming research confirms that it works.

Vagus Nerve Stimulation

A device the size of a thin stopwatch may someday help treat depression in people who can't be helped by drugs, if early research bears out. Called vagus nerve stimulation, the device is FDA-approved for treating epilepsy, according to Dr. Rush, who is one of the researchers testing the device.

"The device itself is called a generator," says Dr. Rush. "It's implanted in the left chest, kind of like a heart pacemaker." People are usually not aware of the generator once it's been surgically implanted. Thin wires run from the generator under the skin to the left vagus nerve in the neck, which communicates information to the brain.

Why is the device being tested for depression, if it was originally developed for epilepsy? "Strong circumstantial evidence," answers Dr. Rush. "In the course of the epilepsy trials, some patients appeared to be having an improvement in their mood, but their epilepsy didn't get a whole lot better. And of course when the epilepsy gets better, you would expect an improvement in mood, but the improvement in mood, here, seemed not to be accounted for entirely by the improvement in the epilepsy. That was one observation," he notes.

In addition, the vagus nerve communicates with the limbic system, "Which is the emotional brain," explains Dr. Rush. "Anatomically it's wired into the right portion of the brain."

Finally, studies indicated changes in blood flow to parts of the brain that seem to be involved in depression, as well as changes in levels of serotonin and other neurotransmitters. "So we had a neurotransmitter story, an anatomy story, and a brain function story, and we had clinical observations in epilepsy patients. That body of evidence led people to inquire whether or not this might be helpful in depression."

The device stimulates the vagus nerve intermittently, for 30 seconds once every 5 minutes, 24 hours a day, 7 days a week. "What it appears to be doing is changing the function of different neurotransmitter systems in different parts of the brain," says Dr. Rush.

If research confirms its effectiveness, people with treatment-resistant depression, those who have not done well on several previous medicines, may have another option.

If research confirms its effectiveness, people with treatment-resistant depression, those who have not done well on several previous medicines, may have another option, one that might work for them. Since it requires surgery, however, it's not likely to be the first approach that people try. In fact, researchers are currently studying it only in people who are also taking medication for depression. "Because if the medicine's doing something, we don't want to take it away," says Dr. Rush—even if the medicine isn't doing very much.

Magnetic Seizure Therapy

In a highly experimental new approach, Dr. Sackeim and his colleagues at Columbia University are testing a device that generates seizures in the brain using magnetic coils, a sort of combination of traditional electroconvulsive therapy and the new transcranial magnetic therapy. Unlike transcranial magnetic therapy, which doesn't create a seizure, this new device does so intentionally. This concept is brand new. "The first 10 patients in America were treated in the last 2 months," says Dr. Sackeim.

"With external electrodes on the head in ECT, we have limited control over the paths the current takes inside the brain," says Dr. Sackeim. "We have already shown that where in the brain you stimulate, and at what dosage, really makes a huge difference, so we need much better control."

"We have a long road to travel in terms of developing this type of approach," he notes. If this early study shows good results, he says, "Our next step will be to refine different methods of magnetic seizure therapy to see which is the most effective."

Dawn Simulation for Winter Depression

Research has found that exposure to bright light on fall and winter mornings boosts energy levels in people with seasonal affective disorder (SAD). Most research has involved lightboxes, the currently established therapy for this condition. People need to sit in front of lightboxes for a period ranging from 30 minutes to 2 hours each morning, a time-consuming activity for people who must be at work by sunrise in winter. But there's another, novel approach to getting morning light on short days: dawn simulation.

In dawn simulation, light from a specially wired bedside lamp gradually rises in intensity over a 45- to 90-minute period while people sleep, mimicking the naturally increasing brightness of dawn. The light reaches its brightest at the time people are scheduled to wake up.

Dawn simulation has at least one advantage over lightbox treatment. Since it takes place while people sleep, it doesn't require devoting any extra time to the therapy.

Early research on the technique is mixed. Two small studies found that it decreased symptoms of depression in people with SAD, compared to a placebo.[10] A more recent studied of 61 people found that, while it helped some people, it didn't work as well as lightbox treatment.[11] But it's a bit early to form any real conclusions, since the best timing and intensity of light in dawn simulation are still uncertain. Quite possibly, treatment will need to be individualized. One factor affecting the amount of light people receive is the thickness of their eyelids!

> *Dawn simulation has at least one advantage over lightbox treatment. Since it takes place while people sleep, it doesn't require devoting any extra time to the therapy.*

Dawn simulation is not completely free of side effects. In early studies, a scattering of people developed hypomania—an abnormal "high" characteristic in bipolar type II—a situation which can also occur with standard antidepressants.

PAVING THE WAY FOR THE FUTURE: NEW UNDERSTANDINGS OF DEPRESSION

Advancing our understanding of the causes of depression—whether social, psychological, or physiological—may lead to new preventive techniques. Advancing our understanding of the mechanisms of depression—what specifically happens in the body, mind, and spirit when someone is depressed—may lead to better treatments.

Dr. El-Mallakh cites TMS as an example of advances in treatment arising from a greater understanding of what is happening in the body. "People looked at glucose metabolism in the brain," he says. "How much sugar, how much energy does the brain burn up, how much energy specifically do different parts of the brain burn up, when a person is depressed versus when a person is not depressed?" Imaging studies suggested that one part of the brain, the prefrontal cortex, typically consumed less fuel in depression. Researchers then found a way to direct energy specifically to the prefrontal cortex, using transcranial magnetic stimulation, and found that it helped."

In the past decades, several astounding discoveries have occurred that have tremendous implications for understanding and treating depression: laying out the human genetic code, for example, and research showing that brains change in structure as they learn. Perhaps, one day, such research will bear fruit in the form of new treatments and means of prevention.

Plasticity of the Brain

Describing our brains as plastic sounds unappealing, to say the least. When talking about the brain, however, the word *plastic* means *malleable*—able to learn, change, and grow. An example of the brain's plasticity is that, throughout our lives, we are able to grow new cells in parts of our brains. And just a few decades ago, scientists believed that this was impossible.

Researchers have already discovered one way in which the brain's plasticity may aid in recovery from depression. An area of the brain potentially damaged by depression is the hippocampus, the part of the cerebrum that processes and sorts memories for storage. In long-standing untreated depression, some of the cells in the hippocampus can atrophy. Recent research suggests that ECT may promote the growth of new cells in the hippocampus of people with depression.[12] Other researchers have found early evidence that antidepressants may

Research on Suicide

Historically, research on suicide and its prevention has been relatively scant, for at least two reasons. Typically, researchers on depression have excluded people with suicidal depression from studies on treatments, particularly those studies involving placebos. If people are actively suicidal, they reasoned, how could researchers ethically place them in situations in which they might receive a placebo rather than real treatment? This is, indeed, a good argument for excluding the most depressed individuals from certain studies, as long as researchers can find other ways to determine which treatment methods work best.

Another factor discouraging research is that suicide is relatively rare among people with depression. Although the lifetime risk of suicide may be as high as 8 percent or even 15 percent in certain groups of people, depending on the study, an individual's chance of suicide in a given year is quite small. This circumstance is indisputably positive. Nonetheless, it means that studies of suicide pre-

do the same.[13] Confirmation of this information would, indeed, be grounds for new hope.

Second Messenger Systems

Another area that holds the potential for exciting new discoveries is located within our nerve cells. Scientists are studying what happens inside the nerve cell after a neurotransmitter attaches to the outside. They are finding that in response to the neurotransmitter, considered the "first messenger," other chemicals within the cell take action, leading to further biochemical changes inside the cell. These so-called *second messengers* are the subject of active investigation today, and—who knows?—might one day inspire new treatments.

vention require long time periods and very large numbers of people to show any effects. Relatively few researchers have had the resources or motivation to undertake studies of this type. The result is a dearth of information on what really works to prevent suicide.

When Surgeon General David Satcher, M.D., Ph.D., issued his Call to Action on Suicide in 1999, he recommended increasing research in this area. Currently, NIMH is funding several dozen research projects pertaining to suicidal behavior. One is studying the effectiveness of short-term cognitive therapy after a suicide attempt. Another is seeking to clarify the risk of suicide among lesbians and gay men. Several studies are investigating neurotransmitter function and other aspects of brain biochemistry. Still others are focusing on suicide and its prevention in young people and the elderly.

With the National Strategy for Suicide Prevention indicating a continued federal emphasis on this topic and a push for more research, we should know much more in a few years.

One second messenger is called *cyclic adenosine monophosphate*, or cAMP. When an antidepressant attaches to a nerve cell receptor, it appears to send cAMP into action, triggering a series of other biochemical changes within the nerve cell. These may include "switching on" genes that help the cell maintain its function.

Genetic Research

"Think about the progress in genetic research in the 30 to 40 years since DNA was discovered," says Dr. Dunner. He believes genetic research may ultimately yield new treatments for depression. First, he says, researchers must "identify which genes might be involved in certain forms of depression, and then attack the disorder from a molecular basis." To do so would involve developing drugs that attack the very mechanism of depression, the molecular changes that occur when specific genes are switched on or off. It may turn out that genes cause a considerable portion of depression, says Dr. Dunner. If so, he says, "That may be the way depression is treated at some point in the future."

Besides treatments, genetic research might lead to tests that could help people determine their risk of depression or bipolar disorder—a prospect that some people find heartening, and others terrifying. Having such information could potentially help high-risk people take steps to ward off depression, by learning cognitive-behavioral techniques, for example, to decrease their tendency toward negative thinking. On the other hand, there's always the possibility that such information could be used to stigmatize people, if it got into the wrong hands. Social protections must accompany advances in research.

> *Besides treatments, genetic research might lead to tests that could help people determine their risk of depression or bipolar disorder—a prospect that some people find heartening, and others terrifying.*

Psychosocial Research

If our upbringing and experiences can increase the likelihood of depression—as most experts, today, believe they can—then gaining insight into the exact mechanisms of this process may help future researchers find ways to forestall it. Studies of preschoolers and older children, for example, may help determine which kinds of interactions with parents or others increase a child's susceptibility to depression later in life. "There's a lot of research on the precursors of depression, the things that lead up to it," says Dr. Beutler. "It's not treatment per se. It's indirectly related to treatment." Yet this type of research holds the potential to give us important information for prevention.

Different Types of Depression:
Different Opinions

Are the different types of nonbipolar depression really distinctly different disorders, or is it more accurate to see depression as a continuum of symptoms ranging from major to minor? Researchers are striving to illuminate this area of controversy. In a related question, some researchers wonder if the current diagnoses lump too many people together. Might there really be several different types of major depression, for example, which require different types of medications? If so, this might explain why no antidepressant seems to work on everyone. Researchers are attempting to elucidate this question as well.

RESEARCH AND HOPE

Truly, research holds promise for revolutionizing the treatment of depression, and perhaps its prevention as well. The newspaper brings news of significant research advances almost weekly. Yet the vast majority of people need not wait a year or a decade for effective treatment: They can get help right now. Numerous effective medications, psychotherapies, and other proven treatments exist, including some as simple and as inexpensive as regular exercise.

The prospect of further scientific advances is thrilling. Yet research alone is not sufficient to improve the treatment of depression. Of equal importance is education. If everyone learned, from an early age, the symptoms of depression; if more people understood enough about the disorder to reduce its stigma; and if more doctors learned to search for it routinely among their patients—think how many more people would receive the treatment they need.

If depression affects you or a loved one, you're not alone. There are indeed many effective approaches available, and much reason for hope. If something you're trying isn't helping, numerous alternatives exist. Many people have been down this road before you. Don't give up. Life without depression awaits.

Appendix A: Resources

Y‌OU CAN OBTAIN more information about depression or related conditions by contacting the following organizations. Most of these organizations provide some information to the public for free, either on their Web sites or by mail. Many also provide other services, including advocacy. If the organization offers information on support groups or referrals to mental health care professionals, that is noted after the contact information.

ORGANIZATIONS

**American Academy of Child
and Adolescent Psychiatry**
3615 Wisconsin Avenue NW
Washington, D.C. 20016
Phone: 202-966-7300
Web site: www.aacap.org
*Provides referrals

**American Association for
Geriatric Psychiatry**
7910 Woodmont Avenue
Bethesda, MD 20814
Phone: 301-654-7850
Web site: www.aagpgpa.org
*Provides referrals

**American Association for
Marriage and Family Therapy**
1133 15th Street NW, Suite 300
Washington, D.C. 20005
Phone: 202-452-0109
Web site: www.aamft.org
*Provides referrals

**American Association of
Suicidology**
4201 Connecticut Avenue NW,
Suite 408
Washington, D.C. 20008
Phone: 202-237-2280
Web site: www.suicidology.org
*Provides information on support
groups
*Provides referrals to crisis centers

**American Foundation for
    Suicide Prevention**
120 Wall Street, 22nd Floor
New York, NY 10005
Phone: 888-333-2377 or
    212-363-3500
Web site: www.afsp.org

American Psychiatric Association
1400 K Street NW
Washington, D.C. 20005
Phone: 202-682-6000
Web site: www.psych.org
*Provides referrals

**American Psychological
    Association**
750 First Street NE
Washington, D.C. 20002
Phone: 800-374-3120 or
    202-336-5500
Web site: www.apa.org
*Provides referrals

**Anxiety Disorders Association
    of America**
11900 Parklawn Drive, Suite 100
Rockville, MD 20852
Phone: 301-231-9350
Web site: www.adaa.org
*Provides referrals

**Child and Adolescent Bipolar
    Foundation**
Web site: www.cabf.org
*Provides referrals
*Provides information on support
    groups

Depression After Delivery
P.O. Box 1282
Morristown, PA 19607
Phone: 800-944-4773
Web site: infotrail.com/dad
    /dad.html
*Provides information on support
    groups

**Depression and Related
    Affective Disorders
    Association**
The Johns Hopkins Hospital,
    Meyer 3-181
600 North Wolfe Street
Baltimore, MD 21287
Phone: 410-955-4647 or
    202-955-5800
Web site: www.med.jhu.edu/drada
*Provides information on support
    groups

**Knowledge Exchange
    Network**
Center for Mental Health Services
Web site: www.mentalhealth.org

**Mental Health Recovery
    (Mary Ellen Copeland's
    Web site)**
P.O. Box 301
West Dummerston, VT 05357
Phone: 802-254-2092
Web site: www.mentalhealth
    recovery.com
Wellness Recovery Action Plan and
    other materials available by
    phone or Web site

National Alliance for the Mentally Ill

Colonial Place Three, 2107 Wilson Blvd., Suite 300
Arlington, VA 22201
Phone: 800-950-6264 or 703-524-7600
Web site: www.nami.org
*Provides information on support groups

National Alliance for Research on Schizophrenia and Depression

60 Cutter Mill Road, Suite 404
Great Neck, NY 11021
Phone: 800-829-8289 or 516-829-0091
Web site: www.narsad.org

National Association of Social Workers

750 First Street NE, Suite 700
Washington, D.C. 20002
Phone: 800-638-8799
Web site: www.socialworkers.org
*Provides referrals

National Depressive and Manic-Depressive Association

730 North Franklin Street, Suite 501
Chicago, IL 60610
Phone: 800-826-3632 or 312-642-0049
Web site: www.ndmda.org
*Provides information on support groups

National Foundation for Depressive Illness

P.O. Box 2257
New York, NY 10116
Phone: 800-239-1265
Web site: www.depression.org
*Provides referrals

National Institute of Mental Health

6001 Executive Blvd.
Bethesda, MD 20892
Phone: 800-421-4211 (for mailed information)
Web site: www.nimh.nih.gov

National Institute on Alcohol Abuse and Alcoholism

6000 Executive Blvd., Willco Building
Bethesda, MD 20892
Web site: www.niaaa.nih.gov

National Institute on Drug Abuse

6001 Executive Blvd.
Bethesda, MD 20892
Phone: 800-644-6432
Web site: www.nida.nih.gov

National Mental Health Association

1021 Prince Street
Alexandria, VA 22314
Phone: 800-969-6642 or 703-684-7722
Web site: www.nmha.org

*Provides information on support
groups
*Provides referrals to local mental
health associations, not to
individual doctors

**National Organization of People
of Color Against Suicide**
Web site: www.nopcas.com

**National Strategy for Suicide
Prevention**
A collaborative effort of the federal
Substance Abuse and Mental
Health Services Administration,
Centers for Disease Control and
Prevention, National Institutes
of Health, and Health Resources
and Services Administration
Web site: www.mentalhealth.org
/suicideprevention/

**Postpartum Support
International**
927 North Kellogg Avenue
Santa Barbara, CA 93111
Phone: 805-967-7636
Web site: www.postpartum.net

*Provides information on support
groups
*Provides referrals

**Society for Light Therapy and
Biological Rhythms**
P.O. Box 591687
174 Cook Street
San Francisco, CA 94159
Web site: www.sltbr.org

**Suicide Prevention
Advocacy Network**
5034 Odin's Way
Marietta, GA 30068
Phone: 888-649-1366
Web site: www.spanusa.org

**Support Group.com
Home Page**
Web site: www.support-group.com
/index.htm
*Provides information on support
groups

**Surgeon General of the
United States**
Web site: www.surgeongeneral.gov

ANNUAL EVENTS

National Childhood Depression Awareness Day: May 8
Web site: www.nmha.org

National Depression Screening Day: October 11
Screening for Mental Health, Inc.
One Washington Street, Suite 304
Wellesley Hills, MA 02481
Web site: www.mentalhealthscreening.org

OTHER RESOURCES

1-800-SUICIDE

Connects with the closest available suicide hotline

1-800-662-HELP

Provides referrals for drug and alcohol treatment

Appendix B: Further Reading

American Medical Association. *Essential Guide to Depression*. NY: Pocket Books, 1998.

American Psychiatric Association. *Diagnostic and Statistical Manual of Mental Disorders, Fourth Edition, Text Revision*. Washington, DC: American Psychiatric Association, 2000.

American Psychiatric Association. *Practice Guideline for the Treatment of Patients with Major Depressive Disorder*. 2nd ed. [pamphlet] Washington, DC: American Psychiatric Association, 2000. Available from the American Psychiatric Press (www.appi.org).

American Psychiatric Association. *Treatment Works: Major Depressive Disorder. A Patient and Family Guide*. [pamphlet] Washington, DC: American Psychiatric Association, 2000. Available from the American Psychiatric Press (www.appi.org).

Appleton, William S. *Prozac and the New Antidepressants*. New York: Plume, 2000.

Baumel, Syd. *Dealing with Depression Naturally*. Lincolnwood, IL: Keats, 2000.

Beutler, Larry E., Bruce Bongar, and Joel N. Shurkin. *A Consumer's Guide to Psychotherapy: A Complete Guide to Choosing the Therapist and Treatment That's Right for You*. New York: Oxford University Press, 2000.

Bratman, Steven. *The Natural Pharmacist: Treating Depression*. Roseville, CA: Prima, 2000.

Burns, David A. *Feeling Good: The New Mood Therapy*. New York: Avon Books, 1999.

Cobain, Bev. *When Nothing Matters Anymore: A Survival Guide for Depressed Teens*. Minneapolis, MN: Free Spirit Publishing, 1998.

Copeland, Mary Ellen. *Living Without Depression and Manic-Depression: A Workbook for Maintaining Mood Stability*. Oakland, CA: New Harbinger, 1994.

Copeland, Mary Ellen. *Wellness Recovery Action Plan*. [pamphlet]. Brattleboro, VT:Peach Press, 2000. Available from www.mentalhealthrecovery.com.

Copeland, Mary Ellen. *Winning Against Relapse: A Workbook of Action Plans for Reoccurring Health and Emotional Problems*. Oakland, CA: New Harbinger, 1999.

Cronkite, Kathy. *On the Edge of Darkness*. New York: Dell, 1994.

Davidson, J.R.T. and K.M. Connor. *Herbs for the Mind*. New York: Guilford Press, 2000.

Davis, Martha, et al. *The Relaxation and Stress Reduction Workbook, 3rd Ed*. Oakland, CA: New Harbinger, 1988.

Duke, Patty, and Gloria Hochman. *A Brilliant Madness: Living with Manic-Depressive Illness*. New York: Bantam, 1992.

Fawcett, Jan, Bernard Golden, and Nancy Rosenfeld. *New Hope for People with Bipolar Disorder*. Roseville, CA: Prima, 2000.

Ferber, Jane S. *A Woman Doctor's Guide to Depression*. New York: Hyperion, 1997.

Goodrick, G. Ken. *Energy, Peace, Purpose*: *A Step-by-Step Guide to Optimal Living*. New York: Berkley Books, 1999.

Gorman, Jack M. *The New Psychiatry*. New York: St. Martin's Press, 1996.

Grollman, Earl, and Max Malikow. *Living When a Young Friend Commits Suicide or Even Starts Talking About It*. Boston: Beacon Press, 1999.

Hedaya, Robert. *The Antidepressant Survival Program*. New York: Crown, 2000.

Ingersoll, Barbara D., and Sam Goldstein. *Lonely, Sad and Angry: How to Help Your Unhappy Child*. Plantation, FL: Specialty Press, 2001.

Jack, Dana Crowley. *Silencing the Self: Women and Depression*. Cambridge, MA: Harvard University Press, 1991.

Jamison, Kay Redfield. *Night Falls Fast: Understanding Suicide*. New York: Vintage Books. 1999.

Jamison, Kay Redfield. *An Unquiet Mind*. New York: Knopf, 1996.

Kramer, Peter D. *Listening to Prozac*. New York: Penguin, 1997.

Lewinsohn, Peter, et al. *Control Your Depression*. New York: Simon & Schuster, 1992.

Manning, Martha. *Undercurrents: A Therapist's Reckoning with Her Own Depression*. San Francisco, CA: HarperCollins, 1994.

Mondimore, Francis Mark. *Bipolar Disorder: A Guide for Patients and Families*. Baltimore: Johns Hopkins University Press, 1999.

Mondimore, Francis Mark. *Depression: The Mood Disease*. Baltimore: Johns Hopkins University Press, 1993.

Papolos, Demitri, and Janice Papolos. *The Bipolar Child*. New York: Broadway Books, 1999.

Papolos, Demitri, and Janice Papolos. *Overcoming Depression*. New York: HarperPerennial, 1997.

Ratey, John. *A User's Guide to the Brain*. New York: Pantheon Books, 2001.

Rosenthal, Norman. *Winter Blues*. New York: Guilford Press, 1998.

Schuchter, Stephen R., Nancy Downs, and Sidney Zisook. *Biologically Informed Psychotherapy for Depression*. New York: Guilford Press, 1996.

Snyder, Judith. *I Told You a Million Times: Building Self-Esteem in Young Children Through Discipline*. Cary, IL: Family Connection Publications, 1994.

Styron, William. *Darkness Visible: A Memoir of Madness*. New York: Random House, 1990.

U.S. Department of Health and Human Services. *Mental Health: A Report of the Surgeon General*. Rockville, MD: U.S. Department of Health and Human Services, Substance Abuse and Mental Health Services Administration, Center for Mental Health Services, National Institutes of Health, and National Institute of Mental Health, 1999.

U.S. Department of Health and Human Services. *National Strategy for Suicide Prevention: Goals and Objectives for Action*. Rockville, MD: U.S. Department of Health and Human Services, Substance Abuse and Mental Health Administration, Center for Mental Health Services, National

Institutes of Health, National Institute of Mental Health, Centers for Disease Control, and Health Resources Services Administration, 2001.

U.S. Public Health Service. *The Surgeon General's Call to Action to Prevent Suicide*. Washington, DC: U.S. Public Health Service, 1999.

Weissman, Myrna M. *Mastering Depression Through Interpersonal Psychotherapy: Patient Workbook*. Psychological Corp., 1995.

Yapko, Michael. *Breaking the Patterns of Depression*. New York: Doubleday, 1997.

Yapko, Michael. *Hand-Me-Down Blues: How to Stop Depression from Spreading in Families*. New York: Golden Books, 1999.

Notes

Introduction

1. National Institute of Mental Health (NIMH), *The Numbers Count: Mental Disorders in America*, NIH Publication No. 99-4584 (September 2000); Available at www.nimh.nih.gov/publicat/numbers.cfm.
2. Ibid.

Chapter 1

1. S.B. Oates, *Abraham Lincoln: The Man Behind the Myths*, New York: Harper & Row, 1984: 43.
2. William Styron, *Darkness Visible: A Memoir of Madness*, New York: Random House, 1990: 58.
3. National Institute of Mental Health (NIMH), *The Numbers Count: Mental Disorders in America*, NIH Publication No. 99-4584 (September 2000); Available at www.nimh.nih.gov/publicat/numbers.cfm.
4. Adapted from: American Psychiatric Association, *Diagnostic and Statistical Manual of Mental Disorders, Fourth Edition, Text Revision*, Washington, DC: American Psychiatric Association, 2000.
5. D.J. Kupfer and E. Frank, "The interaction of drug and psychotherapy in the long-term treatment of depression," *Journal of Affective Disorders* 62 (2001): 131–137.
6. Ibid.
7. William Styron, *Darkness Visible: A Memoir of Madness*, New York: Random House, 1990: 43, 46, 63.
8. National Institute of Mental Health (NIMH), *The Numbers Count: Mental Disorders in America*, NIH Publication No. 99-4584 (September 2000); Available at www.nimh.nih.gov/publicat/numbers.cfm.

9. Patty Duke and G. Hochman, *A Brilliant Madness: Living with Manic-Depressive Illness*, New York: Bantam Books, 1992: xxi.

10. Ibid. 245.

11. National Institute of Mental Health (NIMH), *The Numbers Count: Mental Disorders in America*, NIH Publication No. 99-4584 (September 2000); Available at www.nimh.nih.gov/publicat/numbers.cfm.

12. M.W. O'Hara, *Postpartum Depression: Causes and Consequences.* New York: Springer-Verlag, 1995: 14.

13. Yeates Conwell, "Suicide among older people," Available at www.afsp.org/research/articles/conwell.htm.

14. National Institute of Mental Health (NIMH), *The Numbers Count: Mental Disorders in America*, NIH Publication No. 99-4584 (September 2000); Available at www.nimh.nih.gov/publicat/numbers.cfm.

15. J.M. Bostwick and V.S. Pankratz, "Affective disorders and suicide risk: A reexamination," *American Journal of Psychiatry* 157 (2000): 1925-32.

16. National Institute of Mental Health (NIMH), *The Numbers Count: Mental Disorders in America*, NIH Publication No. 99-4584 (September 2000); Available at www.nimh.nih.gov/publicat/numbers.cfm.

17. Ibid.

18. J. Miranda and B.L. Green, "The need for mental health services research focusing on poor young women," *Journal of Mental Health Policy and Economics* 2 (1999): 73–89; In U.S. Department of Health and Human Services, *Mental Health: A Report of the Surgeon General*, Rockville, MD: U.S. Department of Health and Human Services, Substance Abuse and Mental Health Services Administration, Center for Mental Health Services, National Institutes of Health, National Institute of Mental Health, 1999.

19. G.W. Brown and P.M. Moran, "Single mothers, poverty and depression," *Psychological Medicine* (1997): 27, 21–33.

20. J.M. Cyranowski, et al., "Adolescent onset of the gender difference in lifetime rates of major depression: a theoretical model," *Arch Gen Psychiatry* 57 (2000): 21–27.

21. P.M. Lewinsohn, et al., "Natural course of adolescent major depressive disorder in a community sample: predictors of recurrence in young adults," *American Journal of Psychiatry* 157 (2000): 1584–1591. "Major depressive disorder in older adolescents: prevalence, risk factors, and clinical implications," *Clinical Psychology Review* 18 (1998), 765–794.

22. S.E. Son and J.T. Kirchner, "Depression in children and adolescents," *American Family Physician* 62 (2000): 2297–2308.

23. R. Hirschfeld, "History and evolution of the monoamine hypothesis of depression," *Journal of Clinical Psychiatry* 61: suppl 6 (2000): 4–6.

24. U.S. Department of Health and Human Services, *Mental Health: A Report of the Surgeon General*, Rockville, MD: U.S. Department of Health and Human Services, Substance Abuse and Mental Health Services Administration, Center for Mental Health Services, National Institutes of Health, National Institute of Mental Health, 1999: 256.

25. Ibid.

Chapter 2

1. Alexander Young, "The quality of care for depressive and anxiety disorders in the United States," *Archives of General Psychiatry* 58 (2001): 55–61.

2. Kay Redfield Jamison, *An Unquiet Mind*, New York: Knopf, 1996.

Chapter 3

1. American Psychiatric Association, *Practice Guideline for the Treatment of Patients with Major Depressive Disorder, 2nd ed*, Washington DC: American Psychiatric Association, 2000: 9.

2. Ibid. 15, 17.

3. Ibid. 14.

4. U.S. Department of Health and Human Services, *Mental Health: A Report of the Surgeon General*, Rockville, MD: U.S. Department of Health and Human Services, Substance Abuse and Mental Health Services Administration, Center for Mental Health Services, National Institutes of Health, National Institute of Mental Health, 1999: 266–267. BMJ Publishing Group, *Clinical Evidence, Issue 4*. London: BMJ Publishing Group, December 2000: 521. M.B. Keller, et al., "A comparison of nefazodone, the cognitive behavioral-analysis system of psychotherapy, and their combination for the treatment of chronic depression," *New England Journal of Medicine* 342 (2000): 1462–1470.

5. Patty Duke and Gloria Hochman, *A Brilliant Madness: Living with Manic-Depressive Illness*, New York: Bantam, 1992.

6. National Depressive and Manic-Depressive Association, *Beyond Diagnosis: Depression and Treatment*, Chicago: National Depressive and Manic-Depressive Association, 2000.

7. T.A.M. Kramer, "Mechanisms of action," *Medscape Mental Health* 6:1 (2001); Available at www.medscape.com.

8. Peter D. Kramer, *Listening to Prozac*. New York: Penguin, 1997.

9. *Drug Facts and Comparisons*, St. Louis, MO: Facts and Comparisons, 2001: 922.

10. W.S. Appleton, *Prozac and the New Antidepressants*, New York: Plume, 2000: 178.

11. K.R. Jamison, "Suicide and bipolar disorder," *Journal of Clinical Psychiatry* 61: suppl 9 (2000): 47–51.

12. A. Coppen and J. Bailey, "Enhancement of the antidepressant action of fluoxetine by folic acid: a randomised, placebo controlled trial," *Journal of Affective Disorders* 60 (2000): 121–130.

13. Stephen R. Shuchter, Nancy Downs, and Sidney Zisook, *Biologically Informed Psychotherapy for Depression*, New York: Guilford Press, 1996: 124–125.

14. I.M. Blackburn, et al., "A two-year naturalistic follow-up of depressed patients treated with cognitive therapy, pharmacotherapy and a combination of both," *Journal of Affective Disorders* 10 (1986): 67–75. M.D. Evans, et al., "Differential relapse following cognitive therapy and pharmacotherapy for depression," *Arch Gen Psychiatry* 49 (1992): 802–808. A.D. Simons, et al., "Cognitive therapy and pharmacotherapy for depression: sustained improvement over one year," *Arch Gen Psychiatry* 43 (1986): 43–48. J.D. Teasdale, et al., "Prevention of relapse/recurrence in major depression by mindfulness-based cognitive therapy," *Journal of Consulting and Clinical Psychology* 68 (2000): 615–623.

15. L. Tondo, K.R. Jamison, and R.J. Baldessarini, "Effect of lithium maintenance on suicidal behavior in major mood disorders," *Annals of the New York Academy of Sciences* 836 (1997): 339–351.

16. E. Frank, et al., "Three-year outcomes for maintenance therapies in recurrent depression," *Arch Gen Psychiatry* 47 (1990): 1093–1099.

17. Martha Manning, *Undercurrents: A Therapist's Reckoning with Her Own Depression*, San Francisco: HarperSanFrancisco, 1994.

18. S.E. Son and J.T. Kirchner, "Depression in children and adolescents," *American Family Physician* 62 (2000): 2311–2312.

19. P.W. Dimmock, et al., "Efficacy of selective serotonin-reuptake inhibitors in premenstrual syndrome: a systematic review. *Lancet* 356 (2000): 1131–1136.

20. T. Pearlstein and M. Steiner, "Non-antidepressant treatment of premenstrual syndrome," *Journal of Clinical Psychiatry* 61:suppl 12 (2000): 22–27.

L.L. Altshuler, et. al., "Pharmacological Management of Premenstrual Disorder," *Harvard Rev Psychiatry* 2 (1995): 233–245.

Chapter 4

1. R.C. Kessler, et al., "The use of complementary and alternative therapies to treat anxiety and depression in the United States," *American Journal of Psychiatry* 158 (2001): 289–294.

2. Ibid.

3. P.R. Knaudt, et al., "Alternative therapy use in psychiatric outpatients," *Journal of Nerv Ment Dis* 187 (1999): 692–695.

4. J.W. Williams, et al., "A systematic review of newer pharmacotherapies for depression in adults: evidence report summary," *Annals of Intern Med* 132 (2000): 743–756.

5. E. Schrader, "Equivalence of St. John's wort extract (Ze 117) and fluoxetine: a randomized, controlled study in mild–moderate depression," *Int Clin Psychopharmacol* 15 (2000): 61–68.

6. R.C. Shelton, et al., "Effectiveness of St. John's wort in major depression: a randomized controlled trial," *Journal of the American Medical Association* 285 (2001): 1978–1986.

7. S. Meyers, "Use of neurotransmitter precursors for treatment of depression," *Alternative Medicine Review* 5 (2000): 64–71.

8. W.F. Byerley, "5-hydroxytryptophan: a review of its antidepressant efficacy and adverse effects," *Journal of Clinical Psychopharmacology* 7 (1987): 127–137.

9. Food and Drug Administration, "FDA Talk Paper: Impurities confirmed in dietary supplement 5-hydroxy-l-tryptophan," Rockville, MD: FDA, August 31, 1998.

10. E.M. Sternberg, et al., "Development of a scleroderma-like illness during therapy with l-5-hydroxytryptophan and carbidopa," *New England Journal of Medicine* 303 (1980): 782–787. P. Joly, et al., "Development of pseudobullous morphea and scleroderma-like illness during therapy with L-5-hydroxytryptophan and carbidopa," *Journal of the American Academy of Dermatol* 25 (1991): 332–333.

11. H. Schubert and P. Halama, "Depressive episode primarily unresponsive to therapy in elderly patients: efficacy of *Ginkgo biloba* extract EGb 761 in combination with antidepressants," *Geriatrie Forschung* 3 (1993): 45–53 [in German].

12. J.R.T. Davidson and K.M. Connor, *Herbs for the Mind*, New York: Guilford Press, 2000.

13. S. Meyers, "Use of neurotransmitter precursors for treatment of depression," *Alternative Medicine Review* 5 (2000): 64–71.

14. Helmut Beckmann, et al. "Dl-phenylalanine versus imipramine: A double-blind controlled study," *Archiv für Psychiatrie und Nervenkrankheiten* 227 (1979): 49–58.

15. G. M. Bressa, "S-adenosyl-l-methionine (SAMe) as antidepressant: meta-analysis of clinical studies," *Acta Neurologica Scandinavica*, Supplement 154 (1994): 7–14.

16. D. Christensen, "Medical mimicry: sometimes, placebos work—but how?" *Science News* 159 (2001): 74–75, 78.

17. A. Coppen and J. Bailey, "Enhancement of the antidepressant action of fluoxetine by folic acid: a randomised, placebo controlled trial," *Journal of Affective Disorders* 60 (2000): 121–130.

18. P.S.A. Godfrey, et al., "Enhancement of recovery from psychiatric illness by methylfolate," *Lancet* 336 (1990): 392–395.

19. J.E. Alpert and M. Fava, "Nutrition and depression: the role of folate," *Nutrition Reviews* 55 (1997): 145–149.

20. B.W.J.H. Penninx, et al., "Vitamin B_{12} deficiency and depression in physically disabled older women: epidemiologic evidence from the women's health and aging study," *American Journal of Psychiatry* 157 (2000): 715–721.

21. M. Maggioni, et al., "Effects of phosphatidyl serine therapy in geriatric patients with depressive disorders," *Acta Psychiatr Scand* 81 (1990): 165–270. F. Brambilla, et al., "Beta-endorphine concentration in peripheral blood mononuclear cells of elderly depressed patients—effects of phosphatidylserine therapy," *Neuropsychobiology* 34 (1996): 18–21.

22. A.L. Stoll, et al., "Omega 3 fatty acids in bipolar disorder: a preliminary double-blind, placebo-controlled trial," *Arch Gen Psychiatry* 56 (1999): 407–412.

23. E. Ernst, et al., "Complementary therapies for depression: an overview," *Arch Gen Psychiatry* 55 (1998): 1026–1032.

24. S. Thys-Jacobs, et al., "Calcium carbonate and the premenstrual syndrome: effects on premenstrual and menstrual symptoms," *American Journal of Obstet Gynecol* 179 (1998): 444–452.

25. K.M. Wyatt, et al., "Efficacy of vitamin B_6 in the treatment of premenstrual syndrome: systematic review," *BMJ* 318 (1999): 1375–1381.

26. L.L. Altshuler, et al., "Pharmacological management of premenstrual disorder," *Harvard Rev Psychiatry* 2 (1995): 233–245.

27. T. Pearlstein and M. Steiner, "Non-antidepressant treatment of premenstrual syndrome," *Journal of Clinical Psychiatry* 61:suppl 12 (2000): 22–27. L.L. Altshuler, et al., "Pharmacological management of premenstrual disorder," *Harvard Rev Psychiatry* 2 (1995): 233–245.

28. L.S. Eller, "Guided imagery interventions for symptom management," *Annual Review of Nursing Research* 17 (1999): 57–84. Wayne A. Bowers, "Treatment of depressed in-patients: cognitive therapy plus medication, relaxation plus medication, and medication alone," *British Journal of Psychiatry* 156 (1990): 73–78.

29. T. Field, et al., "Massage reduces anxiety in child and adolescent psychiatric patients," *Journal of the American Academy Child Adolesc Psychiatry* 31 (1992): 125–131; In E. Ernst, et al., "Complementary therapies for depression: an overview," *Arch Gen Psychiatry* 55 (1998): 1026–1032.

30. J.D. Teasdale, et al., "Prevention of relapse/recurrence in major depression by mindfulness-based cognitive therapy," *Journal of Consulting and Clinical Psychology* 68 (2000): 615–623.

Chapter 5

1. J.A. Blumenthal, et al., "Effects of exercise training on older patients with major depression," *Arch Intern Med* 159 (1999): 2349–2356.

2. Ibid.

3. M. Babyak, et al., "Exercise treatment for major depression: maintenance of therapeutic benefit at 10 months," *Psychosomatic Medicine* 62 (2000): 633–638.

4. E.J. Doyne, et al., "Running versus weight lifting in the treatment of depression," *Journal of Consulting and Clinical Psychology* 55 (1987): 748–754.

5. B.G. Berger and D.R. Owen, "Mood alteration with yoga and swimming: aerobic exercise may not be necessary," *Percept Mot Skills* 75 (1992): 1331–1343.

6. G.P. Pappas, et al., "Reducing symptoms of depression with exercise," (letter) *Psychosomatics* 31 (1990): 112–113.

7. E. Ernst, et al., "Complementary therapies for depression: an overview," *Arch Gen Psychiatry* 55 (1998): 1026–1032.

8. P.W. Curatolo and D. Robertson, "The health consequences of caffeine," *Annals of Internal Medicine* 5 (1983): 641–653.

9. D. Michelson, et al., "Bone mineral density in women with depression," *New England Journal of Medicine* 335 (1996): 1176–1181.

10. K.A. Bruinsma and D.L. Taren, "Dieting, essential fatty acid intake, and depression," *Nutrition Reviews* 58 (2000): 98–108.

11. A. Tanskanen, et al., "Fish consumption and depressive symptoms in the population," Program and abstracts from the 153rd Annual American Psychiatric Association Meeting (May 13–18, 2000), Chicago, Illinois. Abstract 34.

12. T. Hirayama, *Life-Style and Mortality: A Large Census-Based Cohort Study in Japan*, Basel: Karger, 1990; In K.R. Jamison, *Night Falls Fast*, New York: Random House, 1999: 249–250, 393.

13. K.A. Bruinsma and D.L. Taren, "Dieting, essential fatty acid intake, and depression," *Nutrition Reviews* 58 (2000): 98–108.

14. A.L. Stoll, et al., "Omega 3 fatty acids in bipolar disorder: a preliminary double-blind, placebo-controlled trial," *Arch Gen Psychiatry* 56 (1999): 407–412.

15. R. Manfredini, et al., "The association of low serum cholesterol with depression and suicidal behaviours: new hypotheses for the missing link," *J Int Med Res* 28 (2000): 247–257.

16. J.R. Hibbeln and N. Salem, "Dietary polyunsaturated fatty acids and depression: when cholesterol does not satisfy," *American Journal of Clinical Nutrition* 62 (1995): 1–9. M. Garland, et al., "Total serum cholesterol in relation to psychological correlates in parasuicide," *British Journal of Psychiatry* 177 (2000): 77–83.

17. Robert Hedaya, *The Antidepressant Survival Program*, NY: Crown, 2000.

18. G.K. Goodrick, *Energy, Peace, Purpose: A Step-By-Step Guide to Optimal Living*. New York: Berkley Books, 1999.

19. P. Cuijpers, "Bibliotherapy in unipolar depression: a meta-analysis," *Journal of Behav Ther and Exp Psychiat* 28 (1997): 139–147.

20. BMJ Publishing Group, *Clinical Evidence, Issue 4*. London: BMJ Publishing Group, December 2000: 529.

21. H.G. Koenig, et al., "Religious coping and health status in medically ill hospitalized older adults," *Journal of Nerv Ment Dis* 186 (1998): 513–521. "Religiosity and remission of depression in medically ill older patients," *American Journal of Psychiatry* 155 (1998): 536–542.

22. S.B. Hanser and L.W. Thompson, "Effects of a music therapy strategy on depressed older adults," *J. Gerontol.* 49 (1994): 265–269.

23. M. Babyak, et al., "Exercise treatment for major depression: maintenance of therapeutic benefit at 10 months," *Psychosomatic Medicine* 62 (2000): 633–638.

Chapter 6

1. J. Petrila and T. Brink, "Mental illness and changing definitions of disability under the Americans with Disabilities Act," *Psychiatric Services* 52 (2001): 626–630.
2. U.S. Department of Health and Human Services, *Mental Health: A Report of the Surgeon General*, Rockville, MD: U.S. Department of Health and Human Services, Substance Abuse and Mental Health Services Administration, Center for Mental Health Services, National Institutes of Health, National Institute of Mental Health, 1999.

Chapter 7

1. S.L. Murphy, "Deaths: Final Data for 1998," *National Vital Statistics Reports* 48:11 (July 24, 2000). DHHS Publication No. (PHS) 2000-1120. Hyattsville, MD: National Center for Health Statistics; Adapted from data from Table 8, p. 26; Available at www.iusb.edu/~jmcintos /SuicideStats.html.
2. National Mental Health Association, "Millions of Americans contemplate suicide" (May 2, 2001); Available at www.nmha.org/newsroom /system/news.vw.cfm?do=vw&rid=285.
3. D.G. Jacobs, et al., "Suicide assessment: an overview and protocol," In D.G. Jacobs, ed., *Harvard Medical School Guide to Assessment and Intervention in Suicide*, San Francisco: Jossey-Bass, 1998: 7.
4. L. Tondo and R.J. Baldessarini, "Suicide: an overview," *Medscape Psychiatry Clinical Management Modules* (March 15, 2001); Available at www .medscape.com/Medscape/psychiatry/ClinicalMgmt/CM.v03/pnt-CM .v03.html.
5. Ibid.
6. U.S. Public Health Service, *The Surgeon General's Call to Action to Prevent Suicide*, Washington, DC: U.S. Public Health Service, 1999: 3.
7. Adapted from J.L. McIntosh, "Tabled data compiled and calculated from 1998 National Center for Health Statistics figures and population estimates from the U.S. Bureau of the Census," (2001); Available at www.iusb.edu/~jmcintos/SuicideStats.html. Used with permission.

8. U.S. Public Health Service, *The Surgeon General's Call to Action to Prevent Suicide*, Washington, DC: U.S. Public Health Service, 1999: 10.

9. K.R. Jamison, *Night Falls Fast: Understanding Suicide*, New York: Vintage Books, 1999: 114.

10. J.J. Mann, "How should suicidal behavior be managed?" *Harvard Mental Health Letter* 16:9 (March 2000): 8.

11. L. Tondo and R.J. Baldessarini, "Suicide: an overview," *Medscape Psychiatry Clinical Management Modules* (March 15, 2001); Available at www.medscape.com/Medscape/psychiatry/ClinicalMgmt/CM.v03/pnt-CM.v03.html.

12. J.L. McIntosh, "1998 Official Final Statistics: U.S.A. Suicide," Available at www.iusb.edu/~jmcintos/USA98Summary.htm.Accessed 5/1/01.J.

13. D. Shaffer and L. Craft, "Methods of adolescent suicide prevention," *Journal of Clinical Psychiatry* 60:suppl 2 (1999): 70–74.

14. J.L. McIntosh, "1998 Official Final Statistics: U.S.A. Suicide," Available at www.iusb.edu/~jmcintos/USA98Summary.htm.Accessed 5/1/01.

15. U.S. Public Health Service, *The Surgeon General's Call to Action to Prevent Suicide*, Washington, DC: U.S. Public Health Service, 1999: 3.

16. B.L. Mishara, "Conceptions of death and suicide in children ages 6–12 and their implications for suicide prevention," *Suicide and Life-Threatening Behavior* 29 (1999): 105–118.

17. D. Shaffer and L. Craft, "Methods of adolescent suicide prevention," *Journal of Clinical Psychiatry* 60:suppl 2 (1999): 70–74.

18. Ibid.

19. National Mental Health Association and National Council for Community Behavioral Healthcare, "What's the Matter? Depression and Suicide," *National Health Matters*; Available at: www.nmha.org./children/green/child_suicide.cfm.

20. D.A. Jobes, et al., "The Kurt Cobain suicide crisis: perspectives from research, public health, and the news media," *Suicide and Life-Threatening Behavior* 26 (1996): 260–271.

21. D.G. Jacobs and J. Reizes, "Danger signs of suicide" (May 2001) Wellesley Hills, MA: Screening for Mental Health; www.mentalhealthscreening.org. Used with permission.

22. J.L. McIntosh, "Suicide Rates in the Young, Elderly, and the Nation, USA, 1933–1998," *1998 Official Final Statistics: U.S.A. Suicide* (2001); Available at www.iusb.edu/~jmcintos/SuicideStats.html. Used with permission.

23. Joseph Telushkin, *The Book of Jewish Values*. New York: Bell Tower, 2000: 406.

Chapter 8

1. C.D. Sherbourne, et al., "Long-term effectiveness of disseminating quality improvement for depression in primary care," *Archives of General Psychiatry* 58 (2001): 696–703.

2. Alexander Young, "The quality of care for depressive and anxiety disorders in the United States," *Archives of General Psychiatry* 58 (2001): 55–61.

3. C.D. Sherbourne, et al., "Long-term effectiveness of disseminating quality improvement for depression in primary care," *Archives of General Psychiatry* 58 (2001): 696-703.

4. H.A. Sackeim, et al., "Continuation pharmacotherapy in the prevention of relapse following electroconvulsive therapy: a randomized controlled trial," *Journal of the American Medical Association* 285 (2001): 1299–1307.

5. J.D. Amsterdam and J.A. Bodkin, "Transdermal selegiline in the treatment of patients with major depression: a double-blind, placebo-controlled trial," National Institute of Mental Health. NCDEU Poster Abstracts, 40th Annual NCDEU Meeting, Poster No. 15; Available at www.nimh.nih.gov/ncdeu/abstracts2000/ncdeu015.cfm.

6. C.B. Nemeroff, "The neurobiology of depression," *Scientific American* (June 1998); Available at www.sciam.com/1998/0698issue/0698nemeroff.html.

7. T. Hökfelt, et al., "Substance P: a pioneer amongst neuropeptides," *Journal of Internal Medicine* 249 (2001): 27–40.

8. T.A. Kramer, "Transcranial magnetic stimulation and its effectiveness in affective disorders," XXIInd Congress of the Collegium Internationale Neuro-Psychopharmacologicum, *Medscape*, 2000; Available at http://psychiatry.medscape.com/medscape/cno/2000/CINP/Story.cfm?story_id=1498.

9. Ibid.

10. D.A. Avery, et al., "Dawn simulation compared with a dim red signal in the treatment of winter depression," *Biological Psychiatry* 36 (1994): 181–188.

11. O. Lingjærde, et al., "Dawn simulation vs. lightbox treatment in winter depression: a comparative study," *Acta Psychiatr Scand* 98 (1998): 73–80.

12. T.A. Kramer, "Transcranial magnetic stimulation and its effectiveness in affective disorders," XXIInd Congress of the Collegium Internationale Neuro-Psychopharmacologicum, *Medscape*, 2000; Available at http://psychiatry.medscape.com/medscape/cno/2000/CINP/Story .cfm?story_id=1498.

13. R.S. Duman and E.J. Nessler, "Role of gene expression in stress and drug-induced neural plasticity," *TEN* 2 (2000): 53–70.

Glossary

adjustment disorder with depressed mood   *DSM-IV* term for a mild form of depression occurring in response to external events.

alternative medicine   System of diagnosis and treatment, such as herbal medicine, homeopathy, or faith healing, not usually offered by conventional medical doctors.

amygdala   Almond-shaped mass of cells in the brain that is important in generating emotion in response to stimuli.

antagonist   In pharmacology, a chemical that counters the actions of another drug or substance.

antidepressant   Drug used to treat depression.

antipsychotic   Drug used to treat psychosis.

ants on a log   Celery filled with peanut butter or cream cheese and covered with raisins.

atypical depression   Major or bipolar depression in which people can still respond to positive events. People with atypical depression often have a long-standing pattern of being highly sensitive to perceived rejection by others, and are likely to overeat and oversleep when depressed.

baby blues   Transitory period of tearfulness, confusion, and irritability within the first few weeks after childbirth.

bipolar disorder   Chronic mood disorder characterized by one or more episodes of abnormally elevated mood such as mania as well as episodes of depression.

borderline personality disorder   Psychiatric diagnosis given to individuals with severe impulsiveness, chaotic relationships, changeable and volatile moods, and self-destructive behaviors.

bright light therapy   *See* light therapy.

cerebral cortex   Thin gray layer of nerve cells covering the wrinkled surface of the cerebrum.

cerebrum   Largest and most advanced part of the brain.

cognition   Thinking processes.

cognitive-behavioral therapy   Form of psychotherapy focused on identifying and changing negative thoughts and behaviors.

cognitive therapy   Form of psychotherapy focused on identifying and changing negative thought patterns.

complementary medicine   Combined use of alternative and conventional medicine.

cortex   *See* cerebral cortex.

corticotropin releasing factor (CRF)   Also called corticotropin releasing hormone, a substance secreted by the hypothalamus that triggers the release of the hormone ACTH from the pituitary gland, which in turn stimulates the release of cortisol by the adrenal gland. CRF also acts as a neurotransmitter in the brain.

cortisol   Sometimes called "stress hormone," a substance produced by the adrenal glands.

CRF   *See* corticotropin releasing factor.

cyclothymia   *See* cyclothymic disorder.

cyclothymic disorder   Chronic mood disorder involving frequent highs and lows that are shorter and/or milder than those in bipolar disorder.

delusion   False belief held despite evidence to the contrary.

dopamine   Neurotransmitter that may play a role in depression.

double depression   Dysthymic disorder plus major depression.

DSM-IV *Diagnostic and Statistical Manual of Mental Disorders, Fourth Edition*, the American Psychiatric Association's standard manual for the classification of mental disorders.

dysthymia   *See* dysthymic disorder.

dysthymic disorder   *DSM-IV* term for a chronic, low-grade depression.

ECT   *See* electroconvulsive therapy.

electroconvulsive therapy   Formerly known as electroshock treatment, a treatment for depression in which electrodes create the electrical equivalent of seizure activity in the brain.

Employee Assistance Program   Worksite-based program designed to assist organizations in addressing productivity issues and employee clients in identifying and resolving personal concerns.

glucocorticoids   Hormones, including cortisol, produced by the adrenal gland, that normally help the body cope with stress.

hallucination   A sensory experience without basis in reality that the perceiver nonetheless believes to be real; can involve sight, sound, smell, taste, or touch.

hypomania   Mild form of mania.

hypothalamus   Part of the brain that controls appetite, libido, and mood, and releases hormones, including CRF, that regulate the pituitary gland.

hypothyroidism   Condition in which the thyroid gland produces too little thyroid hormone, leading to symptoms of fatigue, feeling chilled, slowed thinking, constipation, weight gain, and depression.

interpersonal therapy   Type of time-limited psychotherapy for depression, focused on four areas: prolonged grief, disputes, role transitions, and social isolation.

light therapy   Treatment for seasonal affective disorder (SAD) involving daily (usually morning) exposure to a source of bright light.

limbic system   Parts of the brain that together sense and produce emotions.

lithium   Mineral that can help prevent and treat mania and, to a lesser extent, depression, in many people with bipolar disorder.

major depression   *See* major depressive disorder.

major depressive disorder   *DSM-IV* term for one-time or recurrent major depressive episodes not caused by other conditions such as bipolar disorder.

major depressive episode   *DSM-IV* term for single occurrence of significant depression lasting at least 2 weeks and meeting certain specific criteria.

managed behavioral health provider   Insurance industry term for an organization responsible for managing people's mental health benefits; sometimes called a managed behavioral health program.

managed care   Insurance industry term for several different types of systems designed to direct people to appropriate levels of care and control health care costs; sometimes called managed health care. Most managed care plans require a primary care provider or other "gatekeeper" to approve any referrals to specialists.

mania   Episode of extreme excitement, rapid speech, and other indications of abnormally elevated mood.

manic-depression   *See* bipolar disorder.

monoamine oxidase inhibitors   *See* MAOIs.

MAOIs (monoamine oxidase inhibitors)   Also called MAO inhibitors, a family of antidepressants that includes Nardil and Parnate.

mental health care provider or professional   *See* mental health care specialist.

mental health care specialist   Professional with specialized training in treating mental disorders; may be a psychiatrist, psychologist, social worker, nurse specialist, or mental health counselor.

mental status exam   The psychiatric equivalent of the physical exam in which the patient's thinking and emotions are evaluated.

mood disorder   Mental disorder involving abnormally elevated or depressed moods; includes major depressive disorder, bipolar disorder, dysthymic disorder, and substance-induced mood disorder.

mood stabilizer   Drug such as lithium used to prevent mania as well as depression.

norepinephrine   Neurotransmitter that tends to cause physical and mental arousal and is involved in mood regulation in an as yet poorly understood way.

neurotransmitter   Chemical carrying a message between nerve cells.

omega-3 fatty acids   Essential fatty acids found in cold-water fish and flaxseed oil.

oxytocin   Hormone produced by the pituitary with multiple functions, including contracting uterus during labor and acting as a neurotransmitter. As a neurotransmitter, it may play a role in emotional bonding.

PCP   *See* primary care provider.

pernicious anemia   Severe form of blood disease requiring treatment with vitamin B_{12}.

personality disorder   One of several chronic mental disorders involving patterns of deeply-ingrained personality traits that cause either distress or problems in social functioning.

PET scan   *See* positron emission tomography.

phototherapy   *See* light therapy.

placebo   Dummy treatment indistinguishable from a real treatment; often used in research for a control group of subjects, which is compared to the test group.

positron emission tomography   Imaging technique using injections of a radioactive marker to identify the parts of the brain using the most blood sugar and thus working the hardest.

postpartum depression   Depression beginning relatively soon after giving birth (definitions range from 4 weeks to 6 months); more severe than baby blues.

posttraumatic stress disorder   Disorder caused by exposure to an extremely stressful experience (often involving serious injury or the threat of death). Symptoms include nightmares, flashbacks of the event, and avoidance of stimuli related to the event.

prefrontal cortex   Area at the front of the cerebrum involved with complex thought processing.

premenstrual dysphoric disorder   *DSM-IV* term for severe premenstrual depression that disrupts work, school, and/or relationships.

primary care provider (PCP)   Doctor, nurse practitioner, or physician assistant who diagnoses and treats most health problems, coordinating referrals to specialists as needed. PCPs can be family practitioners, internists, pediatricians, and sometimes obstetrician/gynecologists.

psychopharmacology   Study of drugs used to treat mental disorders.

psychosis   Severe mental disorder involving loss of contact with reality, as with hallucinations or delusions.

psychotherapy "Talk" therapy in which a health care professional treats mental disorders through psychological techniques rather than medication or other physical means.

qi Term used in Chinese medicine indicating the energy that animates the universe and permeates everything.

receptor site Location on the surface of the cell where a neurotransmitter, drug, or another molecule attaches, leading to changes within the cell.

recurrence A new episode of illness.

relapse Reactivation of an episode of illness.

reuptake Reabsorption of neurotransmitters by the nerve cell that originally released them. The nerve cell gathers them back into storage until the cell receives another message to release them.

SAD *See* seasonal affective disorder.

seasonal affective disorder (SAD) Symptoms such as low energy, depression, and increased eating and sleeping that recur annually at a particular time of year, generally during late fall and winter in response to low light levels.

serotonin Neurotransmitter that may function to maintain normal patterns of appetite, sleep, sexual activity, and mood.

SSRIs (selective serotonin reuptake inhibitors) Family of antidepressants that includes Prozac, Zoloft, and Paxil.

synapse Tiny gap between two nerve cells across which neurotransmitters convey nerve impulses.

treatment-resistant depression Depression in which the first treatment(s) tried didn't work or caused too many side effects to continue.

tricyclics A family of antidepressants that includes Elavil, Tofranil, and Pamelor.

TSH (thyroid stimulating hormone) A hormone that is often elevated in cases of hypothyroidism.

winter depression *See* seasonal affective disorder.

Index

A

Action-oriented therapies, 99
Acupuncture, 130, 133–136
Adjustment disorder with depressed
    mood, 12
Adolescents
    bipolar disorder in, 25, 107–108
    Claire's story, 188–189, 228–230
    cognitive-behavioral therapy for,
        107, 168–169, 247
    college students, 198–199
    helping depressed, 185–186
    signs of depression in, 24–26
    suicide attempts by, 214
    suicide contagion and, 224–225,
        226–227
    suicide prevention in, 222–225
    suicide rates for, 19, 202, 239
    treatment for, 107–108
    Treatment for Adolescents with
        Depression Study (TADS),
        246–247
Aerobic exercise, 145, 147
Alcohol
    abuse, 19–20, 204
    as cause of mood disorder, 14
    prescription drugs and, 70, 79,
        92, 150
    reasons to avoid, 149, 150
    sleep disruption and, 150, 157
Alternative and complementary
    treatments
    acupuncture, 133–136

defined, 115
doctor's supervision and, 114,
    130–131
herbs and supplements, 115–129
homeopathy, 129, 132, 134–135
massage, 136–137
meditation, 137, 139–140, 166–167
popularity of, 113–114
relaxation techniques, 132–133, 158
yoga, 137, 138, 147
Alternative health care providers, 53
Americans with Disabilities Act
    (ADA), 191–192
Amino acids, 120–121
Anatomy, brain, 253–256
Anemia, 17, 48, 124, 151
Antidepressants
    brand names of, 82
    Celexa, 82, 83, 86, 87
    for children, 108–109
    choice of, 77
    duration of treatment with, 92–93,
        93–94
    Effexor, 81, 82, 85, 86–87, 89
    exercise versus, 144–148
    fears about taking, 90
    folic acid with, 91, 124
    generic names for, 82
    Ginkgo biloba and, 119–120
    mania and, 89
    monoamine oxidase inhibitors
        (MAOIs), 80, 81, 82, 85
    neurotransmitters and, 78–81

About the Author

Marian Broida, R.N., has been writing and teaching about health issues for more than 20 years. A former family nurse practitioner, she has provided primary health care in community clinics and in a mental health care setting. Ms. Broida holds a bachelor's degree in holistic health and a master's degree in nursing. She has written for numerous publications as well as TheNaturalPharmacist.com Web site, and has published an award-winning children's book on ancient history. Ms. Broida lives in Seattle, Washington, where she now devotes herself full-time to writing.

About the Medical Reviewer

Francis Mark Mondimore, M.D., is a graduate of the Johns Hopkins University School of Medicine where he completed his training in psychiatry at the Phipps Psychiatric Clinic of the Johns Hopkins Hospital. An expert in mood disorders, Dr. Mondimore is the author of several award-winning books, including *Bipolar Disorder: A Guide for Patients and Families.* He is on the faculty of Johns Hopkins and a member of the Affective Disorders Consultation Clinic where he cares for patients with depression and bipolar disorders, is a medical educator, and pursues research on the genetics of mood disorders. Dr. Mondimore lives in Baltimore, Maryland.